# THE WORST

# TOWNS IN THE U.S.A

## MAURICE CROW

# THE WORST

# TOWNS IN THE U.S.A

MAURICE CROW

# Contents

The United States of America is a great place to live and a lousy place to live. It just depends…

It depends on whether you're rich or poor, healthy or sick, smart or stupid, critically alert or just dumbly accepting. Above all, it depends on WHERE you live.

Life in the richest country on earth can be an impoverished nightmare –and we don't just mean in terms of wealth – or a rich and fulfilling experience. As we say, it all depends.

There are coffee tables across the land groaning under the weight of books that portray in glossy pictures and even glossier words the shining virtues of each and every corner of our 50 states. And in an age when even the tiniest town seems to have a Visitors and Convention Bureau, an unlimited budget to pump out its particular propaganda and a website on which to disseminate it, it would be easy to accept that everywhere across this fair land is uniformly wonderful.

Well, it ain't. We know it. You know it. A blind man sleeping in the back of a blacked-out van speeding across the country with earplugs in knows it. And this book aims to put the record straight.

Our country is dotted with dumps. With crap towns that deserve to be shaken awake and forced into the 21st Century. Places where a brief stopover feels like an afterlife in purgatory.

We've been there, and we can assure you we are not exaggerating. That's how this book came about. We were sick of being told: 'Welcome to our wonderful city… a great place to work and live… be greeted with a warm smile… undergoing an unparalleled renaissance… a wealth of historic sites…' Then we'd arrive to witness the truth – the nightmare.

Crime, drugs, poverty, pollution, dereliction and decrepitude are all obvious signs that you are entering an all-American hell-hole. But, as we shall see, there are other, more subtle reasons for fleeing from towns that are, truly, the pits.

We have chosen 50 towns throughout the United States and given them a good going-over. Because there is no real science to the study of utterly rubbishy places, the selection has been somewhat arbitrary. We have not chosen to rank the 50 towns in the interests of fairness they appear alphabetically by state. We readily admit it, and we know we're in for a rubbishing ourselves from the proud and undoubtedly protesting inhabitants of many of them.

But each town has been picked for a reason. Some are simply uninhabitable urban prisons in which no human deserves to suffer the sentence of subsisting. Others are the victims of shameless political and corporate neglect.

Some have been destroyed by the poisonous emissions of industry or government and have seemingly been abandoned to a lingering toxic death. Some have been poisoned in a different way – by the miasma of ignorance or bigotry.

At the other end of the scale, some towns may at first seem to be perfect examples of the American dream. Yet sleeping sickness would a truer diagnosis. Mind-numbing monotony or self-satisfied tedium can propel a town into our catalogue of shame just as surely as more physical signs of civic contagion.

But, you might well ask, are we being scrupulously fair in maligning the 50 towns that appear in the following pages. The answer, we give with firm voice, is a resounding: 'No. Nothing fair about it.'

Let's be honest. There must be many, MANY towns out there which richly deserve inclusion in Worst Towns of the USA. Which equally means that there are at least a few among those we have chosen that deserve to be allowed out. So, if you think your town has been grievously wronged, this is how we plan to make amends…

Tell us briefly why your town is a great place and why it should be removed from future editions of Worst Towns of the USA. We promise we'll listen sympathetically. But to encourage us to expunge your town in favour of another, it will help prove your case if you can nominate somewhere that truly does deserve inclusion in the next edition.

And, of course, we're on the lookout for that next line up of Worst Towns from all of you out there. Do you live in a sad city? Is your hometown the tawdriest? Have you just passed through a place that's the pits? Have you spent student days or a business trip or even a vacation somewhere so execrably vile that you feel we ought to pay it a visit and expose it?

Tell us about it by logging on to our website:

**www.worsttownsusa.com**

You could be doing civilization a favour – by warning the world against ever setting foot in the Worst Towns of the USA.

### AND THESE DIDN'T EVEN MAKE OUR LIST...

## *"America's Secret City"*
### - OAK RIDGE, TN

## *"Appalachian Square Dance Capital of the World"*
### - LEBANON, TN

## *"Barbed Wire Capital of the World "*
### - LA CROSSE, KS

## *"Bigfoot Capital of the World"*
### - WILLOW CREEK, CA

## *"Bird Dog Capital of the World"*
### - WAYNESBORO, GA

## *"Birthplace of Kool-Aid"*
### - HASTINGS, NE

## *"Cherry Pit Spitting Capital of the World"*
### - EAU CLAIRE, MI

## *"Christmas Pickle Capital of the World"*
### - BERRIEN SPRINGS, MI

## *"Clogging Capital of the World"*
### - MAGGIE VALLEY, NC

## *"Corn Cob Pipe Capital of the World"*
### - WASHINGTON, MO

## *"Covered Dish Capital of the World"*
### - WINDOM, KS

## *"Cow Chip Capital of Kansas"*
### - RUSSELL SPRINGS, KS

## *"Cow Chip Capital of the World"*
### - BEAVER, OK

## *"Cowboy Capital of the World"*
### - BANDERA, TX

## *"Dandelion Capital of the World"*
### - VINELAND, NJ

## *"Farm Toy Capital of the World"*
### - DYERSVILLE, IA

## *"Flower Box City"*
### - NEOSHO, MO

## *"Frog Jump Capital of Ohio"*
### - VALLEY CITY, OH

## *"Hubcap Capital of the World"*
### - PEARSONVILLE, CA

## *"Jackalope Capital of the World"*
### - DOUGLAS, WY

## *"Jackrabbit Capital of Texas"*

### - ODESSA, TX

## *"Peak of Good Living"*

### - APEX, NC

## *"Spamtown USA"*

### - AUSTIN, MN

## *"The Town Without a Frown"*

### - HAPPY, TX

## *"Town of Oil Repute"*

### - DRUMRIGHT, OK

Two close wells, about 10 feet apart, in Drumright OK  c. 1930's

## *"Town Without a Toothache"*

### - HEREFORD, TX

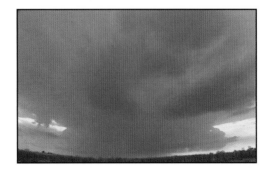

## *"Turf Grass Capital of the World"*

### - SAVANNAH, GA

## *"Western Swing Capital of the World"*

### - TURKEY, TX

# DP: Selected Characteristics: 2003

## Data Set: 2003 American Community Survey Summary Tables

## Geographic Area: United States

NOTE. Data are limited to the household population and exclude the population living in institutions, college dormitories, and other group quarters.

| Selected Economic Characteristics: 2003 | Estimate | Lower Bound | Upper Bound |
|---|---|---|---|
| **Employment Status** | | | |
| Population 16 years and over | 218,256,211 | 218,203,094 | 218,309,328 |
| In labor force | 144,022,380 | 143,804,029 | 144,240,731 |
| Civilian labor force | 143,374,440 | 143,155,405 | 143,593,475 |
| Employed | 132,422,387 | 132,198,493 | 132,646,281 |
| Unemployed | 10,952,053 | 10,847,697 | 11,056,409 |
| Percent unemployed | 7.6 | 7.6 | 7.7 |
| Armed Forces | 647,940 | 603,491 | 692,389 |
| Not in labor force | 74,233,831 | 74,019,099 | 74,448,563 |
| Females 16 years and over | 112,903,779 | 112,857,839 | 112,949,719 |
| In labor force | 66,625,293 | 66,481,119 | 66,769,467 |
| Civilian labor force | 66,535,259 | 66,390,904 | 66,679,614 |
| Employed | 61,468,467 | 61,312,945 | 61,623,989 |
| Own children under 6 years | 22,498,477 | 22,430,754 | 22,566,200 |
| All parents in family in labor force | 13,458,046 | 13,355,142 | 13,560,950 |
| Own children 6 to 17 years | 45,943,969 | 45,853,384 | 46,034,554 |
| All parents in family in labor force | 31,513,549 | 31,351,783 | 31,675,315 |
| Population 16 to 19 years | 14,768,985 | 14,702,025 | 14,835,945 |
| Not enrolled in school and not a H.S. graduate | 1,130,575 | 1,089,031 | 1,172,119 |
| Unemployed or not in the labor force | 687,515 | 656,148 | 718,882 |
| **Commuting To Work** | | | |
| Workers 16 years and over | 129,141,982 | 128,905,839 | 129,378,125 |
| Car, truck, or van -- drove alone | 100,416,861 | 100,167,389 | 100,666,333 |
| Car, truck, or van -- carpooled | 13,483,102 | 13,347,344 | 13,618,860 |
| Public transportation (including taxicab) | 6,230,997 | 6,155,284 | 6,306,710 |
| Walked | 2,934,433 | 2,857,488 | 3,011,378 |
| Other means | 1,558,206 | 1,512,372 | 1,604,040 |
| Worked at home | 4,518,383 | 4,441,432 | 4,595,334 |

# ECONOMIC

| Selected Economic Characteristics: 2003 | Estimate | Lower Bound | Upper Bound |
|---|---|---|---|
| Mean travel time to work (minutes) | 24.3 | 24.2 | 24.4 |
| Employed civilian population 16 years and over | 132,422,387 | 132,198,493 | 132,646,281 |
| **Occupation** | | | |
| Management, professional, and related occupations | 45,215,214 | 44,965,829 | 45,464,599 |
| Service occupations | 21,351,389 | 21,212,420 | 21,490,358 |
| Sales and office occupations | 34,752,972 | 34,555,398 | 34,950,546 |
| Farming, fishing, and forestry occupations | 935,847 | 897,015 | 974,679 |
| Construction, extraction, and maintenance occupations | 12,612,711 | 12,482,980 | 12,742,442 |
| Production, transportation, and material moving occupations | 17,554,254 | 17,381,287 | 17,727,221 |
| **Industry** | | | |
| Agriculture, forestry, fishing and hunting, and mining | 2,338,703 | 2,244,324 | 2,433,082 |
| Construction | 9,591,021 | 9,478,150 | 9,703,892 |
| Manufacturing | 16,302,557 | 16,094,698 | 16,510,416 |
| Wholesale trade | 4,938,833 | 4,874,236 | 5,003,430 |
| Retail trade | 15,356,518 | 15,219,691 | 15,493,345 |
| Transportation and warehousing, and utilities | 6,666,049 | 6,577,232 | 6,754,866 |
| Information | 3,466,754 | 3,406,335 | 3,527,173 |
| Finance, insurance, real estate, and rental and leasing | 9,441,454 | 9,347,146 | 9,535,762 |
| Professional, scientific, management, administrative, and waste management services | 12,870,057 | 12,770,459 | 12,969,655 |
| Educational, health, and social services | 27,292,718 | 27,104,439 | 27,480,997 |
| Arts, entertainment, recreation, accommodation, and food services | 11,070,816 | 10,957,748 | 11,183,884 |
| Other services (except public administration) | 6,484,803 | 6,414,731 | 6,554,875 |
| Public Administration | 6,602,104 | 6,496,325 | 6,707,883 |
| **Class Of Worker** | | | |
| Private wage and salary workers | 102,579,670 | 102,311,434 | 102,847,906 |
| Government workers | 20,098,282 | 19,896,130 | 20,300,434 |
| Self-employed workers in own not incorporated business | 9,361,640 | 9,244,412 | 9,478,868 |
| Unpaid family workers | 382,795 | 365,685 | 399,905 |
| **Income And Benefits (In 2003 Inflation-adjusted Dollars)** | | | |
| Total households | 108,419,506 | 108,167,885 | 108,671,127 |
| *Less than $10,000* | 9,764,122 | 9,641,030 | 9,887,214 |

| Selected Economic Characteristics: 2003 | Estimate | Lower Bound | Upper Bound |
|---|---|---|---|
| $10,000 to $14,999 | 6,941,697 | 6,863,025 | 7,020,369 |
| $15,000 to $24,999 | 13,759,052 | 13,631,502 | 13,886,602 |
| $25,000 to $34,999 | 13,197,069 | 13,081,001 | 13,313,137 |
| $35,000 to $49,999 | 17,090,897 | 16,967,511 | 17,214,283 |
| $50,000 to $74,999 | 20,705,116 | 20,560,815 | 20,849,417 |
| $75,000 to $99,999 | 11,784,523 | 11,674,507 | 11,894,539 |
| $100,000 to $149,999 | 9,699,638 | 9,600,556 | 9,798,720 |
| $150,000 to $199,999 | 2,906,155 | 2,864,168 | 2,948,142 |
| $200,000 or more | 2,571,237 | 2,530,267 | 2,612,207 |
| Median household income (dollars) | 43,564 | 43,336 | 43,792 |
| Mean household income (dollars) | 58,036 | 57,827 | 58,245 |
| With earnings | 86,890,034 | 86,635,709 | 87,144,359 |
| Mean earnings (dollars) | 59,349 | 59,148 | 59,550 |
| With Social Security | 28,818,496 | 28,678,322 | 28,958,670 |
| Mean Social Security income (dollars) | 12,651 | 12,615 | 12,687 |
| With retirement income | 18,435,251 | 18,284,169 | 18,586,333 |
| Mean retirement income (dollars) | 17,005 | 16,865 | 17,145 |
| With Supplemental Security Income | 4,183,060 | 4,118,903 | 4,247,217 |
| Mean Supplemental Security Income (dollars) | 6,731 | 6,668 | 6,794 |
| With cash public assistance income | 2,751,446 | 2,701,966 | 2,800,926 |
| Mean cash public assistance income (dollars) | 3,084 | 3,016 | 3,153 |
| With Food Stamp benefits in the past 12 months | 7,286,735 | 7,180,190 | 7,393,280 |
| Families | 73,057,960 | 72,802,717 | 73,313,203 |
| Less than $10,000 | 3,980,675 | 3,910,841 | 4,050,509 |
| $10,000 to $14,999 | 3,054,654 | 3,001,644 | 3,107,664 |
| $15,000 to $24,999 | 7,597,476 | 7,502,875 | 7,692,077 |
| $25,000 to $34,999 | 8,309,508 | 8,212,572 | 8,406,444 |
| $35,000 to $49,999 | 11,686,750 | 11,583,991 | 11,789,509 |
| $50,000 to $74,999 | 15,717,228 | 15,586,288 | 15,848,168 |
| $75,000 to $99,999 | 9,730,836 | 9,623,421 | 9,838,251 |
| $100,000 to $149,999 | 8,279,403 | 8,185,253 | 8,373,553 |
| $150,000 to $199,999 | 2,488,607 | 2,445,912 | 2,531,302 |
| $200,000 or more | 2,212,823 | 2,173,350 | 2,252,296 |
| Median family income (dollars) | 52,273 | 52,068 | 52,478 |
| Mean family income (dollars) | 66,920 | 66,655 | 67,185 |

| Selected Economic Characteristics: 2003 | Estimate | Lower Bound | Upper Bound |
|---|---|---|---|
| *Per capita income (dollars)* | 23,110 | 23,030 | 23,190 |
| Nonfamily households | 35,361,546 | 35,189,205 | 35,533,887 |
| *Median nonfamily income (dollars)* | 26,492 | 26,341 | 26,643 |
| *Mean nonfamily income (dollars)* | 37,232 | 37,042 | 37,421 |
| Median earnings (dollars): | 26,236 | 26,157 | 26,315 |
| *Male full-time, year-round workers* | 40,556 | 40,456 | 40,656 |
| *Female full-time, year-round workers* | 30,599 | 30,507 | 30,691 |
| **Number Below Poverty In The Past 12 Months** | | | |
| Families | 7,143,075 | 7,055,895 | 7,230,255 |
| *With related children under 18 years* | 5,640,409 | 5,564,398 | 5,716,420 |
| *With related children under 5 years only* | 1,199,849 | 1,163,110 | 1,236,588 |
| Families with female householder, no husband present | 3,860,916 | 3,799,565 | 3,922,267 |
| *With related children under 18 years* | 3,474,563 | 3,417,544 | 3,531,582 |
| *With related children under 5 years only* | 756,171 | 727,026 | 785,316 |
| Individuals | 35,846,289 | 35,421,421 | 36,271,157 |
| *18 years and over* | 23,173,006 | 22,900,630 | 23,445,382 |
| *65 years and over* | 3,319,167 | 3,258,263 | 3,380,071 |
| *Related children under 18 years* | 12,341,089 | 12,139,666 | 12,542,512 |
| *Related children 5 to 17 years* | 8,358,763 | 8,210,213 | 8,507,313 |
| *Unrelated individuals 15 years and over* | 10,868,688 | 10,706,853 | 11,030,523 |
| **Percent Below Poverty In The Past 12 Months** | | | |
| Individuals | 12.7 | 12.6 | 12.9 |
| *18 years and over* | 11 | 10.9 | 11.2 |
| *65 years and over* | 9.8 | 9.6 | 10 |
| *Related children under 18 years* | 17.3 | 17.1 | 17.6 |
| *Related children under 5 years* | 20.5 | 20.1 | 21 |
| *Related children 5 to 17 years* | 16.1 | 15.8 | 16.4 |
| *Unrelated individuals 15 years and over* | 22.3 | 22 | 22.5 |

Source: U.S. Census Bureau, 2003 American Community Survey

| Selected Housing Characteristics: 2003 | Estimate | Lower Bound | Upper Bound |
|---|---|---|---|
| Total housing units | 120,879,390 | ***** | ***** |
| **Units In Structure** | | | |
| 1-unit, detached | 73,551,424 | 73,273,017 | 73,829,831 |
| 1-unit, attached | 6,707,518 | 6,619,315 | 6,795,721 |
| 2 units | 5,039,138 | 4,961,973 | 5,116,303 |
| 3 or 4 units | 5,805,366 | 5,712,324 | 5,898,408 |
| 5 to 9 units | 6,053,427 | 5,951,357 | 6,155,497 |
| 10 to 19 units | 5,506,410 | 5,415,644 | 5,597,176 |
| 20 or more units | 9,431,243 | 9,330,492 | 9,531,994 |
| Mobile home | 8,697,578 | 8,470,893 | 8,924,263 |
| Boat, RV, van, etc. | 87,286 | 76,789 | 97,783 |
| **Year Structure Built** | | | |
| 2000 or later | 5,690,900 | 5,599,616 | 5,782,184 |
| 1995 to 1999 | 10,667,615 | 10,555,114 | 10,780,116 |
| 1990 to 1994 | 8,743,885 | 8,638,270 | 8,849,500 |
| 1980 to 1989 | 17,893,449 | 17,751,277 | 18,035,621 |
| 1970 to 1979 | 21,112,229 | 20,960,080 | 21,264,378 |
| 1960 to 1969 | 15,068,483 | 14,931,467 | 15,205,499 |
| 1950 to 1959 | 14,989,398 | 14,843,559 | 15,135,237 |
| 1940 to 1949 | 8,134,126 | 8,035,655 | 8,232,597 |
| 1939 or earlier | 18,579,305 | 18,364,484 | 18,794,126 |
| **Rooms** | | | |
| 1 room | 1,918,514 | 1,873,170 | 1,963,858 |
| 2 rooms | 4,410,702 | 4,344,815 | 4,476,589 |
| 3 rooms | 11,783,358 | 11,643,386 | 11,923,330 |
| 4 rooms | 21,003,290 | 20,823,818 | 21,182,762 |
| 5 rooms | 26,163,152 | 25,984,568 | 26,341,736 |
| 6 rooms | 22,635,586 | 22,482,889 | 22,788,283 |
| 7 rooms | 14,462,296 | 14,329,594 | 14,594,998 |
| 8 rooms | 9,372,110 | 9,276,961 | 9,467,259 |
| 9 rooms or more | 9,130,382 | 9,009,348 | 9,251,416 |
| Median (rooms) | 5.3 | 5.1 | 5.5 |
| Occupied housing units | 108,419,506 | 108,167,885 | 108,671,127 |
| **Year Householder Moved Into Unit** | | | |
| 2000 or later | 40,316,237 | 40,112,728 | 40,519,746 |
| 1995 to 1999 | 24,458,047 | 24,311,692 | 24,604,402 |

| Selected Housing Characteristics: 2003 | Estimate | Lower Bound | Upper Bound |
|---|---|---|---|
| 1990 to 1994 | 12,760,443 | 12,660,051 | 12,860,835 |
| 1980 to 1989 | 13,722,704 | 13,605,231 | 13,840,177 |
| 1970 to 1979 | 8,874,294 | 8,788,998 | 8,959,590 |
| 1969 or earlier | 8,287,781 | 8,185,170 | 8,390,392 |
| **Vehicles Available** | | | |
| No vehicles available | 9,788,183 | 9,689,565 | 9,886,801 |
| *1* | 36,135,604 | 35,973,777 | 36,297,431 |
| *2* | 41,671,007 | 41,465,232 | 41,876,782 |
| *3 or more* | 20,824,712 | 20,678,995 | 20,970,429 |
| **House Heating Fuel** | | | |
| Utility gas | 55,084,675 | 54,634,173 | 55,535,177 |
| Bottled, tank, or LP gas | 6,684,131 | 6,482,692 | 6,885,570 |
| Electricity | 33,903,973 | 33,586,007 | 34,221,939 |
| Fuel oil, kerosene, etc. | 9,377,649 | 9,133,282 | 9,622,016 |
| Coal or coke | 156,622 | 136,369 | 176,875 |
| Wood | 1,840,178 | 1,745,574 | 1,934,782 |
| Solar energy | 35,186 | 30,420 | 39,952 |
| Other fuel | 422,634 | 400,848 | 444,420 |
| No fuel used | 914,458 | 888,319 | 940,597 |
| **Selected Characteristics** | | | |
| Lacking complete plumbing facilities | 437,100 | 417,648 | 456,552 |
| Lacking complete kitchen facilities | 564,170 | 541,651 | 586,689 |
| No telephone service available | 4,076,804 | 3,977,888 | 4,175,720 |
| **Occupants Per Room** | | | |
| 1.00 or less | 104,279,392 | 104,024,940 | 104,533,844 |
| 1.01 to 1.50 | 2,811,798 | 2,765,847 | 2,857,749 |
| 1.51 or more | 1,328,316 | 1,289,428 | 1,367,204 |
| Specified owner-occupied units | 58,808,660 | 58,410,255 | 59,207,065 |
| **Value** | | | |
| Less than $50,000 | 3,978,242 | 3,869,388 | 4,087,096 |
| $50,000 to $99,999 | 13,422,819 | 13,248,645 | 13,596,993 |
| $100,000 to $149,999 | 12,676,645 | 12,515,310 | 12,837,980 |
| $150,000 to $199,999 | 9,009,762 | 8,893,345 | 9,126,179 |
| $200,000 to $299,999 | 8,807,310 | 8,692,207 | 8,922,413 |
| $300,000 to $499,999 | 7,311,114 | 7,230,480 | 7,391,748 |
| $500,000 to $999,999 | 3,018,958 | 2,966,892 | 3,071,024 |

| Selected Housing Characteristics: 2003 | Estimate | Lower Bound | Upper Bound |
|---|---|---|---|
| $1,000,000 or more | 583,810 | 561,230 | 606,390 |
| Median (dollars) | 147,275 | 146,508 | 148,042 |
| **Mortgage Status And Selected Monthly Owner Costs** | | | |
| Housing units with a mortgage | 41,176,939 | 40,866,268 | 41,487,610 |
| Less than $300 | 217,089 | 203,110 | 231,068 |
| $300 to $499 | 1,532,437 | 1,489,965 | 1,574,909 |
| $500 to $699 | 3,912,422 | 3,850,152 | 3,974,692 |
| $700 to $999 | 9,071,210 | 8,968,381 | 9,174,039 |
| $1,000 to $1,499 | 12,932,211 | 12,793,014 | 13,071,408 |
| $1,500 to $1,999 | 6,903,398 | 6,809,739 | 6,997,057 |
| $2,000 or more | 6,608,172 | 6,528,863 | 6,687,481 |
| Median (dollars) | 1,204 | 1,200 | 1,208 |
| Housing units without a mortgage | 17,631,721 | 17,481,947 | 17,781,495 |
| Less than $100 | 208,509 | 196,744 | 220,274 |
| $100 to $199 | 2,391,486 | 2,340,275 | 2,442,697 |
| $200 to $299 | 4,767,267 | 4,699,837 | 4,834,697 |
| $300 to $399 | 4,035,102 | 3,977,053 | 4,093,151 |
| $400 or more | 6,229,357 | 6,161,043 | 6,297,671 |
| Median (dollars) | 333 | 331 | 335 |
| **Selected Monthly Owner Costs As A Percentage Of Household Income** | | | |
| Housing unit with a mortgage | 41,176,939 | 40,866,268 | 41,487,610 |
| Less than 20 percent | 16,275,361 | 16,128,118 | 16,422,604 |
| 20.0 to 24.9 percent | 7,098,282 | 7,011,070 | 7,185,494 |
| 25.0 to 29.9 percent | 5,153,522 | 5,070,363 | 5,236,681 |
| 30.0 to 34.9 percent | 3,371,413 | 3,315,572 | 3,427,254 |
| 35.0 percent or more | 9,116,407 | 9,023,649 | 9,209,165 |
| Not computed | 161,954 | 148,700 | 175,208 |
| Housing unit without a mortgage | 17,631,721 | 17,481,947 | 17,781,495 |
| Less than 10 percent | 7,609,771 | 7,519,153 | 7,700,389 |
| 10.0 to 14.9 percent | 3,587,687 | 3,536,010 | 3,639,364 |
| 15.0 to 19.9 percent | 2,059,710 | 2,022,802 | 2,096,618 |
| 20.0 to 24.9 percent | 1,265,907 | 1,235,579 | 1,296,235 |
| 25.0 to 29.9 percent | 770,234 | 748,696 | 791,772 |
| 30.0 to 34.9 percent | 516,567 | 496,830 | 536,304 |
| 35.0 percent or more | 1,666,217 | 1,628,272 | 1,704,162 |
| Not computed | 155,628 | 144,394 | 166,862 |

# HOUSING

| Selected Housing Characteristics: 2003 | Estimate | Lower Bound | Upper Bound |
|---|---|---|---|
| Specified renter-occupied units | 35,545,466 | 35,288,267 | 35,802,665 |
| **Gross Rent** | | | |
| Less than $200 | 1,364,843 | 1,324,581 | 1,405,105 |
| $200 to $299 | 1,441,346 | 1,402,731 | 1,479,961 |
| $300 to $499 | 5,892,050 | 5,792,576 | 5,991,524 |
| $500 to $749 | 11,076,257 | 10,953,825 | 11,198,689 |
| $750 to $999 | 7,437,683 | 7,349,363 | 7,526,003 |
| $1,000 to $1,499 | 4,662,773 | 4,597,702 | 4,727,844 |
| $1,500 or more | 1,660,830 | 1,617,081 | 1,704,579 |
| No cash rent | 2,009,684 | 1,957,730 | 2,061,638 |
| Median (dollars) | 679 | 677 | 681 |
| **Gross Rent As A Percentage Of Household Income** | | | |
| Less than 15 percent | 4,766,195 | 4,691,439 | 4,840,951 |
| 15.0 to 19.9 percent | 4,497,771 | 4,435,520 | 4,560,022 |
| 20.0 to 24.9 percent | 4,409,666 | 4,347,845 | 4,471,487 |
| 25.0 to 29.9 percent | 3,897,232 | 3,830,889 | 3,963,575 |
| 30.0 to 34.9 percent | 2,860,715 | 2,806,950 | 2,914,480 |
| 35.0 percent or more | 12,497,290 | 12,357,884 | 12,636,696 |
| Not computed | 2,616,597 | 2,556,109 | 2,677,085 |

Source: U.S. Census Bureau, 2003 American Community Survey

| Selected Social Characteristics: 2003 | Estimate | Lower Bound | Upper Bound |
|---|---|---|---|
| **School Enrollment** | | | |
| Population 3 years and over enrolled in school | 75,128,957 | 74,942,693 | 75,315,221 |
| Nursery school, preschool | 4,611,102 | 4,548,783 | 4,673,421 |
| Kindergarten | 3,993,377 | 3,941,606 | 4,045,148 |
| Elementary school (grades 1–8) | 32,706,140 | 32,613,088 | 32,799,192 |
| High school grade (grades 9–12) | 16,599,058 | 16,513,339 | 16,684,777 |
| College or graduate school | 17,219,280 | 17,057,863 | 17,380,697 |
| **Educational Attainment** | | | |
| Population 25 years and over | 184,395,128 | 184,330,531 | 184,459,725 |
| Less than 9th grade | 11,892,176 | 11,733,773 | 12,050,579 |
| 9th to 12th grade, no diploma | 18,321,443 | 18,160,724 | 18,482,162 |
| High school graduate (including equivalency) | 54,954,343 | 54,691,370 | 55,217,316 |
| Some college, no degree | 37,407,246 | 37,215,920 | 37,598,572 |
| Associate degree | 12,882,642 | 12,770,076 | 12,995,208 |
| Bachelor's degree | 31,138,178 | 30,901,997 | 31,374,359 |
| Graduate or professional degree | 17,799,100 | 17,617,274 | 17,980,926 |
| Percent high school graduate or higher | 83.6 | 83.5 | 83.8 |
| Percent bachelor's degree or higher | 26.5 | 26.3 | 26.7 |
| **Marital Status** | | | |
| Males 15 years and over | 107,432,675 | 107,389,696 | 107,475,654 |
| Never married | 32,670,276 | 32,533,427 | 32,807,125 |
| Now married, except separated | 60,772,654 | 60,598,968 | 60,946,340 |
| Separated | 1,824,752 | 1,774,144 | 1,875,360 |
| Widowed | 2,642,475 | 2,597,246 | 2,687,704 |
| Divorced | 9,522,518 | 9,439,649 | 9,605,387 |
| Females 15 years and over | 114,911,030 | 114,868,734 | 114,953,326 |
| Never married | 28,453,285 | 28,323,326 | 28,583,244 |
| Now married, except separated | 59,293,345 | 59,128,290 | 59,458,400 |
| Separated | 2,989,683 | 2,930,360 | 3,049,006 |
| Widowed | 11,182,170 | 11,106,070 | 11,258,270 |
| Divorced | 12,992,547 | 12,888,540 | 13,096,554 |
| **Fertility** | | | |
| Number of women 15 to 50 years old who had a birth in the past 12 months | 3,966,840 | 3,900,879 | 4,032,801 |
| Unmarried women (widowed, divorced, and never married) | 1,160,510 | 1,120,257 | 1,200,763 |
| Per 1,000 unmarried women | 34 | 33 | 35 |

# SOCIAL

| Selected Social Characteristics: 2003 | Estimate | Lower Bound | Upper Bound |
|---|---|---|---|
| As a percent of all women with a birth | 29.3 | 28.5 | 30 |
| Per 1,000 women 15 to 50 years old | 54 | 53 | 55 |
| Per 1,000 women 15 to 19 years old | 30 | 28 | 32 |
| Per 1,000 women 20 to 34 years old | 103 | 101 | 105 |
| Per 1,000 women 35 to 50 years old | 20 | 20 | 21 |
| **Grandparents** | | | |
| Number of grandparents with own grandchildren under 18 years in households | 5,505,115 | 5,417,509 | 5,592,721 |
| Responsible for grandchildren | 2,348,758 | 2,286,921 | 2,410,595 |
| less than 1 year | 521,339 | 496,244 | 546,434 |
| 1 or 2 years | 534,956 | 505,042 | 564,870 |
| 3 or 4 years | 380,923 | 355,062 | 406,784 |
| 5 or more years | 911,540 | 876,683 | 946,397 |
| Percent who are female | 63.3 | 62.7 | 63.9 |
| Percent who are married | 71.1 | 70 | 72.1 |
| Percent who are in labor force | 57.8 | 56.8 | 58.7 |
| Percent who are in poverty | 19.8 | 18.9 | 20.7 |
| **Veteran Status** | | | |
| Civilian population 18 years and over | 209,628,197 | 209,579,130 | 209,677,264 |
| Civilian veterans | 24,008,355 | 23,863,265 | 24,153,445 |
| **Disability Status Of The Civilian Noninstitutionalized Population** | | | |
| Population 5 to 20 years | 63,505,309 | 63,433,377 | 63,577,241 |
| With a disability | 4,059,794 | 3,978,423 | 4,141,165 |
| Population 21 to 64 years | 165,180,683 | 165,092,107 | 165,269,259 |
| With a disability | 19,871,681 | 19,715,577 | 20,027,785 |
| Percent employed | 37.8 | 37.5 | 38.2 |
| No disability | 145,309,002 | 145,138,818 | 145,479,186 |
| Percent employed | 77.5 | 77.4 | 77.6 |
| Population 65 years and over | 33,896,172 | 33,867,171 | 33,925,173 |
| With a disability | 13,526,817 | 13,434,569 | 13,619,065 |
| **Residence 1 Year Ago** | | | |
| Population 1 year and over | 279,117,736 | 279,060,275 | 279,175,197 |
| Same house | 237,077,406 | 236,637,149 | 237,517,663 |
| Different house in the U.S. | 40,499,414 | 40,087,950 | 40,910,878 |
| Same county | 26,182,072 | 25,845,110 | 26,519,034 |
| Different county | 14,317,342 | 14,125,261 | 14,509,423 |

| Selected Social Characteristics: 2003 | Estimate | Lower Bound | Upper Bound |
|---|---|---|---|
| *Same state* | 8,116,428 | 7,964,461 | 8,268,395 |
| *Different state* | 6,200,914 | 6,071,590 | 6,330,238 |
| *Abroad* | 1,540,916 | 1,483,397 | 1,598,435 |
| **Place Of Birth, Citizenship, And Year Of Entry** | | | |
| Total population | 282,909,885 | ***** | ***** |
| Native | 249,375,940 | 249,157,941 | 249,593,939 |
| Born in United States | 245,896,339 | 245,671,739 | 246,120,939 |
| State of residence | 168,656,391 | 168,013,673 | 169,299,109 |
| Different state | 77,239,948 | 76,644,506 | 77,835,390 |
| Born in Puerto Rico, U.S. Island areas, or born abroad to American parent(s) | 3,479,601 | 3,408,684 | 3,550,518 |
| Foreign born | 33,533,945 | 33,315,946 | 33,751,944 |
| Naturalized citizen | 13,893,436 | 13,755,311 | 14,031,561 |
| Not a citizen | 19,640,509 | 19,440,636 | 19,840,382 |
| Entered 1990 or later | 16,571,998 | 16,376,830 | 16,767,166 |
| Entered before 1990 | 16,961,947 | 16,803,590 | 17,120,304 |
| **Region Of Birth Of Foreign Born** | | | |
| Foreign-born population with region of birth reported | 33,533,945 | 33,315,946 | 33,751,944 |
| *Europe* | 4,775,586 | 4,689,236 | 4,861,936 |
| *Asia* | 9,146,958 | 9,055,262 | 9,238,654 |
| *Africa* | 1,039,489 | 992,436 | 1,086,542 |
| *Oceania* | 191,320 | 174,926 | 207,714 |
| *Latin America* | 17,533,710 | 17,332,869 | 17,734,551 |
| *Northern America* | 846,882 | 811,158 | 882,606 |
| **Language Spoken At Home** | | | |
| Population 5 years and over | 263,230,104 | 263,204,319 | 263,255,889 |
| English only | 214,809,283 | 214,512,791 | 215,105,775 |
| *Language other than English* | 48,420,821 | 48,130,410 | 48,711,232 |
| *Speak English less than "very well"* | 22,001,256 | 21,794,389 | 22,208,123 |
| *Spanish* | 29,698,115 | 29,507,647 | 29,888,583 |
| *Speak English less than "very well"* | 14,432,957 | 14,250,141 | 14,615,773 |
| Other Indo-European languages | 9,509,828 | 9,302,307 | 9,717,349 |
| *Speak English less than "very well"* | 3,275,644 | 3,170,133 | 3,381,155 |
| Asian and Pacific Islander languages | 7,449,893 | 7,374,368 | 7,525,418 |
| *Speak English less than "very well"* | 3,749,195 | 3,685,286 | 3,813,104 |
| Other languages | 1,762,985 | 1,689,895 | 1,836,075 |

| Selected Social Characteristics: 2003 | Estimate | Lower Bound | Upper Bound |
|---|---|---|---|
| *Speak English less than "very well"* | 543,460 | 508,159 | 578,761 |
| **Ancestry (Total Reported)** | | | |
| Total Population | 282,909,885 | ***** | ***** |
| *Arab* | 1,258,319 | 1,204,286 | 1,312,352 |
| *Czech* | 1,426,354 | 1,359,350 | 1,493,358 |
| *Danish* | 1,435,000 | 1,375,738 | 1,494,262 |
| *Dutch* | 5,059,238 | 4,892,024 | 5,226,452 |
| *English* | 28,402,887 | 28,136,521 | 28,669,253 |
| *French (except Basque)* | 9,677,776 | 9,504,033 | 9,851,519 |
| *French Canadian* | 2,187,922 | 2,122,106 | 2,253,738 |
| *German* | 47,842,275 | 47,428,020 | 48,256,530 |
| *Greek* | 1,229,023 | 1,180,048 | 1,277,998 |
| *Hungarian* | 1,494,953 | 1,444,150 | 1,545,756 |
| *Irish* | 33,992,086 | 33,723,758 | 34,260,414 |
| *Italian* | 16,726,217 | 16,497,632 | 16,954,802 |
| *Lithuanian* | 719,575 | 688,360 | 750,790 |
| *Norwegian* | 4,494,107 | 4,263,209 | 4,725,005 |
| *Polish* | 9,303,599 | 9,119,880 | 9,487,318 |
| *Portuguese* | 1,349,161 | 1,296,154 | 1,402,168 |
| *Russian* | 2,974,942 | 2,908,110 | 3,041,774 |
| *Scotch-Irish* | 5,098,850 | 5,003,813 | 5,193,887 |
| *Scottish* | 5,811,085 | 5,719,579 | 5,902,591 |
| *Slovak* | 811,172 | 767,959 | 854,385 |
| *Subsaharan African* | 1,884,454 | 1,810,079 | 1,958,829 |
| *Swedish* | 4,253,810 | 4,122,351 | 4,385,269 |
| *Swiss* | 984,443 | 922,656 | 1,046,230 |
| *Ukrainian* | 869,799 | 834,075 | 905,523 |
| *United States or American* | 19,676,981 | 19,307,544 | 20,046,418 |
| *Welsh* | 1,890,237 | 1,842,844 | 1,937,630 |
| *West Indian (excluding Hispanic origin groups)* | 2,129,199 | 2,054,871 | 2,203,527 |

Source: U.S. Census Bureau, 2003 American Community Survey

| General Demographic Characteristics: 2003 | Estimate | Lower Bound | Upper Bound |
|---|---|---|---|
| Total population | 282,909,885 | ***** | ***** |
| **Sex And Age** | | | |
| Male | 138,396,524 | 138,345,711 | 138,447,337 |
| Female | 144,513,361 | 144,462,548 | 144,564,174 |
| Under 5 years | 19,679,781 | 19,653,996 | 19,705,566 |
| 5 to 9 years | 19,741,730 | 19,636,901 | 19,846,559 |
| 10 to 14 years | 21,144,669 | 21,038,575 | 21,250,763 |
| 15 to 19 years | 18,856,479 | 18,810,858 | 18,902,100 |
| 20 to 24 years | 19,092,098 | 19,024,525 | 19,159,671 |
| 25 to 34 years | 38,777,573 | 38,708,538 | 38,846,608 |
| 35 to 44 years | 43,724,771 | 43,664,619 | 43,784,923 |
| 45 to 54 years | 40,391,039 | 40,332,181 | 40,449,897 |
| 55 to 59 years | 15,484,024 | 15,399,480 | 15,568,568 |
| 60 to 64 years | 12,121,549 | 12,036,087 | 12,207,011 |
| 65 to 74 years | 18,050,132 | 18,020,846 | 18,079,418 |
| 75 to 84 years | 12,317,084 | 12,262,609 | 12,371,559 |
| 85 years and over | 3,528,956 | 3,480,688 | 3,577,224 |
| Median age (years) | 36 | 35.8 | 36.2 |
| 18 years and over | 210,275,463 | 210,248,306 | 210,302,620 |
| 21 years and over | 199,698,589 | 199,625,188 | 199,771,990 |
| 62 years and over | 40,626,693 | 40,553,362 | 40,700,024 |
| 65 years and over | 33,896,172 | 33,867,171 | 33,925,173 |
| Male | 14,380,551 | 14,359,090 | 14,402,012 |
| Female | 19,515,621 | 19,494,235 | 19,537,007 |
| **Race** | | | |
| One race | 277,555,200 | 277,434,226 | 277,676,174 |
| White | 215,451,392 | 215,211,807 | 215,690,977 |
| Black or African American | 34,313,529 | 34,219,825 | 34,407,233 |
| American Indian and Alaska Native | 2,173,834 | 2,120,420 | 2,227,248 |
| Asian | 11,743,093 | 11,690,751 | 11,795,435 |
| Native Hawaiian and Other Pacific Islander | 404,619 | 381,822 | 427,416 |
| Some other race | 13,468,733 | 13,232,139 | 13,705,327 |
| Two or more races | 5,354,685 | 5,233,711 | 5,475,659 |
| Two races including Some other race | 1,137,995 | 1,091,584 | 1,184,406 |
| Two races excluding Some other race, and Three or more races | 4,216,690 | 4,112,180 | 4,321,200 |

| General Demographic Characteristics: 2003 | Estimate | Lower Bound | Upper Bound |
|---|---|---|---|
| **Race alone or in combination with one or more other races:** | | | |
| White | 220,041,236 | 219,794,732 | 220,287,740 |
| Black or African American | 36,186,830 | 36,107,034 | 36,266,626 |
| American Indian and Alaska Native | 3,895,038 | 3,831,756 | 3,958,320 |
| Asian | 13,103,497 | 13,064,676 | 13,142,318 |
| Native Hawaiian and Other Pacific Islander | 748,933 | 717,238 | 780,628 |
| Some other race | 14,689,042 | 14,445,486 | 14,932,598 |
| **Hispanic Origin And Race** | | | |
| **Total population** | 282,909,885 | ***** | ***** |
| **Hispanic or Latino (of any race)** | 39,194,837 | 39,109,582 | 39,280,092 |
| Mexican | 25,287,619 | 25,111,572 | 25,463,666 |
| Puerto Rican | 3,717,941 | 3,644,483 | 3,791,399 |
| Cuban | 1,363,769 | 1,317,204 | 1,410,334 |
| Other Hispanic or Latino | 8,825,508 | 8,671,007 | 8,980,009 |
| **Not Hispanic or Latino** | 243,715,048 | 243,629,793 | 243,800,303 |
| White alone | 191,768,647 | 191,691,174 | 191,846,120 |
| Black or African American alone | 33,677,190 | 33,593,641 | 33,760,739 |
| American Indian or Alaska Native alone | 1,863,268 | 1,821,381 | 1,905,155 |
| Asian alone | 11,604,208 | 11,552,827 | 11,655,589 |
| Native Hawaiian and Other Pacific Islander alone | 360,462 | 340,887 | 380,037 |
| Some other race alone | 572,237 | 531,388 | 613,086 |
| **Two or more races:** | 3,869,036 | 3,774,422 | 3,963,650 |
| Two races including Some other race | 192,055 | 173,317 | 210,793 |
| Two races excluding Some other race, and Three or more races | 3,676,981 | 3,583,805 | 3,770,157 |
| **Relationship** | | | |
| **Household population** | 282,909,885 | ***** | ***** |
| Householder | 111,899,369 | 111,724,520 | 112,074,218 |
| Spouse | 56,506,554 | 56,334,633 | 56,678,475 |
| Child | 84,618,892 | 84,415,427 | 84,822,357 |
| Other relatives | 16,299,904 | 16,118,075 | 16,481,733 |
| Nonrelatives | 13,585,166 | 13,411,321 | 13,759,011 |
| Unmarried partner | 5,753,955 | 5,677,652 | 5,830,258 |

| General Demographic Characteristics: 2003 | Estimate | Lower Bound | Upper Bound |
|---|---|---|---|
| **Households By Type** | | | |
| Total households | 108,419,506 | 108,167,885 | 108,671,127 |
| Family households (families) | 73,057,960 | 72,802,717 | 73,313,203 |
| *With own children under 18 years* | 34,878,416 | 34,741,908 | 35,014,924 |
| Married-couple families | 54,688,008 | 54,414,206 | 54,961,810 |
| *With own children under 18 years* | 24,272,929 | 24,119,388 | 24,426,470 |
| Female householder, no husband present | 13,632,172 | 13,524,568 | 13,739,776 |
| *With own children under 18 years* | 8,294,092 | 8,218,038 | 8,370,146 |
| Nonfamily households | 35,361,546 | 35,189,205 | 35,533,887 |
| Householder living alone | 29,090,016 | 28,926,660 | 29,253,372 |
| *65 years and over* | 9,852,761 | 9,775,679 | 9,929,843 |
| Households with one or more people under 18 years | 38,429,174 | 38,281,921 | 38,576,427 |
| Households with one or more people 65 years and over | 24,967,316 | 24,858,983 | 25,075,649 |
| Average household size | 2.61 | 2.59 | 2.63 |
| Average family size | 3.19 | 3.18 | 3.2 |
| **Housing Occupancy** | | | |
| Total housing units | 120,879,390 | ***** | ***** |
| *Occupied housing units* | 108,419,506 | 108,167,885 | 108,671,127 |
| *Vacant housing units* | 12,459,884 | 12,208,263 | 12,711,505 |
| Homeowner vacancy rate (percent) | 1.7 | 1.6 | 1.7 |
| Rental vacancy rate (percent) | 8 | 7.9 | 8.2 |
| **Housing Tenure** | | | |
| Occupied housing units | 108,419,506 | 108,167,885 | 108,671,127 |
| *Owner-occupied* | 72,418,662 | 72,044,742 | 72,792,582 |
| *Renter-occupied* | 36,000,844 | 35,748,823 | 36,252,865 |
| Average household size of owner-occupied unit | 2.72 | 2.7 | 2.74 |
| Average household size of renter-occupied unit | 2.39 | 2.38 | 2.4 |

Source: U.S. Census Bureau, 2003 American Community Survey

# GENERAL DEMOGRAPHICS

| State | Population | Index offenses total | Violent crime total | Murder and non-negligent Manslaughter | Forcible rape | Robbery | Aggravated assault | Property crime total | Burglary | La... |
|---|---|---|---|---|---|---|---|---|---|---|
| Alabama | 4486508 | 200331 | 19931 | 303 | 1664 | 5962 | 12002 | 180400 | 42578 | 123 |
| Alaska | 643786 | 27745 | 3627 | 33 | 511 | 489 | 2594 | 24118 | 3908 | 177 |
| Arizona | 5456453 | 348467 | 30171 | 387 | 1608 | 8000 | 20176 | 318296 | 59087 | 201 |
| Arkansas | 2710079 | 112672 | 11501 | 142 | 754 | 2524 | 8081 | 101171 | 23229 | 711 |
| California | 35116033 | 1384872 | 208388 | 2395 | 10198 | 64968 | 130827 | 1176484 | 238428 | 715 |
| Colorado | 4506542 | 195936 | 15882 | 179 | 2066 | 3579 | 10058 | 180054 | 31678 | 125 |
| Connecticut | 3460503 | 103719 | 10767 | 80 | 730 | 4060 | 5897 | 92952 | 17088 | 642 |
| Delaware | 807385 | 31803 | 4836 | 26 | 358 | 1154 | 3298 | 26967 | 5355 | 185 |
| Columbia (DC) | 570898 | 45799 | 9322 | 264 | 262 | 3834 | 4962 | 36477 | 5170 | 217 |
| Florida | 16713149 | 905957 | 128721 | 911 | 6753 | 32581 | 88476 | 777236 | 177242 | 51 |
| Georgia | 8560310 | 385830 | 39271 | 606 | 2108 | 13432 | 23125 | 346559 | 73932 | 234 |
| Hawaii | 1244898 | 75238 | 3262 | 24 | 372 | 1210 | 1656 | 71976 | 12722 | 49 |
| Idaho | 1341131 | 42547 | 3419 | 36 | 497 | 240 | 2646 | 39128 | 7441 | 290 |
| Illinois | 12600620 | 506086 | 78214 | 949 | 4298 | 25272 | 47695 | 427872 | 81123 | 30 |
| Indiana | 6159068 | 230966 | 22001 | 362 | 1843 | 6612 | 13184 | 208965 | 42605 | 146 |
| Iowa | 2936760 | 101265 | 8388 | 44 | 797 | 1169 | 6378 | 92877 | 18643 | 68 |
| Kansas | 2715884 | 110997 | 10229 | 78 | 1035 | 2165 | 6951 | 100768 | 19679 | 738 |
| Kentucky | 4092891 | 118799 | 11418 | 184 | 1088 | 3063 | 7083 | 107381 | 27855 | 70 |
| Louisiana | 4482646 | 228528 | 29690 | 593 | 1529 | 7123 | 20445 | 198838 | 45350 | 13 |
| Maine | 1294464 | 34381 | 1396 | 14 | 377 | 270 | 735 | 32985 | 6965 | 24 |
| Maryland | 5458137 | 259120 | 42015 | 513 | 1370 | 13417 | 26715 | 217105 | 39765 | 14 |
| Massachusetts | 6427801 | 198890 | 31137 | 173 | 1777 | 7169 | 22018 | 167753 | 33243 | 10 |
| Michigan | 10050446 | 389366 | 54306 | 678 | 5364 | 11847 | 36417 | 335060 | 70970 | 21 |
| Minnesota | 5019720 | 177454 | 13428 | 112 | 2273 | 3937 | 7106 | 164026 | 28034 | 12 |
| Mississippi | 2871782 | 119442 | 9858 | 264 | 1127 | 3356 | 5111 | 109584 | 29593 | 70 |
| Missouri | 5672579 | 261077 | 30557 | 331 | 1465 | 7024 | 21737 | 230520 | 42721 | 15 |
| Montana | 909453 | 31948 | 3197 | 16 | 237 | 283 | 2661 | 28751 | 3289 | 23 |
| Nebraska | 1729180 | 73606 | 5428 | 48 | 464 | 1359 | 3557 | 68178 | 10329 | 51 |
| Nevada | 2173491 | 97752 | 13856 | 181 | 928 | 5118 | 7629 | 83896 | 18951 | 47 |
| New Hampshire | 1275056 | 28306 | 2056 | 12 | 446 | 413 | 1185 | 26250 | 4838 | 19 |
| New Jersey | 8590300 | 259789 | 32168 | 337 | 1347 | 13905 | 16579 | 227621 | 43898 | 14 |
| New Mexico | 1855059 | 94196 | 13719 | 152 | 1027 | 2206 | 10334 | 80477 | 19634 | 53 |
| New York | 19157532 | 537121 | 95030 | 909 | 3885 | 36653 | 53583 | 442091 | 76700 | 31 |
| North Carolina | 8320146 | 392826 | 39118 | 548 | 2196 | 12205 | 24169 | 353708 | 99535 | 22 |
| North Dakota | 634110 | 15258 | 496 | 5 | 163 | 58 | 270 | 14762 | 2243 | 11 |

| Motor vehicle theft | Index offense rate | Violent Crime rate | Murder and non-negligent man-slaughter rate | Forcible rape rate | Robbery rate | Aggra-vated assault rate | Property crime rate | Burglary rate | Larceny-theft rate | Motor vehicle theft rate |
|---|---|---|---|---|---|---|---|---|---|---|
| 3890 | 4465.2 | 444.2 | 6.8 | 37.1 | 132.9 | 267.5 | 4020.9 | 949 | 2762.3 | 309.6 |
| 2471 | 4309.7 | 563.4 | 5.1 | 79.4 | 76 | 402.9 | 3746.3 | 607 | 2755.4 | 383.8 |
| 57668 | 6386.3 | 552.9 | 7.1 | 29.5 | 146.6 | 369.8 | 5833.4 | 1082.9 | 3693.6 | 1056.9 |
| 813 | 4157.5 | 424.4 | 5.2 | 27.8 | 93.1 | 298.2 | 3733.1 | 857.1 | 2624.6 | 251.4 |
| 222364 | 3943.7 | 593.4 | 6.8 | 29 | 185 | 372.6 | 3350.3 | 679 | 2038.1 | 633.2 |
| 23183 | 4347.8 | 352.4 | 4 | 45.8 | 79.4 | 223.2 | 3995.4 | 702.9 | 2778 | 514.4 |
| 1572 | 2997.2 | 311.1 | 2.3 | 21.1 | 117.3 | 170.4 | 2686.1 | 493.8 | 1857.9 | 334.4 |
| 5057 | 3939 | 599 | 3.2 | 44.3 | 142.9 | 408.5 | 3340 | 663.3 | 2298.2 | 378.6 |
| 599 | 8022.3 | 1632.9 | 46.2 | 45.9 | 671.6 | 869.2 | 6389.4 | 905.6 | 3802.4 | 1681.4 |
| 8516 | 5420.6 | 770.2 | 5.5 | 40.4 | 194.9 | 529.4 | 4650.4 | 1060.5 | 3060.3 | 529.6 |
| 8036 | 4507.2 | 458.8 | 7.1 | 24.6 | 156.9 | 270.1 | 4048.4 | 863.7 | 2740.4 | 444.3 |
| 910 | 6043.7 | 262 | 1.9 | 29.9 | 97.2 | 133 | 5781.7 | 1021.9 | 3963.7 | 796 |
| 2627 | 3172.5 | 254.9 | 2.7 | 37.1 | 17.9 | 197.3 | 2917.5 | 554.8 | 2166.8 | 195.9 |
| 4857 | 4016.4 | 620.7 | 7.5 | 34.1 | 200.6 | 378.5 | 3395.6 | 643.8 | 2395.9 | 356 |
| 0287 | 3750 | 357.2 | 5.9 | 29.9 | 107.4 | 214.1 | 3392.8 | 691.7 | 2371.7 | 329.4 |
| 823 | 3448.2 | 285.6 | 1.5 | 27.1 | 39.8 | 217.2 | 3162.6 | 634.8 | 2329.5 | 198.3 |
| 212 | 4087 | 376.6 | 2.9 | 38.1 | 79.7 | 255.9 | 3710.3 | 724.6 | 2720.2 | 265.5 |
| 750 | 2902.6 | 279 | 4.5 | 26.6 | 74.8 | 173.1 | 2623.6 | 680.6 | 1729.2 | 213.8 |
| 0186 | 5098.1 | 662.3 | 13.2 | 34.1 | 158.9 | 456.1 | 4435.7 | 1011.7 | 2973.7 | 450.3 |
| 429 | 2656 | 107.8 | 1.1 | 29.1 | 20.9 | 56.8 | 2548.2 | 538.1 | 1899.7 | 110.4 |
| 4020 | 4747.4 | 769.8 | 9.4 | 25.1 | 245.8 | 489.5 | 3977.6 | 728.5 | 2625.8 | 623.3 |
| 6588 | 3094.2 | 484.4 | 2.7 | 27.6 | 111.5 | 342.5 | 2609.8 | 517.2 | 1679 | 413.6 |
| 9723 | 3874.1 | 540.3 | 6.7 | 53.4 | 117.9 | 362.3 | 3333.8 | 706.1 | 2132.9 | 494.7 |
| 3842 | 3535.1 | 267.5 | 2.2 | 45.3 | 78.4 | 141.6 | 3267.6 | 558.5 | 2433.4 | 275.8 |
| 523 | 4159.2 | 343.3 | 9.2 | 39.2 | 116.9 | 178 | 3815.9 | 1030.5 | 2453.8 | 331.6 |
| 7878 | 4602.4 | 538.7 | 5.8 | 25.8 | 123.8 | 383.2 | 4063.8 | 753.1 | 2819.2 | 491.5 |
| 783 | 3512.9 | 351.5 | 1.8 | 26.1 | 31.1 | 292.6 | 3161.4 | 361.6 | 2603.7 | 196.1 |
| 409 | 4256.7 | 313.9 | 2.8 | 26.8 | 78.6 | 205.7 | 3942.8 | 597.3 | 2974.8 | 370.6 |
| 7486 | 4497.5 | 637.5 | 8.3 | 42.7 | 235.5 | 351 | 3860 | 871.9 | 2183.5 | 804.5 |
| 944 | 2220 | 161.2 | 0.9 | 35 | 32.4 | 92.9 | 2058.7 | 379.4 | 1526.8 | 152.5 |
| 5739 | 3024.2 | 374.5 | 3.9 | 15.7 | 161.9 | 193 | 2649.7 | 511 | 1722.7 | 416 |
| 437 | 5077.8 | 739.5 | 8.2 | 55.4 | 118.9 | 557.1 | 4338.2 | 1058.4 | 2878.9 | 400.9 |
| 7366 | 2803.7 | 496 | 4.7 | 20.3 | 191.3 | 279.7 | 2307.7 | 400.4 | 1660.1 | 247.2 |
| 4866 | 4721.4 | 470.2 | 6.6 | 26.4 | 146.7 | 290.5 | 4251.2 | 1196.3 | 2756 | 298.9 |
| 018 | 2406.2 | 78.2 | 0.8 | 25.7 | 9.1 | 42.6 | 2328 | 353.7 | 1813.7 | 160.5 |

| State | Population | Index offenses total | Violent crime total | Murder and non-negligent Manslaughter | Forcible rape | Robbery | Aggravated assault | Property crime total | Burglary | La... |
|---|---|---|---|---|---|---|---|---|---|---|
| Ohio | 11421267 | 469104 | 40128 | 526 | 4809 | 17871 | 16922 | 428976 | 99164 | 287 |
| Oklahoma | 3493714 | 165715 | 17587 | 163 | 1573 | 2966 | 12885 | 148128 | 35171 | 100 |
| Oregon | 3521515 | 171443 | 10298 | 72 | 1238 | 2742 | 6246 | 161145 | 25696 | 118 |
| Pennsylvania | 12335091 | 350446 | 49578 | 624 | 3731 | 17163 | 28060 | 300868 | 55610 | 212 |
| Rhode Island | 1069725 | 38393 | 3051 | 41 | 395 | 916 | 1699 | 35342 | 6415 | 240 |
| South Carolina | 4107183 | 217569 | 33761 | 298 | 1959 | 5774 | 25730 | 183808 | 43745 | 123 |
| South Dakota | 761063 | 17342 | 1350 | 11 | 361 | 117 | 861 | 15992 | 3034 | 121 |
| Tennessee | 5797289 | 290961 | 41562 | 420 | 2290 | 9413 | 29439 | 249399 | 61248 | 161 |
| Texas | 21779893 | 1130292 | 126018 | 1302 | 8508 | 37580 | 78628 | 1004274 | 212602 | 688 |
| Utah | 2316256 | 103129 | 5488 | 47 | 943 | 1140 | 3358 | 97641 | 15124 | 747 |
| Vermont | 616592 | 15600 | 658 | 13 | 126 | 77 | 442 | 14942 | 3489 | 106 |
| Virginia | 7293542 | 229039 | 21256 | 388 | 1839 | 6961 | 12068 | 207783 | 31757 | 157 |
| Washington | 6068996 | 309931 | 20964 | 184 | 2734 | 5797 | 12249 | 288967 | 54948 | 193 |
| West Virginia | 1801873 | 45320 | 4221 | 57 | 328 | 657 | 3179 | 41099 | 9677 | 275 |
| Wisconsin | 5441196 | 176987 | 12238 | 154 | 1237 | 4713 | 6134 | 164749 | 27926 | 123 |
| Wyoming | 498703 | 17858 | 1364 | 15 | 148 | 93 | 1108 | 16494 | 2448 | 133 |
| United States-Total | 288368698 | 11877218 | 1426325 | 16204 | 95136 | 420637 | 894348 | 10450893 | 2151875 | 705 |

| Motor vehicle theft | Index offense rate | Violent Crime rate | Murder and non-negligent man-slaughter rate | Forcible rape rate | Robbery rate | Aggra-vated assault rate | Property crime rate | Burglary rate | Larceny theft rate | Motor vehicle theft rate |
|---|---|---|---|---|---|---|---|---|---|---|
| 2767 | 4107.3 | 351.3 | 4.6 | 42.1 | 156.5 | 148.2 | 3755.9 | 868.2 | 2513.3 | 374.5 |
| 2772 | 4743.2 | 503.4 | 4.7 | 45 | 84.9 | 368.8 | 4239.8 | 1006.7 | 2867.6 | 365.6 |
| 6524 | 4868.4 | 292.4 | 2 | 35.2 | 77.9 | 177.4 | 4576 | 729.7 | 3377.1 | 469.2 |
| 2817 | 2841 | 401.9 | 5.1 | 30.2 | 139.1 | 227.5 | 2439.1 | 450.8 | 1722.2 | 266 |
| 876 | 3589.1 | 285.2 | 3.8 | 36.9 | 85.6 | 158.8 | 3303.8 | 599.7 | 2248.3 | 455.8 |
| 6867 | 5297.3 | 822 | 7.3 | 47.7 | 140.6 | 626.5 | 4475.3 | 1065.1 | 2999.5 | 410.7 |
| 19 | 2278.7 | 177.4 | 1.4 | 47.4 | 15.4 | 113.1 | 2101.3 | 398.7 | 1595 | 107.6 |
| 6541 | 5018.9 | 716.9 | 7.2 | 39.5 | 162.4 | 507.8 | 4302 | 1056.5 | 2787.7 | 457.8 |
| 02680 | 5189.6 | 578.6 | 6 | 39.1 | 172.5 | 361 | 4611 | 976.1 | 3163.4 | 471.4 |
| 722 | 4452.4 | 236.9 | 2 | 40.7 | 49.2 | 145 | 4215.5 | 653 | 3229.1 | 333.4 |
| 69 | 2530 | 106.7 | 2.1 | 20.4 | 12.5 | 71.7 | 2423.3 | 565.9 | 1732.8 | 124.7 |
| 8478 | 3140.3 | 291.4 | 5.3 | 25.2 | 95.4 | 165.5 | 2848.9 | 435.4 | 2160.1 | 253.3 |
| 0493 | 5106.8 | 345.4 | 3 | 45 | 95.5 | 201.8 | 4761.4 | 905.4 | 3188.8 | 667.2 |
| 898 | 2515.2 | 234.3 | 3.2 | 18.2 | 36.5 | 176.4 | 2280.9 | 537.1 | 1527.5 | 216.3 |
| 3458 | 3252.7 | 224.9 | 2.8 | 22.7 | 86.6 | 112.7 | 3027.8 | 513.2 | 2267.2 | 247.3 |
| 43 | 3580.9 | 273.5 | 3 | 29.7 | 18.6 | 222.2 | 3307.4 | 490.9 | 2667.5 | 149 |
| 246096 | 4118.8 | 494.6 | 5.6 | 33 | 145.9 | 310.1 | 3624.1 | 746.2 | 2445.8 | 432.1 |

**MONTGOMERY, ALABAMA.**
*Motto: 'We dare defend our rights'*

Not even the fact that it has a celebrated civil rights history can save Montgomery from being known as the place that tries and fails. It had to have four attempts before succeeding to become the capital of Alabama – a state, incidentally, which ranks amongst America's 'least livable'.

Montgomery is named after General Richard Mongomery who died in the American Revolutionary War attempting to capture Quebec, Canada. Still on the 'tries hard but fails' line, Montgomery has been described as: 'Trying hard to be the state capital but not succeeding very well.'

One of its landmarks should certainly be Rosa Parks Highway, named after the black civil rights leader who refused to give up her bus seat to a white man on a Montgomery route. Her actions triggered the national civil rights movement and Rosa Parks became a civil rights heroine. Despite the fact that Rev Dr Martin Luther King also marched from Selma,

Alabama, to Montgomery, this historic district's contribution to past memorable events is to boast a road of old bungalows.

Downtown Montgomery is always deserted – aside from a few vagrants hanging outside a crumbling old hotel that now serves as a homeless shelter. In the suburbs – and for that read road after road of identical small ranch houses, all with

| Population (year 2000) | 201,568 |
|---|---|
| Males | 94,573 (46.9%) |
| Females | 106,995 (53.1%) |
| Elevation | 250 feet |
| County | Montgomery |
| Land area | 155.4 square miles |
| Zip code | 36104 - 36117. |
| Median resident age | 32.9 years |
| Median household income | $35,627 (year 2000) |
| Median house value | $86,800 (year 2000) |

| Races in Montgomery | |
|---|---|
| White Non-Hispanic | 47.1% |
| Hispanic | 1.2% |
| Other race | 0.6% |
| American Indian | 0.5% |
| Two or more races | 1.0% |
| Black | 49.6% |
| **Ancestries** | |
| United States (9.4%), English (6.7%), Irish (5.4%), German (4.5%), Scotch-Irish (2.2%), Scottish (1.8%) | |

| For population 25 years and over in Montgomery | |
|---|---|
| High school or higher | 80.7% |
| Bachelor's degree or higher | 29.4% |
| Graduate or professional degree | 11.3% |
| Unemployed | 6.9% |
| Mean travel time to work | 19.6 minutes |

| For population 15 years and over in Montgomery | |
|---|---|
| Never married | 30.7% |
| Now married | 47.3% |
| Separated | 2.5% |
| Widowed | 7.5% |
| Divorced | 12.0% |
| 2.1% Foreign born (0.8% Asia, 0.6% Europe, 0.4% Latin America) | |

| Crime | |
|---|---|
| Violent Crime risk | 26 murders (12.8 per 100,000) |
| Property Crime risk | 3,252 burglaries (1607.1 per 100,000) |

signs warning of 24-hour security patrols – it's the same. A stranger in town could well be forgiven for thinking the place was devoid of civilised human life. In fact, Montgomery is so uncivilised that it boasts just one Starbucks, and that's tucked away in a small shopping mall surrounded by freeways.

One of the few things in Montgomery that could be interesting- – if anyone could find it- – is the F. Scott and Zelda Fitzgerald Museum. The Twenties flapper girl turned roaring lunatic was born on South Street but spent much of her short life wandering aimlessly around Europe with her author husband getting drunk. We'd like to say that Scott wrote some of his greatest work while renting a house on Felder Street, Montgomery. Sadly, he didn't. The couple soon got bored with Alabama and went back to their wandering ways. Scott died of a heart attack in Hollywood in 1940 while Zelda perished in a lunatic asylum fire eight years later. The Felder Street house is now a museum but – typical of Montgomery – the only clue that it exists is just one wooden sign post on a suburban road.

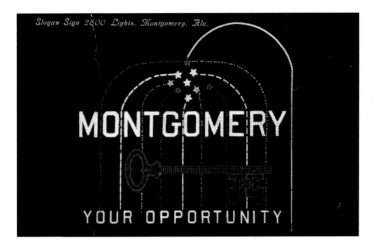

At least Rosa Parks got a road named after her. But few in their right mind would venture along it. Amongst the occasional sad and tired-looking bit of greenery along Rosa Parks Highway are equally sad and tired-looking crack addicts – which is probably one of the reasons why Alabama needs its 11,378 Law Enforcement Officers. That and the fact that, among 'medium sized' cities with populations between 200,000 and 500,000, Montgomery ranks second in the crime list of shame, due to its significantly high rates of murder, robbery and assaults. In one year alone, 473 kgs of cocaine were seized and 10,640 thefts of varying degrees were perpetrated.

Dubious notable facts about Montgomery are that the average temperature in December is 60 degrees and that the world's first Electric Trolley System was introduced here in 1886.

People with the misfortune of having to have put Montgomery, Alabama, on their birth certificate include singers Nat King Cole and Hank Williams and baseball stars Hank Aaron and Willie Mays.

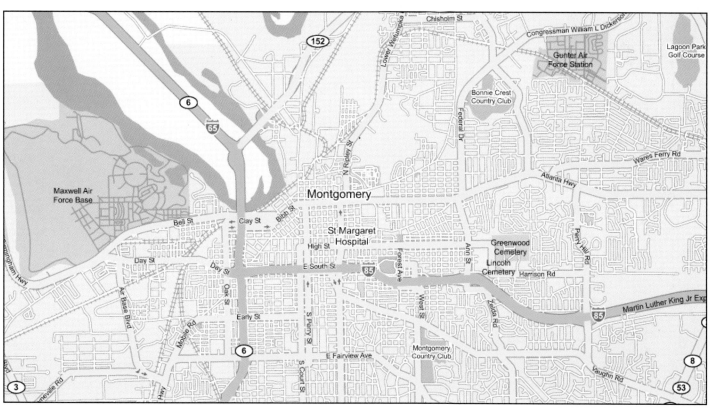

## LAKE HAVASU CITY, ARIZONA
*God enriches (state motto of Arizona)*

Lake Havasu City is one of those places where you think you're going to laugh at the locals – 'hey wouldn't it be great to visit the town that bought London Bridge by mistake' – but it turns out the joke's on you. You drive for an eternity to discover it's a blisteringly hot, unshaded little pimple on the

edge of an artificial lake in the middle of Arizona.

The locals thought they were getting Tower Bridge, with the cool hydraulics that lift the middle section and the Victorian frilly bits. They got a great grey lump of unremarkable London stone which squats unhappily in the glaring sunshine looking... boring.

But the hapless Havasuvians got their own back. You come to laugh – you stay to suffer. It's so isolated that once in, you have to stay at least one night in what is really one of the tackiest, most plastic, garish, ghastly, tourist traps in the world.

At the foot of the poor old bridge is so-called English Village, a nightmare interpretation of Merrie Olde England as designed by a Burger King architect on acid.

We sent along an English-born spy to enjoy a full appreciation of the place and she returned shocked and saddened to report: 'It is a travesty.

'Lake Havasu is certainly the only place in Arizona where you can see a red telephone box (it wasn't working, so at least that was authentic) and a pretend Beefeater in full costume, poor sweaty sucker, alongside a busty serving wench and a Ye Olde Pubbe with no beer.

| Population (year 2000) | 41,938 |
|---|---|
| Males | 20,624 (49.2%) |
| Females | Females: 21,314 (50.8%) |
| Elevation | 735 feet |
| County | Mohave |
| Land area | 43.0 square miles |
| Zip code | 86403, 86404, 86406. |
| Median resident age | 47.5 years |
| Median household income | $36,499 |
| Median house value | $98,500 |

| Races in Lake Havasu City | |
|---|---|
| White Non-Hispanic | 89.5% |
| Hispanic | 7.9% |
| Other race | 2.5% |
| American Indian | 1.3% |
| Two or more races | 1.5% |
| Black | - |
| **Ancestries** | |
| German (21.3%), English (15.9%), Irish (14.5%), Italian (7.2%), United States (6.6%), French (4.8%) | |

| For population 25 years and over in Lake Havasu City | |
|---|---|
| High school or higher | 83.8% |
| Bachelor's degree or higher | 13.1% |
| Graduate or professional degree | 4.9% |
| Unemployed | 5.5% |
| Mean travel time to work | 16.9 minutes |

| For population 15 years and over in Lake Havasu City | |
|---|---|
| Never married | 14.8% |
| Now married | 63.2% |
| Separated | 1.6% |
| Widowed | 9.0% |
| Divorced | 11.4% |
| 5.6% Foreign born (2.4% Latin America, 1.7% Europe, 0.9% North America) | |

| Crime | |
|---|---|
| Violent Crime risk | 1 murder (2.2 per 100,000) |
| Property Crime risk | 323 burglaries (724.2 per 100,000) |

'However, there's nothing to eat but greasy burger-joint food in places with names like Shakespeare's Rib Shack, and nothing to drink but terrifying cocktails in pint glasses with parasols. The beer is non-alcoholic or American – which to anyone who is there because they love English ale, is almost the same thing. There are even Pearly Kings and Queens wandering about trying to make quaint Cockney remarks in rhyming slang. God, it's painful.'

That's what Lake Havasu is famous for. But what else does the place have to offer that lures tourists and has swelled its permanent population to 47,000? Well, it caters for trailer-dwelling sun-lovers (there's a huge RV park) and conventions looking for fun on the cheap, so you can imagine the motels. Our researcher's had smelly sheets, broken air conditioning, no water – 'only Pepsi or Coke, it's more hygienic, was the excuse – and a 24-hour casino. There is no shortage of casinos here, but not the sort that you'd find James Bond in, of course.

It's all so artificial. Lake Havasu, 45 miles long, is not a natural lake; it was created on the Colorado River when the

Parker Dam was built in the 1930s. Its name is borrowed from the Mohave for 'Green Water'. And the bridge, as we know, was purchased from the city of London, where it was about to be dismantled because it was sinking into the mud of the River Thames.

Engineering magnate and property developer Robert P. McCulloch bought it and rebuilt it stone by stone in Lake Havasu, opening it in 1971. Until they saw the finished product, would-be investors had believed they were getting the much more famous and more attractive Tower Bridge, but that remains firmly astride the Thames.

What summed it up for our spy was a visit to the one bar that set itself the task of attracting the more swinging Lake Havasu set. On the wall was a slogan that rather reflected the tone. 'Have a Brew. Have a Screw. Havasu.' Lovely sentiment, eh? And only a few yards to Ye Olde Curiosity Shoppe Merrie England trinket store.

Lake Havasu City got second best. As it has with everything else. Engineer McCulloch, whose most famous product was the brand of chainsaw that bore his name, has succeeded in creating an Arizona Chainsaw Massacre of good taste in this once-peaceful desert.

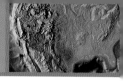

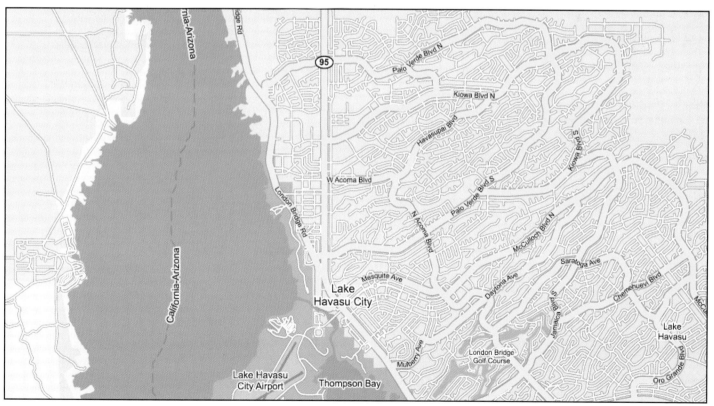

### PHOENIX, ARIZONA
*Ditat Deus (God enriches)*
*(State motto of Arizona)*

Phoenix and Arizona run off the tongue when you're singing the song after a few beers. In reality, there really is nothing to sing about. We love this summing up of Phoenix in one highly reputable guide book: 'Phoenix in particular can

be seen as the bloated spider at the center of the web, sucking the juices from the rest of the state. By far the largest city in Arizona, it holds only minimal appeal for tourists.'

It goes on to describe Phoenix and Tucson as 'two of the most ludicrous cities on earth because there's no logical reason for their existence'.

The state motto is 'Ditat Deus'. It means 'God enriches' – but since Phoenix has stolen most of the state's riches, it is pretty meaningless.

In southern Arizona, there isn't any scenery, just a grotesquely swollen population in those two towns. Water supplies are poor. Both residential and tourist appeal is minimal. Adds our favourite guide book, The Rough Guide to the South West: 'Phoenix's fragile grip on reality is highlighted by the fact that it was built on the ruins of a long-lost desert civilisation...'

Until 1350, the valleys of southern Arizona were home to the Hokoham people who took so much from the land there was nothing left to survive on. When it really began life in the 1860s, Phoenix was a little farming town in the heart of the Salt River Valley, with a bright future thanks to the irrigation

| Population (year 2000) | 1,321,045 |
|---|---|
| Males | 671,760 (50.9%) |
| Females | 649,285 (49.1%) |
| Elevation | 1072 feet |
| County | Maricopa |
| Land area | 474.9 square miles |
| Zip code | 85003 - 85085. |
| Median resident age | 30.7 years |
| Median household income | $41,207 |
| Median house value | $112,600 |

| Races in Phoenix | |
|---|---|
| White Non-Hispanic | 55.8% |
| Hispanic | 34.1% |
| Other race | 16.4% |
| American Indian | 2.7% |
| Two or more races | 3.3% |
| Black | 5.1% |
| Ancestries | |
| German (13.7%), Irish (9.4%), English (8.0%), Italian (4.4%), United States (4.0%), Polish (2.4%) | |

| For population 25 years and over in Phoenix | |
|---|---|
| High school or higher | 76.6% |
| Bachelor's degree or higher | 22.7% |
| Graduate or professional degree | 7.6% |
| Unemployed | 5.6% |
| Mean travel time to work | 26.1 minutes |

| For population 15 years and over in Phoenix | |
|---|---|
| Never married | 29.9% |
| Now married | 51.0% |
| Separated | 2.4% |
| Widowed | 4.8% |
| Divorced | 11.9% |
| 19.5% Foreign born (15.5% Latin America) | |

| Crime | |
|---|---|
| Violent Crime risk | 177 murders (12.6 per 100,000) |
| Property Crime risk | 16,855 burglaries (1199.7 per 100,000) |

systems left by the ancient Indians. Within a century, however, Phoenix was well on the way to its 'bloated spider' existence. Or, as writer Edward Abbey described it, 'the blob that is eating Arizona' because of its skill in acquiring financial and political clout to ensure self-survival - no matter the cost to any other communities. In short, Phoenix takes what it wants and to hell with anyone else.

Today, Arizona is America's eight largest city, with over a million people living within its sprawling boundaries. And it is still growing with obscene speed, swallowing up the entire valley, and almost revelling in its reputation as the most unpleasant city in the South West.

'Las Vegas with no casinos, LA with no beach' is how Phoenix can be summed up.

On top of all this are high crime statistics – with Phoenix having the fourth highest number of car thefts out of the US's big cities – and high temperatures. Can you imagine anything worse than being in a steaming, stinking sprawl where temperatures can reach 105 degrees?

In 2005 Phoenix was named the nation's 'Sweatiest City' in a survey by the Old Spice company that produces men's fragrances to cover up such body odors. The rankings were based on the average U.S. male/female height/weight and the average high temperature during June, July and August. The sweat level was analyzed based on the assumption that an individual was walking for one hour. It was found that the average Phoenix resident produced .76 liters of sweat per hour during a typical summer day in 2004 – the equivalent of more than two 12-ounce glasses of lemonade. In a two-hour period, residents of Phoenix collectively produced more than enough sweat to equal a 12-ounce glass of lemonade for everyone in the state of Arizona. In recognition of the dubious award, Old Spice delivered a year's supply of Old Spice Red Zone antiperspirant to Phoenix Mayor Phil Gordon.

None of this stops the good people of Phoenix complaining, of course. If a place is hot, it's hot and not even a lifetime's supply of deodorant is going to save you. The place is dry, scorched and dead. Some say that description could also fit some of the inhabitants of Phoenix (those who don't give out a lemonade bottle's worth of sweat in an embarrassingly short time) but even we think that's going too far. Well, OK, no we don't. A 'Hell's Kitchen', 'Devil's Oven' and 'Satan's Sandpit' are all aptly suggested alternative names of Phoenix, where even the moon seems to emanate searing heat.

'It's a humid but dusty sprawling wasteland burnt brown by the heat,' one visitor reported to us. 'The notion that this part of the world languishes in sun-kissed "dry heat" is nonsense. For most of the year, it is as sweaty as a bear's armpit.' In short, said our researcher, there's only one thing worse than a high-rise landscape and that's the low-rise sprawl of Phoenix.

It is a good job so few wish to visit Phoenix because there is no Amtrak service and travelling across town takes hours. One who dared to pay Phoenix a visit was terrified of committing some small misdemeanour. This is because of the zealous sheriff who has ruled there for years, with most of the population scared to oppose him. It's jail if you are caught drink-driving. In fact, it's jail for most things, which is why there's an overflow prison tent city, neatly located next to the town dump. A day's cruising around Phoenix will be rewarded with the sight of male and female chain gangs picking up litter.

Incredibly, people do drop into Phoenix, but only to spend vast fortunes at the luxury resorts and spas. Sightseeing is not on the agenda. As the guide-books say, apart from the Heard Museum's Native American displays, the cactuses at the Desert Botanical Garden and Frank Lloyd-Wright's architecture at Taliesin West, you wouldn't miss much if you wiped Phoenix off your travel map altogether.

## LITTLE ROCK, ARKANSAS
*The Natural State, and*
*Regnat Populus (The People Rule)*
*(State mottos of Arkansas)*

Litttle Rock is famous but for all the wrong reasons. It first got on the map as a bastion of the Confederacy in the America Civil War, with an arsenal churning out weaponry to enable those Southern sophisticates to enjoy their traditional lifestyle – and their low-cost labor market – without interference from them damn Yankees.

Then in 1957, just to prove that this sweltering fleapit of oppression and bigotry could maintain worthwhile traditions, there was the famous 'Central High School' incident. President Eisenhower, who had seen enough of the ethos of racial superiority when he crushed Nazi Germany, instituted a law which annoyed the tobacco chewers in places like Little Rock: namely that uppity negro kids had the same right to schooling as any bone-headed, bigoted, white kids.

National Guards had to be called in to the state capital to protect a handful of black students from being torn limb from limb as they strode past the hissing, spitting defenders of white supremacy. The TV newsreel pictures were said to shock the world but no-one in Little Rock saw what the problem was.

Its third claim to Warholian glory came with the election of former Arkansas governor William Jefferson Blythe IV Clinton as forty-second President of the United States. Clinton – born in Hope (that's Hope, Arkansas) and raised in nearby Hot Springs – brought fleeting hope to the state but ended up in hot water, being only the second president to be impeached. But he is credited with overseeing the economic miracle of his age… Under him, Arkansas became the biggest supplier of chicken parts in the whole of the United States.

Look at the map and you'll notice that Little Rock is located in the geographical center of the state, in the center of what is commonly referred to as 'the Sunbelt', and in the

| | |
|---|---|
| Population (year 2000) | 183,133 |
| Males | 86,322 (47.1%) |
| Females | 96,811 (52.9%) |
| Elevation | 350 feet |
| County | Pulaski |
| Land area | 116.2 square miles |
| Zip code | 72201 - 72227. |
| Median resident age | 34.5 years |
| Median household income | $37,572 |
| Median house value | $89,300 |

| Races in Little Rock | |
|---|---|
| White Non-Hispanic | 54.0% |
| Hispanic | 2.7% |
| Other race | 1.3% |
| American Indian | 0.7% |
| Two or more races | 1.3% |
| Black | 40.4% |
| **Ancestries** | |

Ancestries: English (8.8%), German (8.6%), United States (7.8%), Irish (7.3%), Scotch-Irish (2.6%), French (2.0%).

| For population 25 years and over in Little Rock | |
|---|---|
| High school or higher | 85.9% |
| Bachelor's degree or higher | 35.5% |
| Graduate or professional degree | 13.4% |
| Unemployed | 6.0% |
| Mean travel time to work | 19.5 minutes |

| For population 15 years and over in Little Rock | |
|---|---|
| Never married | 29.7% |
| Now married | 48.8% |
| Separated | 2.3% |
| Widowed | 6.7% |
| Divorced | 12.5% |

3.8% Foreign born (1.5% Asia, 1.3% Latin America, 0.7% Europe)

| Crime | |
|---|---|
| Violent Crime risk | 41 murders (22.1 per 100,000) |
| Property Crime risk | 4,826 burglaries (2599.6 per 100,000) |

center of the USA. It was here in the 18th century that the first European explorers noticed 'La Petite Roche', the little rock on the bank of the Arkansas River that iss the site of this city. They also encountered the friendly Quapaw Indians – too friendly, because their policy of peaceful coexistence was rewarded by the US government forcing them to surrender their Arkansas lands in 1818 and 1824.

As late as 1819, when the Arkansas territory was created, the Little Rock area was still little more than a sweltering wilderness. Not much had changed by 1836 when it became the state capital. Many say that not much has changed since.

OK, so you can get your antebellum mansion fix here in Little Rock if you want,. You can also eat steaks the size of premature babies at Doe's Eat Place; the night one of our correspondents dined there the steaks started at 4lbs. But the civic exhortations to have fun and frolics on the banks of the Arkansas River fall flatter than a can of Dr. Pepper left open for three days. For if, after admiring the cast-iron cannons that once turned union troops into mincemeat, you are tempted

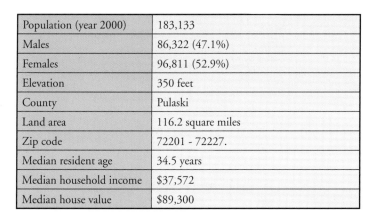

to stray far from downtown, you will be required to turn your watches back 200 years.

Black people still live on the wrong side of the tracks and many of the officers of the law still looks like Boss Hog on steroids. The reasons for this time warp are clear: whenever Arkansas rates highly in something, it's usually bad. The U.S. Census Bureau, for instance, says that Arkansas' poverty rate is the second highest in the nation (after Mississippi). And in recent years, it has actually been rising.

In this environment, many of Little Rock's youth tend to shrug off their worries in a haze of drugs. According to the narcotics agencies, crack and powdered cocaine 'continue to be a significant and long-term problem in the city. But recently the 'primary drug of concern has become methamphetamine'.

The natural result of all of this is an epidemic of crime. A visiting journalist reported: 'A nasty undercurrent cuts through this part of the world like Warfarin shredding the innards of a sewer rat. Best stay away.'

A bit over-dramatic? Not if you have been one of the unfortunate victims of this lawless place. Within one year, the city's population of 185,00 suffered 41 murders, 116

rapes, 884 robberies, 1,370 assaults, 4,826 burglaries, 11,930 larcenies. This put its crime index at 850, against the US average of 330.

The Arkansas state motto is 'Regnat Populus', which means 'The People Rule'. (Rule by fear, we assume.) But Latin references are obviously a bit hi'fallutin' for Arkansas folk. Those worthy sentiments are nowadays generally replaced by the substitute, more easily understood motto 'The Natural State'. And the natural state of Little Rock is not one to be envied.

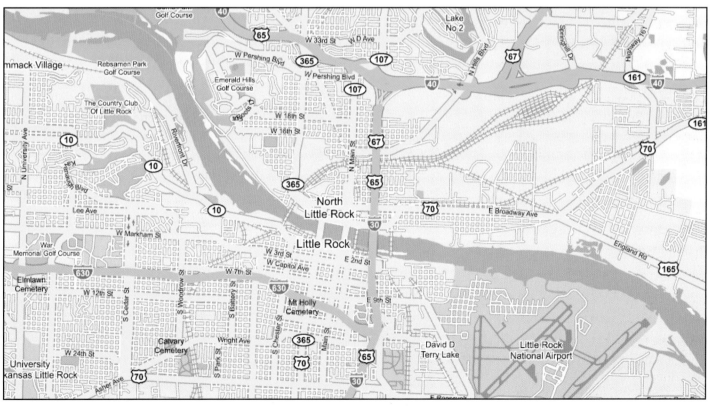

## MODESTO, CALIFORNIA
### *I have found it (state motto of California)*

THE man who put the modest in Modesto knew what he was doing. Somewhere between the Sierra Nevada Mountains and the coast, the California of Beach Boys fun and sun-soaked excess peters out in this Nowheresville of utter mediocrity.

Modesto is like some transplant from the Mid-West. Which is not surprising: its descendants are those Oklahoma refugees from the Great Depression who fled one dustbowl to come and try to work in another. Half a million Oakies migrated via Route 66, and one-eighth of California's population now claim Oakie ancestry.

Many of the two million descendents of this economic exodus remain in the San Joaquin Valley, where their forebears ended up after their arduous journey west. Their lasting legacy is their churches, politics, music, tastes, values and conversational limitations. The people are as closed as

the downtown shops after 6.00pm, with none of the free-and-breezy gentleness and affability associated with other Californians.

Modesto itself, with its 200,000-plus inhabitants, has little to distinguish it except for a rather pompous civic pride that is proclaimed on a 100-year-old steel arch on the main road into town. 'Water, wealth, contentment, health,' it says. Well, one out of four ain't bad, because there aren't many rich people here, water is in short supply and the area harbors some peculiarly local ailments.

According to the normally generous Insight Guides for visitors to California: 'The San Joaquin Valley is known for some unpleasant natural phenomena. "Valley fever", a little known respiratory illness, is spread when strong winds stir up the spores of a fungus indigenous to the arid soil in some parts of the valley. And in December and January dense "tule fog" blankets the area for days at a time, making driving

hazardous.'

But who cares? This is intensive farming country, where the alluvial soil of the valley has made it the biggest producer in California. So it's flat and boring and, if you can see little of it because of the 'tule fog', there's little you're missing.

Modesto is a 'nearby' sort of place – that's to say, everything that is interesting is nearby, not there. The official town website boasts 'nearby' golf, water sports and hiking. And it talks of 'day trip options from Modesto that include San Francisco, Sacramento, and Yosemite National Park'. All true, and one the one good thing about Modesto is the array of signposts that point you straight through it and out of it, in the direction of places far more appealing.

American Graffiti, that celebration of bored American

| Population (year 2000) | 188,856 |
|---|---|
| Males | 91,572 (48.5%) |
| Females | 97,284 (51.5%) |
| Elevation | 87 feet |
| County | Stanislaus |
| Land area | 35.8 square miles |
| Zip code | 95350 - 95358. |
| Median resident age | 32.7 years |
| Median household income | $40,394 |
| Median house value | $126,000 |

| Races in Modesto | |
|---|---|
| White Non-Hispanic | 59.6% |
| Hispanic | 25.6% |
| Other race | 18.8% |
| American Indian | 2.6% |
| Two or more races | 5.9% |
| Black | 4.0% |
| Ancestries | |
| German (11.5%), Irish (8.8%), English (8.4%), United States (4.7%), Italian (4.5%), Portuguese (3.4%) | |

| For population 25 years and over in Modesto | |
|---|---|
| High school or higher | 75.0% |
| Bachelor's degree or higher | 16.5% |
| Graduate or professional degree | 5.3% |
| Unemployed | 10.1% |
| Mean travel time to work | 25.7 minutes |

| For population 15 years and over in Modesto | |
|---|---|
| Never married | 25.6% |
| Now married | 53.6% |
| Separated | 2.5% |
| Widowed | 6.4% |
| Divorced | 11.8% |
| 15.8% Foreign born (7.8% Latin America, 5.1% Asia, 1.6% Europe) | |

| Crime | |
|---|---|
| Violent Crime risk | 5 murders (2.6 per 100,000) |
| Property Crime risk | 1,819 burglaries (929.0 per 100,000) |

youth taking to their cars to parade up and down the main drag because they can't quite escape the place, was set in Modesto. The city celebrates this notoriety every single year – urging visitors to 'pull out those poodle skirts and hoola hoops and join us for the festivities!' Wow.

George Lucas, of Star Wars fame, was born here too. Needless to say, he left as soon as he could.

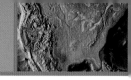

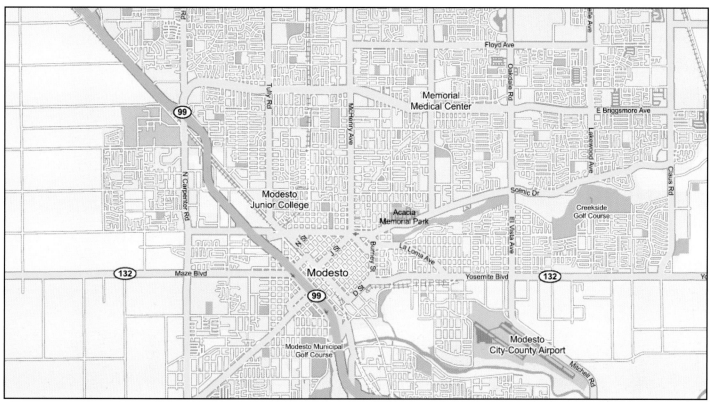

### OXNARD, CALIFORNIA
*Motto: 'The City that Cares'*

There's no wrong side and right side of the tracks in Oxnard. Both sides of the railroad line, that slices through the tired heart of this paint-peeling, soul-sapping California coastal city like a knife through a stale old cake, are equally grungy.

Oxnard's perfume is the stench of cheap cooking oil and the pungent odor of locomotive Diesel. Its anthem is the mournful wail of the cab whistles from the freight trains and passenger liners that rattle and trundle through on their way up from San Diego to San Francisco.

Oxnard, named for its founder Henry T. Oxnard, is a 40-minute drive but a million light years away from the glamour of Malibu, Beverly Hills and Hollywood. If Los Angeles is the Cinderella who married her glamorous Prince and lived happily ever after; then Oxnard is the permanently Ugly Sister.

Its 25 square miles is a collection of beaten up stores, used car lots, dirt-poor Tex-Mex fast food joints, gun marts, trailer

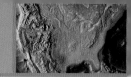

| Population (year 2000) | 170,358 |
| --- | --- |
| Males | 87,090 (51.1%) |
| Females | 83,268 (48.9%) |
| Elevation | 52 feet |
| County | Ventura |
| Land area | 25.3 square miles |
| Zip code | 93030, 93033, 93035. |
| Median resident age | 28.9 years |
| Median household income | $48,603 |
| Median house value | $189,400 |

| Races in Oxnard | |
| --- | --- |
| White Non-Hispanic | 20.6% |
| Hispanic | 66.2% |
| Other race | 46.7% |
| American Indian | 2.0% |
| Two or more races | 4.7% |
| Black | 3.8% |
| Ancestries | |
| German (4.5%), Irish (3.6%), English (3.5%), United States (2.4%), Italian (1.6%), French (1.1%) | |

| For population 25 years and over in Oxnard | |
| --- | --- |
| High school or higher | 59.5% |
| Bachelor's degree or higher | 13.7% |
| Graduate or professional degree | 4.6% |
| Unemployed | 7.5% |
| Mean travel time to work | 23.3 minutes |

| For population 15 years and over in Oxnard | |
| --- | --- |
| Never married | 31.9% |
| Now married | 53.3% |
| Separated | 2.7% |
| Widowed | 4.5% |
| Divorced | 7.5% |
| 36.9% Foreign born (30.6% Latin America, 5.4% Asia) | |

| Crime | |
| --- | --- |
| Violent Crime risk | 10 murders (5.7 per 100,000) |
| Property Crime risk | 913 burglaries (516.9 per 100,000) |

parks and rundown thrift shops. Even the name is about as elegant as a pig's snout. Say: 'O –Nard'. It comes out like a belch rather than a name. An Ox is big and dumb, and Nard sounds too much like nerd for comfort.

This shabby city, with all the poise and confidence of a battered housewife, is an elephants' graveyard for Hollywood losers. This is where failed actors, writers and directors come to die, first shoving their drooling mouths into the $4.50 seniors' Early Bird Meat Loaf Dinner and boring their fellow diners with tales of past glories.

Drive through Oxnard and you glimpse the grubby underside of the miraculous and glittering gold coin that is the American Dream. In the diners, dispirited waitresses pour stewed coffee. Migrant workers who toil in the fields on the edge of town slump exhausted at the counter, poking listless forks at tired breakfast burritos.

Not surprising. Oxnard is almost 67 per cent Hispanic. The average age of the 180,000 population is just under 30. But that can only be because most of the inhabitants seem to

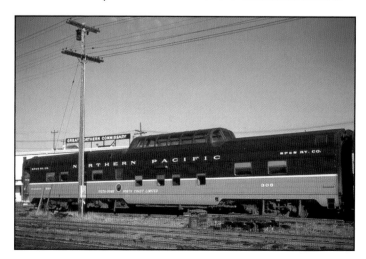

be either under five or over 60. The main mode of transport is pushchair or wheeled Zimmer frame.

Oxnard has an airport, but you can forget exotic flights to Alaska, Hawaii, or Mexico; there's only one destination: Los Angeles Airport. Don't look for cinnamon bagels or Wolfgang Puck mini-pizzas at the one tiny terminal. Instead it boasts (or apologises for) a 'Western barbecue'. Just the thing you want on your stomach for the bumpy 15-minute ride down to LA.

On countless days, the city is covered in a gray sea-haze from the Pacific, giving the place a washed-out pallor like a patient on his deathbed. But when the sun shines you'd think you'd wandered onto the banks of the Rio Grande. Dark-skinned moustachioed men sit on benches wearing cowboy Panamas, high-heeled boots and belt-buckles the size of Rhode Island.

It's not that Oxnard doesn't try. They got the Dallas Cowboys to come up for training sessions two years running. And if you want entertainment, how about 'Hula fun' at the Wilson Senior Center?

It isn't all Oxnard's fault. Its fate is that of all places en route to somewhere else. No-comes to Oxnard. They pass through it; North to Santa Barbara, Monterey, San Francisco. Or South, to Los Angeles and San Diego.

Oxnard is the city time didn't simply forget, it ignored It's the homely and rejected girl at the dance. It's the blink-you-missed-it, one-horse town you sped through to get to the 101 Freeway.

Oxnard is not an ambition; it's a denial. It's not a destination, it's a way station. It's not a place you aspire to live in, it's a hometown you strive to get out of. And if you are from Oxnard and do make it, you never admit where you came from. As the Biblical cock crows thrice, you deny your roots, and say you're actually from LA or Montecito, or Santa Barbara. Would-be CEOs don't want Oxnard on their CV.

It tries hard but fails by comparison. It was born in the wrong place in the wrong state. It's the runt of a litter of pedigree Californian coastal beauties.

Poor Oxnard. But it has a jewel in its plastic ten-cent crown. In Casablanca, Bogie said to Ingrid Bergman: 'We'll always have Paris.' Well, on the edge of Oxnard as you head up from Malibu, there's a brand, spanking new Marie Callender's House of Pies with a salad bar to die for. Sorry Oxnard, there can never be any romance between us. But we'll always have Marie Callender's and that divine honey-mustard dressing. Here's lookin' at you, kid.

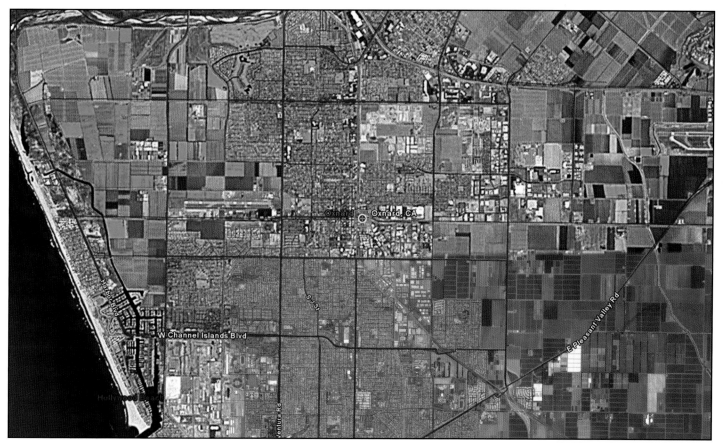

## VISALIA AND PORTERVILLE, CALIFORNIA

*I have found it*
*(state motto of California)*

Los Angeles is the most polluted city in the United States. Well, we all know that. But LA has many reasons to love it, which is why so many people choose to live under its cloud of smog. So we have let the City of Angels off the hook and nominated the town (or in this case towns) which get the official badge of shame as the second most polluted in the US.

No, it's not Houston or Detroit or Knoxville or Dallas or any off the other choking hell-holes we mention elsewhere in this book, although all of those appear in the pollution Top Ten. We are talking here about Visalia-Porterville. Where? You might well ask. They are twin towns in central California, the state over which a cloud hangs, literally and metaphorically.

Visalia and Porterville jointly receive the dishonor of being second, after Los Angeles, in the list of most polluted cities, with more particle pollution and higher smog levels than other metro areas in the US. These were the findings of the American Lung Association, which for the first time measured not only smog but particle pollution – the microscopic soot-like particles produced by power plant emissions, diesel exhausts, wood burning, and other sources.

According to the association's survey, particle pollution is a widespread problem across the country but especially serious in large parts of the East, Midwest, and in California.

Both Visalia and Porterville are in the California Central Valley's Tulare County, the former with a population of about 100,000 and the latter just over 40,000, a high proportion of whom are listed as Hispanic (35 per cent and 50 per cent respectively). There are differences, however: crime in Porterville is about the national average, yet just up the road in

| Population (year 2000) | 91,565 |
|---|---|
| Males | 44,167 (48.2%) |
| Females | 47,398 (51.8%) |
| Elevation | 331 feet |
| County | Tulare |
| Land area | 28.6 square miles |
| Zip code | 93277, 93291, 93292. |
| Median resident age | 31.7 years |
| Median household income | $41,349 |
| Median house value | $115,300 |

| Races in Visalia-Porterville | |
|---|---|
| White Non-Hispanic | 54.9% |
| Hispanic | 35.6% |
| Other race | 21.6% |
| American Indian | 2.4% |
| Two or more races | 4.2% |
| Black | 1.9% |
| Ancestries | |
| German (10.4%), Irish (8.6%), English (8.4%), United States (4.9%), Italian (3.7%), Portuguese (2.5%) | |

| For population 25 years and over in Visalia-Porterville | |
|---|---|
| High school or higher | 76.4% |
| Bachelor's degree or higher | 18.9% |
| Graduate or professional degree | 6.3% |
| Unemployed | 8.3% |
| Mean travel time to work | 19.1 minutes |

| For population 15 years and over in Visalia-Porterville | |
|---|---|
| Never married | 25.9% |
| Now married | 56.3% |
| Separated | 2.1% |
| Widowed | 5.8% |
| Divorced | 10.1% |
| 12.8% Foreign born (7.9% Latin America, 3.8% Asia) | |

| Crime | |
|---|---|
| Violent Crime risk | 12 murders (12.6 per 100,000) |
| Property Crime risk | 1,094 burglaries (1152.4 per 100,000) |

Visalia it is running at almost twice that level.

It may seem unfair to pick out these two small towns as pollution blackspots but they are representative of a problem affecting many California cities, which dominate the lists of most polluted places in the nation for all measures. Ten of the 25 worst cities for short-term levels of particle pollution are in California, as are seven of the worst 25 for year-round particle levels and nine of the worst 25 for ozone. Twenty-three Californian counties have unhealthy short-term levels of particle pollution, while 13 failed the year-round test. And it's even worse than it sounds. For, if measured against California's particle pollution standards, which are tougher than those required by the national Environment Protection Agency, another four counties would have failed the year-round test.

Just so we all know who we're talking about, here are the first four in the American Lung Association's list of most smog-polluted towns in the US: Los Angeles, Visalia-Porterville, Bakersfield and Fresno. And here is the list of the most particle-polluted towns in the US: Los Angeles, Visalia-

Porterville, Bakersfield and Fresno. Yes, they're all round death traps, particularly if you happen to be asthmatic.

It is no wonder that this chronic lung disease is on the rise in California, the prevalence of which has increased by more than 75 per cent since 1980. An above-average 11.9 per cent of Californians – 3.9 million children and adults – have been diagnosed with asthma at some point in their lives, and 667,000 Californian schoolchildren were recorded as experiencing asthma symptoms during a 12-month study period. Air pollution plays a well-documented role in these horrifying statistics.

At least the powers-that-be in the San Joaquin Valley are taking the first steps to alleviate the problem. Three major bills were recently passed to clean up the atmosphere by expanding the authority of valley air officials to regulate vehicle pollution and prevent farm waste burn-offs. San Joaquin Valley Air Pollution Control District gained the power to require ride-share programs for businesses and direct public agencies to add low-emission vehicles to their fleets. The measures also

allowed for the levying of fees for regional trucking centers and ordered the district authority to monitor emissions from diesel-powered irrigation water pumps on farms. Predictably, the Fresno County Farm Bureau and a number of local farmers opposed the measures.

However, we wonder whether there are others causes of pollution that the San Joaquin Valley authorities might have overlooked. Illegal marijuana cultivation takes place throughout the Central Valley, and according to that custodian of the public morality, The Porterville Recorder, Tulare County was ranked fourth on the list for most marijuana plants seized in the entire state of California in 2004. That fact spurred law enforcement authorities to step up their so-called CAMP (Campaign Against Marijuana Planting) eradication program for 2005, with the aim of exceeding the previous year's record haul of 620,000 plants worth $2.5 billion.

In Tulare County, seizures now take place throughout the marijuana growing season (which, for those of a horticultural bent, starts in mid April until harvests end in early October). 'Nearly half of them have been found on public lands,' said a very hurt-sounding Attorney General Bill Lockyer, adding: 'California's landscape is being ravaged by the chemicals and the waste associated with these illegal marijuana gardens.'

So is ride-sharing only part of the answer in this wacky-baccy county? Could it be that the fragrant smoke being exhaled into the atmosphere above Visalia and Porterville somehow explains why these small towns figure so highly in the list of America's most smog-choked?

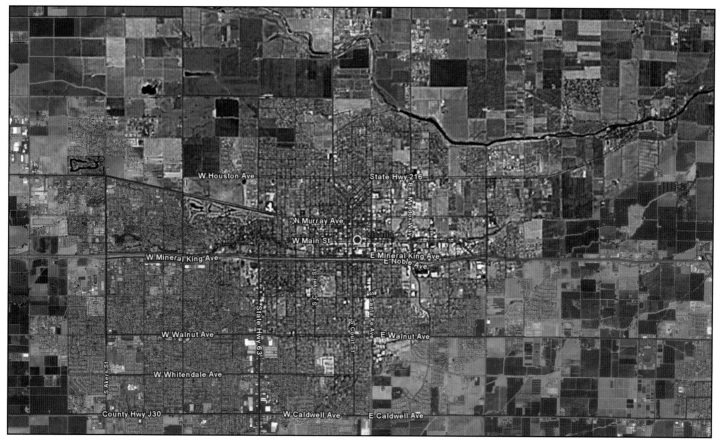

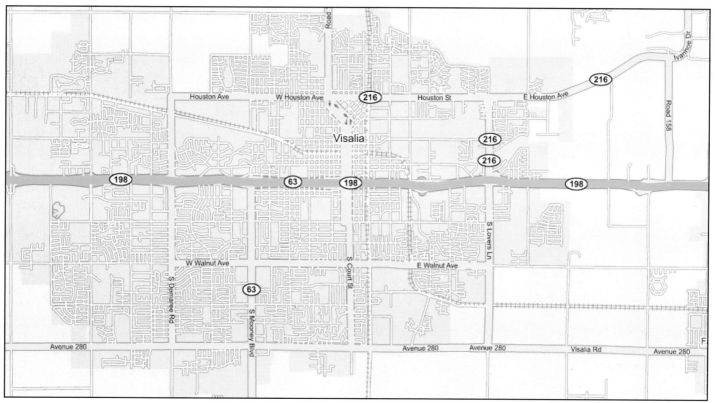

## NEDERLAND, Colorado

*Nothing Without Providence*
*(State motto of Colorado)*

Aah... the chilling Rocky Mountains mortuary that is Nederland – the town that has turned having a dead body on its doorstep into fun, fun, fun. It has become legendary in a frozen, deceased sort of a way, since capitalizing on its infamy of having been home to a preserved corpse. Forever, Nederland will be known as the 'Grandpa in the Tuff Shed Town'.

Every year there is a fascinating festival of Frozen Dead Guy Days, with events such as 'Thaw your bones Chilli Cook-Off', Tuff Shed Coffin Races, Frozen T-Shirt contests, Brain Freeze and 'Say Hello to Grandpa' Ghost Stories (at, where else, but the local ice cream parlour).

Where do we begin with Nederland's tale of a granddaddy on the rocks? In short, Grandpa Bredo Morstoel died at his family's mountain retreat in Norway in 1989, aged 89. At the

behest of his loving grandson, the old man was immediately packed in ice and sent to California, where he was cryogenically preserved – frozen in anticipation of one day being thawed and cured of all his ills to walk this earth again.

Grandpappy resided at the Trans Times facility in Oakland for four years until 1993, when grandson Trygve Bauge decided to make his home in Nederland – with Grandpa In a Tuff Shed, right next door to his house. He even managed to get Grandpa a frozen friend, one Al Campbell from Chicago, to keep him company. The aim was one day to set up a Life Extension Institute of his very own, complete with underground vault in which to store cryogenic capsules and all the other paraphernalia that goes with corpse preservation.

Now, all this would have remained a secret to Bauge, his elderly mother Aud Morstoel and just a handful of Nederland locals if the young man hadn't regarded Green Cards as nothing but a bureaucratic nuisance and publicly labelled the INS 'idiots' when they reminded him that his visa had expired. They took umbrage at this and ordered Bauge back to Norway.

It was only a casual remark by Aud Morstoel, who had been allowed to remain, that made everyone stop in their tracks. Presented with an eviction order for having no proper electricity or plumbing supply, she pointed out that the two frozen bodies would melt if she wasn't on hand to keep them chilled at minus 109 degrees (bodies in cryogenic suspension normally being kept at around minus 320 degrees). Police immediately descended upon Aud's home. The shed was opened and the bodies on ice were discovered. The corpse of Al Campbell was returned to Chicago and a conventional grave but, thanks to a legal loophole, Grandpa Bredo was allowed to stay – as a resident alien. From Norway, Bauge obtained the

# NEDERLAND

| Population (year 2000) | 1,394 |
|---|---|
| Males | 741 (53.2%) |
| Females | 653 (46.8%) |
| Elevation | 8233 feet |
| County | Boulder |
| Land area | 1.5 square miles |
| Zip code | 80466 |
| Median resident age | 32.8 years |
| Median household income | $50,588 |
| Median house value | $218,500 |

| Races in Nederland | |
|---|---|
| White Non-Hispanic | 97.1% |
| Hispanic | 1.6% |
| Other race | 1.6% |
| American Indian | 0.4% |
| Two or more races | 1.3% |
| Black | .2% |

**Ancestries**

Irish (22.9%), English (20.3%), German (20.3%), French (6.5%), Italian (6.1%), Polish (4.9%)

| For population 25 years and over in Nederland | |
|---|---|
| High school or higher | 97.2% |
| Bachelor's degree or higher | 59.4% |
| Graduate or professional degree | 20.4% |
| Unemployed | 3.9% |
| Mean travel time to work | 34.6 minutes |

| For population 15 years and over in Nederland | |
|---|---|
| Never married | 32.9% |
| Now married | 51.3% |
| Separated | 1.2% |
| Widowed | 1.6% |
| Divorced | 13.1% |

Foreign Born 3.1%

| Crime | |
|---|---|
| Violent Crime risk | - |
| Property Crime risk | - |

services of a specialized company called Delta Tech to monitor and maintain the do-it-yourself cryogenic life extension project in Bauge's old backyard.

This Norse saga has had an astonishing effect on the previously sleepy town of Nederland. To the horror of the saner of its inhabitants, the place has descended into a modern-day Ice Age. Instead of handicrafts and curios, the stores are full of 'Frozen Dead Guy Days' hats and T-shirts ($17 each), along with mugs, books, posters, pictures and skeletons.

Everywhere you look during the annual festival, there are ice sculptures, coffins and more skeletons. There are snappy lines such as 'All Good Things must Melt Eventually', songs such as 'It's a Dead Man's Party' by the Dead Guy Chorale, Ice Torch Runners 'bringing Grandpa's spirit to town' and a short film entitled 'Grandpa's Still in the Tuff Shed'.

Revellers from all over the world, would you believe, descend on Nederland for the event, which was first held in 2002. Just for the record, at the 2005 festival, an 'ice-encrusted Belgian' won the Look-a-like Contest. As Teresa Warren, of the

Nederland Area Chamber of Commerce, says: 'Nederland is now on the radar for the place to have fun.'

What effect has all this had on those who came to this once-sane sanctuary to enjoy a quiet life? Perhaps the publicity surrounding Nederland is just too much for some of them because the length of time anyone stays is significantly below the state average. It also happens that the population density is significantly below that of the state average for cities. So who knows, the sparsely populated areas could house many frozen inhabitants and we would be none the wiser.

The picturesque little town, about 45 miles northwest of Denver, boasts a population of around 1,394 with a slight bias towards men than women. Through the 1990s, its population grew by about 27 per cent and in recent years has declined at an annual rate of less than one per cent. Perhaps people are afraid to die in case they end up in a Tuff Shed.

There are no less than 20 FM radio stations broadcasting

loud and clear in Nederland and they must all have a field day during Frozen Dead Guy Days because there is certainly no shortage of events to advertise.

Equally, for some reason, there is no shortage of illegal drugs in Nederland to make life more exciting outside of the Frozen Dead Guys time of year. Mexican poly-drug trafficking organisations control most of the methamphetamine, cocaine, marijuana and heroin distributed in the town. Incidentally, most of the methamphetamine comes from large-scale laboratories in California. A bit like, urmh, Grandpa Bredo's body.

On a serious note, drugs are a big problem in Nederland which has been designated a 'High Density Drug Trafficking Area'. According to the authorities, there is even recognised drug abuse amongst medical professionals in the area. Maybe it's the drugs that attract the younger element to Nederland. For the greatest part of its population is made up of men and women aged 20 to 40. Just a tiny proportion are over 60. Again, perhaps they all flee to another town before the likes of Trygve Bauge can get his hands on them.

The people of Nederland will probably think we are being hard on them, particularly as their Chamber of Commerce has sensible plans afoot, as well as backing the bizarre 'Frozen' weekend. its Vision Statement includes having its own colleges (at the moment it has a middle-senior High School and Elementary School but the nearest colleges and universities are anything from between 13 miles away in Boulder to 38 miles away in Denver). The nearest hospital is 21 miles away.  It is also hoped to bury the town's power lines, repaint buildings, have more organized parking and develop the reservoir front. Worryingly, the Vision Statement lists one of the obstacles to all these plans as: 'Who is really going to do this?' We can only hope the town does rally round to stop itself being a bit of a laughing stock.

Meanwhile, Trygve Bauge is alive and well. He fully endorses Frozen Dead Guy Days. He obviously wants to be frozen himself when the time comes – which he hopes will not be for a while, as he bathes in ice water to prolong his life.

But the havoc that he has caused to a once-proud place is an object lesson in how one act of madness can consign an entire town to the joke book. As a local resident told our researcher: 'I came here to escape the madness of the big city. This was once a sanctuary of sanity, and its most precious resource was the normalcy of its people. Now we feel frozen out.'

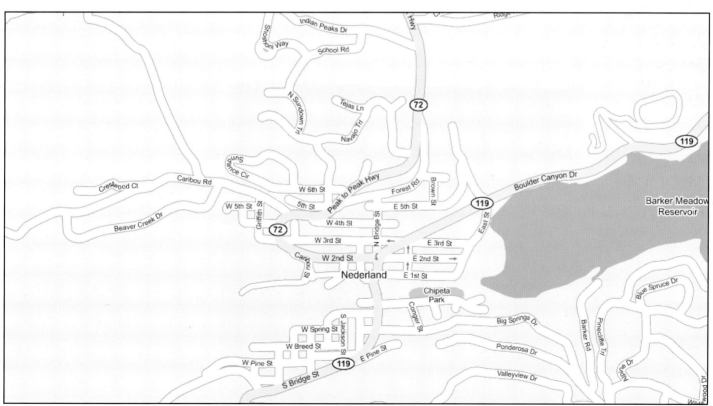

## BELLE GLADE, FLORIDA

*Motto: 'Gateway to the Everglades*

Belle Glade is not a glade and it sure ain't belle. According to the town's own literature, it is famed for its vegetables and its sod farms. Well, it's a good try, folks, but no gloss can disguise the fact that Belle Glade is not a healthy place to live or to visit – because it is really known for only one thing, and that's AIDS.

The central Florida agricultural community has the highest cumulative per capita incidence of AIDS in the United States. Some time ago, an argument developed over why this should be. Two Miami doctors studied and tested sufferers in some of Belle Glade's slums and came up with the controversial theory that mosquitoes and squalor were factors in spreading the disease.

This strange attempt to excuse naughty behaviour with the mantra of 'social deprivation' was popular because Belle Glade has an extremely high immigrant population, with a strong Haitian content. But later studies have clearly shown what everyone knew all along – that the town's AIDS epidemic is caused by unprotected sex and sharing needles. In other words, stupidity.

Most recently, Miami University's Department of Epidemiology and Public Health decided to focus their studies on those members of Belle Glade's population whom they described as 'individuals who were believed to be at the core of the transmission pattern'. These were: 'Injection drug users and their sexual partners. Results suggested that the primary mode of HIV transmission is heterosexual intercourse, mediated by drug taking (particularly crack smoking) and a flourishing sex industry.'

So the good news is that the place is not a modern-day Sodom and Gomorra, because the epidemic is not down to homosexual activity. The bad news is that if you go there and partake of the sins of the flesh in the most normal and natural way, you might die.

Apart from 'AIDS capital', Belle Glade is also known as the 'Sugar fields capital' and is the largest city within the

| Population (year 2000) | 14,906 |
|---|---|
| Males | 7,580 (50.9%) |
| Females | 7,326 (49.1%) |
| Elevation | 20 feet |
| County | Palm Beach |
| Land area | 4.6 square miles |
| Zip code | 33430 |
| Median resident age | 29.9 years |
| Median household income | $22,715 |
| Median house value | $74,600 |

| Races in Belle Glade | |
|---|---|
| White Non-Hispanic | 13.8% |
| Hispanic | 27.6% |
| Other race | 9.7% |
| American Indian | - |
| Two or more races | 8.9% |
| Black | 50.7% |

**Ancestries**

West Indian (13.3%), United States (8.5%), English (3.0%), Irish (1.7%), German (1.4%), Subsaharan African (1.0%)

| For population 25 years and over in Belle Glade | |
|---|---|
| High school or higher | 46.5% |
| Bachelor's degree or higher | 9.9% |
| Graduate or professional degree | 3.6% |
| Unemployed | 12.0% |
| Mean travel time to work | 26.6 minutes |

| For population 15 years and over in Belle Glade | |
|---|---|
| Never married | 38.1% |
| Now married | 44.1% |
| Separated | 4.5% |
| Widowed | 6.4% |
| Divorced | 6.4% |

30.2% Foreign born (29.0% Latin America)

| Crime | |
|---|---|
| Violent Crime risk | 0 murders (0.0 per 100,000) |
| Property Crime risk | 531 burglaries (3406.5 per 100,000) |

Everglades heartland of Florida. Why would anyone name this down-at-heel dump Belle Glade? The story goes that suggestions were written on a hotel blackboard and the one receiving the most votes described the place as 'the belle of the Glades'. Perhaps it was meant as a joke.

The town was incorporated in 1928 – the same year that it almost got wiped out. A fierce storm drove a surging tide from the northern part of Lake Okeechobee and emptied it out into the surrounding countryside. Approximately 2,500 people died in the hurricane and a statue today commemorates those who perished.

A flood control program followed. But the result is a mixed blessing. For, if you imagine that sitting on the southern shore of America's second biggest lake is an appealing prospect, then you should know that the view is not of the glistening waters but of a giant levee called the Hoover Dike, built to stop the place being inundated.

Nevertheless, Belle Glade has become a magnet for fishermen. To quote the town's visitor information: 'The Belle

Glade Marina Campground has become a home away from home for many visitors who want to try their luck catching of the 'Big O's.' (Apparently, that's not some sexual disease but a fish called the wide-mouth bass.)

Any other excitement to be had? Again, to quote: 'From earliest days to the present, agriculture has played an important part in the area's development. Although green beans led the way at one time, today's most important crops are celery, lettuce, sweet corn, and sugar cane. The area is well known for its ornamental and sod farms.'

Fascinating stuff. But we've had a dig around (so to speak) and there are some more relevant statistics about this place. The population of 15,000-plus is made up of roughly 50 per cent Black, 28 per cent Hispanic, 14 per cent White non-Hispanic, and the rest are 'other races' or 'two or more races'. The median household income is $22,000, less than half of Palm Beach County's average. Heading in the opposite direction is the crime index. The US average is 330; Belle Glade's is an unbelievable, skyrocketing 1285.

So while the authorities can at last control the waters of Lake Okeechobee, they can't, it seems, control the criminal and sexual excesses of the locals who live in its mosquito-plagued shadow.

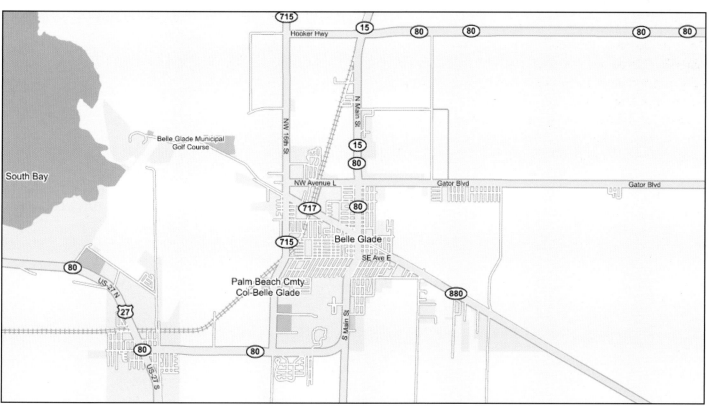

## SYLVESTER, GEORGIA
*'Peanut Capital of the World'*

It was the interaction of ideas among the farming folk of this part of the world that made us investigate the town of Sylvester, Georgia. We had chanced upon the website of the 'Peanut Capital of the World', as the town describes itself, wherein lay an invitation to the inhabitants to tell the city fathers what they think of the place...

'Why do you think Sylvester is a great city?' it asked, followed by the further exhortation: 'Do you have a story about why you think Sylvester is a great, city? If so, click on the comment section and let us know, we would love to hear from you.' Finally, with a hint of desperation, the original invitation was repeated: 'Why do you think Sylvester is a great city?'

After all of that came a window revealing exactly what the response had been in the month since the site had been up and running. It read: 'Replies 0.'

Could the citizens of Sylvester really be so lethargic? Or were they simply being honest? We hotfooted it to this kernel of peanut production to find out – and, by golly, they were being both.

'No wonder they couldn't find anything good to say about it,' reported our undercover researcher. 'It's an odd sort of place. There are peanuts, along with the cotton, growing in the fields, and most of the town seems to be made up of giant peanut packing factories, but the strangest thing I found is that you can't actually buy a packet of peanuts anywhere!'

There is not much else to be bought in Sylvester, either. The dusty downtown area has a couple of twee gift shops (quite who shops there we do not know), a not very good restaurant, and that really is it. For anything else, you have to drive 20 miles to the nearest big town, Albany.

It seems that many of the inhabitants of Sylvester have made that journey and stayed. Incorporated as a town in

1898, Sylvester had grown to a strength of 6,000 before more recently suffering a decade of stagnation and then decline, resulting in a population decrease at a time when the state of Georgia's population increased by more than a quarter.

Sylvester is the county seat of Worth County, and it is this entire area which is officially recognized as 'Peanut Capital of the World'. It hosts the Georgia Peanut Festival, held each October just outside of Sylvester in a place called Possum Poke, where the major attractions include (and we quote), 'the Peanut Parade, a barbecue to honor peanut farmers, peanut cuisine, the Goober Gala, an annual dance, the Miss Georgia Peanut pageant and numerous other events.'

If crowds from far afield ever flocked to this festival, they would have difficulty finding adequate accommodation or

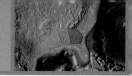

| Population (year 2000) | 5,990 |
|---|---|
| Males | 2,664 (44.5%) |
| Females | 3,326 (55.5%) |
| Elevation | 426 feet |
| County | Worth |
| Land area | 5.7 square miles |
| Zip code | 31791 |
| Median resident age | 32.3 years |
| Median household income | $24,114 |
| Median house value | $64,400 |

| Races in Sylvester | |
|---|---|
| White Non-Hispanic | 38.9% |
| Hispanic | 0.9% |
| Other race | - |
| American Indian | - |
| Two or more races | - |
| Black | 60.0% |

**Ancestries**

United States (8.4%), Irish (4.5%), English (3.3%), German (2.8%), Subsaharan African (2.3%), Italian (1.1%)

| For population 25 years and over in Sylvester | |
|---|---|
| High school or higher | 63.7% |
| Bachelor's degree or higher | 11.9% |
| Graduate or professional degree | 4.8% |
| Unemployed | 11.9% |
| Mean travel time to work | 22.1 minutes |

| For population 15 years and over in Sylvester | |
|---|---|
| Never married | 30.5% |
| Now married | 44.1% |
| Separated | 4.2% |
| Widowed | 12.3% |
| Divorced | 8.9% |

0.7% Foreign born

| Crime | |
|---|---|
| Violent Crime risk | 0 murders (0.0 per 100,000) |
| Property Crime risk | (862.2 per 100,000) |

even refreshment. There are no hotels or motels, as such, in Sylvester, and when we put the magic words 'nearest Starbucks' into the rental car's global satellite positioning thingie, it claimed the nearest was 187 plus miles away in Atlanta.

We're positive there must have been a nearer one than that, but mention coffee to locals and they direct you to a grubby pit stop on the outskirts of Sylvester where assorted bugs were crawling along the window ledge and tables. Locals there were happy to talk about the only topic of interest to them: peanuts. The only other item of conversation when our researcher visited was the arrival somewhere in the locality of a family of 'goddam Ay-rabs' who had bought up an ailing motel business. It transpired that they were actually from India, but then the good people of Peanut Paradise wouldn't want to risk standards slipping or their culture being polluted by an influx of any sort of outsider.

They are, after all, proud of their farming heritage, and why not? Peanut production produced the 39th President of the United States, plain ol' Jimmy Carter from just up the road there in Plains. They are proud of their county courthouse, and justifiably so because it is the only building of architectural merit in Sylvester. They are proud to live in a law-abiding society, although the police department complex looks like several trailers locked together. They are also proud of their homes. A double-fronted trailer is a sign of 'making it' in Sylvester.

In short, the Sylvester citizenry are satisfied with their nondescript little town – even if they can't find the words to extol its virtues on the internet. So let us, on their behalf, sum up in one word everything that Sylvester has to offer: it's peanuts.

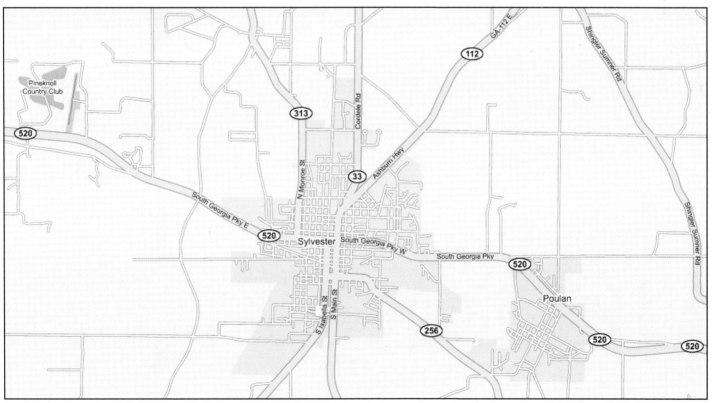

## MARKHAM, ILLINOIS
*State sovereignty, national union
(state motto of Illinois)*

Markham doesn't just demand an entry in this volume; it bludgeons its way into it. It appears here on one notorious basis only – as the most dangerous place in America. Official statistics reveal it as having the highest crime rate of any town in the land.

Markham, Illinois, is five square miles of blighted suburban decrepitude with a population of just 12,600. But its diminutive size hides a big problem. Latest available figures show that in a year it saw four murders, 15 rapes, 50 robberies, 308 burglaries, 650 larceny counts and 1,072 assaults. That means that one in every 12 people walking the streets of this den of criminality will suffer an assault within the next 12 months.

The City-data.com crime index, which compares statistics for each town against a nationwide average of 330.6, put Markham at the top of its list of shame at an astronomical 2405.7.

Other official statistics provide few clues to the cause of this fearful state of affairs. Markham, just 17 miles from the centre of Chicago, has more females (53.6 per cent) than males (46.4 per cent), though here the preponderance of the fairer sex does not seem to provide a moderating influence.

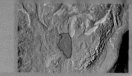

| Population (year 2000) | 12,620 |
|---|---|
| Males | 5,861 (46.4%) |
| Females | 6,759 (53.6%) |
| Elevation | 615 feet |
| County | Cook County |
| Land area | 5.2 square miles |
| Zip code | 60426 |
| Median resident age | 32.9 years |
| Median household income | $41,592 |
| Median house value | $75,200 |

| Races in Markham | |
|---|---|
| White Non-Hispanic | 16.3% |
| Hispanic | 3.1% |
| Other race | 1.6% |
| American Indian | 0.6% |
| Two or more races | 1.5% |
| Black | 78.9% |

**Ancestries**

Irish (5.5%), German (5.1%), Polish (3.1%), Italian (1.8%), English (1.1%), Subsaharan African (1.1%)

| For population 25 years and over in Markham | |
|---|---|
| High school or higher | 77.8% |
| Bachelor's degree or higher | 10.6% |
| Graduate or professional degree | 3.2% |
| Unemployed | 13.3% |
| Mean travel time to work | 30.9 minutes |

| For population 15 years and over in Markham | |
|---|---|
| Never married | 35.9% |
| Now married | 39.8% |
| Separated | 4.8% |
| Widowed | 9.0% |
| Divorced | 10.4% |

2.8% Foreign born (1.2% Asia, 1.0% Latin America, 0.4% Europe)

| Crime | |
|---|---|
| Violent Crime risk | 4 murders (31.7 per 100,000) |
| Property Crime risk | 308 burglaries (2440.6 per 100,000) |

The average age is a relatively youthful 33. Educational achievement is below average too. Incomes are well below average. So are house values, as one would expect. The racial make-up is Black 78.9 per cent, White Non-Hispanic 16.3 per cent and Hispanic 3.1 per cent.

Commenting in the Chicago suburban press on a report that Markham had just recorded an average of 90.4 violent crimes per 1,000 residents, a university criminologist said: 'The suburbs all hiccup when the Chicago economy catches a cold.'

That explanation fails to explain Markham's particular shame. The place is a blight on Illinois which, although previously rated high in comparative crime lists, is now happily slipping down the table of 'Most Dangerous States'. The city of Chicago itself is less crime-ridden than it was in the 1990s.

What has changed is the drug scene. Chicago is the

major transportation hub and distribution center for illegal drugs throughout the Midwest, and street gangs such as the Gangster Disciples, Vice Lords, and Latin Kings control the distribution and retail sale of marijuana, heroin and cocaine. Illinois law enforcement agencies cite the violence associated with gang-related drug trafficking as the most serious criminal threat to the area.

Significantly, a recent report by the nationwide social betterment organization Drug Rehabs may provide the clue to the plight of places like Markham. Referring to the problems of greater Chicago, it says: 'Violent crime associated with street gangs, while declining in major urban areas, is increasing in suburban and rural areas as these gangs expand their drug markets.'

The great worry among law enforcement experts is that youngsters in these suburbs are now being exposed to drugs at an earlier age. Most adults will be baffled by references to 'water', 'hug', 'weed', 'beans' and 'Special K' but, according to the Chicago provincial media, many children and teens in Markham and adjoining suburbs know that they are street names for a variety of illicit drugs. If crime in Markham is out of control now, what hope for its citizens of the future?

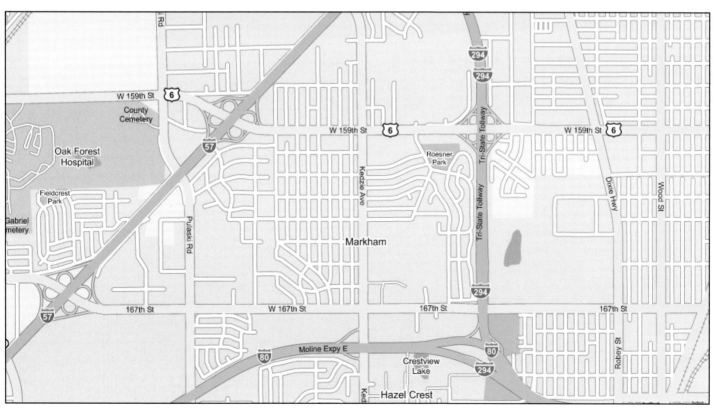

## GARY INDIANA

*The crossroads of America*
*(state motto of Indiana)*

We think it's sad to be so predictable, but this journal of discovery would lose all credibility if it did not include Gary, Indiana. Its listing here is required for all sorts of reasons

– but most importantly because it is a benchmark against which all the other places we've picked on can be judged. After all, by including Gary, we're making lots of other rotten places look good by comparison!

The revered Rough Guide covers Gary fleetingly; to quote: 'The most lasting memories provided by Indiana's 50-mile lakeshore are of the grimy steel mills and poverty-stricken neighbourhoods of Gary.'

The town's infamy has spread worldwide, so that whispering 'Gary, Indiana' is like invoking the bogeyman to frighten naughty children into quiet submission. Yet our researcher bravely ventured into the midst of this industrial Hades to report: 'This is a seriously foul, scary town. Decay and menace hang in the air. Even though you cannot see it, you are aware of the place from miles away, because it is perpetually enveloped in an ugly fog of pollution. And when you arrive, you find the air full of dust which clings to your clothes and hair for days.'

Those are first impressions. What are the facts? Surely

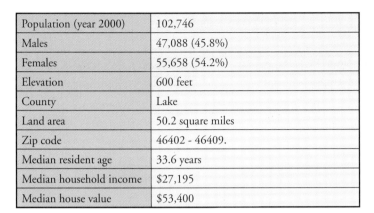

| Population (year 2000) | 102,746 |
|---|---|
| Males | 47,088 (45.8%) |
| Females | 55,658 (54.2%) |
| Elevation | 600 feet |
| County | Lake |
| Land area | 50.2 square miles |
| Zip code | 46402 - 46409. |
| Median resident age | 33.6 years |
| Median household income | $27,195 |
| Median house value | $53,400 |

| Races in Gary | |
|---|---|
| White Non-Hispanic | 10.1% |
| Hispanic | 4.9% |
| Other race | 2.0% |
| American Indian | 0.7% |
| Two or more races | 1.7% |
| Black | 84.0% |

**Ancestries**

United States (2.0%), German (1.9%), Irish (1.7%), Subsaharan African (1.5%)

| For population 25 years and over in Gary | |
|---|---|
| High school or higher | 72.7% |
| Bachelor's degree or higher | 10.1% |
| Graduate or professional degree | 4.0% |
| Unemployed | 14.9% |
| Mean travel time to work | 26.1 minutes |

| For population 15 years and over in Gary | |
|---|---|
| Never married | 38.8% |
| Now married | 34.1% |
| Separated | 4.3% |
| Widowed | 9.4% |
| Divorced | 13.5% |
| 1.6% Foreign born | |

| Crime | |
|---|---|
| Violent Crime risk | 60 murders (57.7 per 100,000) |
| Property Crime risk | 1,543 burglaries (1482.6 per 100,000) |

this lakeside stretch must have been a prettier place in its earliest days. Well, no, because the city was actually planned as an industrial sprawl. It was founded in 1906 by the United States Steel Corporation as the home for its new plant, and was thereby named after the chairman of U.S. Steel, Elbert H. Gary. Its fortunes have ever since risen and fallen with the health of the steel industry, accelerating into a downward spiral of decline in the 1960s.

Gary still suffers unfairly from those lay-offs, and the families thrown on the scrapheap who hadn't the money or gumption to get out of the place have suffered a legacy of difficulties that are a case study in urban decay—unemployment, economic collapse and a high rate of crime.

Gary was once the murder capital of America, and, although it has lost that crown, it is still rampant with crime. The litany from the enforcement agencies is tragically predictable:

'Gary is an active drug transportation and distribution area…'; 'Gary is reckoned to be the main distribution center

there are 84 males, and for every 100 females age 18 and over there are 78 males. The median income for a household in the city is $27,195, with the consequence that 22 per cent of families are living below the poverty line and that an astonishing 38 per cent of those under the age of 18 are below the poverty line. No wonder that the proportion of the population with a graduate or professional degree is only four per cent and that unemployment runs at 15 pert cent.

The racial makeup of the city is 84 per cent black and 12 per cent white, which gets Gary a mention in the record books as having 'the highest percentage of African-American residents among U.S. cities of 100,000 or more'. It had one of the nation's first African-American mayors, Richard G. Hatcher, and hosted the 1972 National Black Political Convention.

Among the black citizens of the place were members of the musical Jackson family. Yes, Michael and Co were born here, and, believe it or not, the Jackson family shack is on Jackson Street (the name came first; it was not changed in their honour). Before his irritating little legal troubles, Michael Jackson had promised to build a performing arts center for Gary, though, being a few millions short in his petty cash box, this has not come to pass.

A pity, because without Michael Jackson, Gary has few claims to fame. There were, of course, The Jacksons albums 2300 Jackson Street and Going Back to Indiana. Indiana is also the subject of a song in the musical The Music Man. And Karl Malden was born in the town – although his Streets of San Francisco has a more appealing ring to it than the crime-ridden streets of Gary.

Surely there must be SOME good news? Well, according to one travel guide, 'five interstates slice their way through Indiana, providing a swift but boring means of getting in, through and out of the place as quickly as possible'.

for drugs to the Midwest…'; 'Powdered cocaine is readily available throughout the city, and crack cocaine primarily available within urban areas…'; 'In northern Gary, Asian white heroin has decreased but has been replaced by Mexican brown and black tar heroin…'; 'The influx of methamphetamine into Gary has increased from year to year...'; 'Most of the heavily populated areas continue to experience shootings and other acts of violence over drug debts.'

The statistics for crimes of violence bear that out. The most recent confirmed figures we could find list 82 murders in 2001 and 60 in 2002. There were 135 rapes in those two years and 500 assaults. This in a town with a population of only 100,000 (and, as you'd imagine, falling).

Who are the poor souls who live in this hell hole? For 'live' read 'subsist'. The most recent census reveals that, among the 38,000 households, about a third are married couples living together, as one would expect, but that another third 'have a female householder with no husband present'. Where have they all gone? The census shows us that for every 100 females

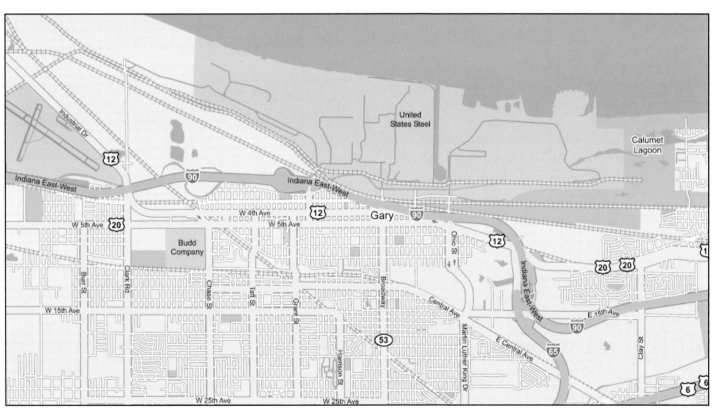

## Des Moines, Iowa

*Our liberties we prize and our rights we will maintain (state motto of Iowa)*

A friend of ours got lost in downtown Des Moines one Friday lunchtime. He looked around in vain for someone to ask directions. There was no-one... at... all. Finally, after pouring over a road map for some minutes, he spotted a lone office worker. Delighted, he leaned out of his car window and shouted a cheery 'Hello'. The woman looked at him in horror and ran for her life. And that was the last person our pal saw outside all day.

Now, he later discovered that there's a three-and-a-half mile skywalk system so people can walk between buildings without ever going outside. So he thought he'd give that a whirl. And, surprise, surprise, there was hardly anyone using it.

Deserted just about sums up Des Moines (pronounced 'da moyne'). Only in August when – yippee – the Iowa State Fair comes to town can you expect to find crowds. Indeed,

the guide books tell us there's no shortage of cheap motels at any time of the year; you only need reservations for those important 10 days of August when the fair arrives. The only other big event on the calendar is the annual World Pork Expo, where we're told the locals go hog wild.

Des Moines describes itself as a meat market, which means something completely different to sophisticated city dwellers. But then even the meaning of Des Moines keeps on changing. French explorers originally called the river 'Riviere des Moingouenas' in honor of the local Native American tribe, and then shortened it to 'des Moings'. Later French settlers changed it slightly to something more familiar – the current name actually means 'of monks'.

So what does this city of monks have to offer? Well, as far as we can establish, there aren't any monasteries of note, but the copper and gold domed state capital building looks quite nice. There's a modern three-storey museum and an arts

center. But our personal favourite is 12 miles out of town: if you can find anyone around to ask directions, head for Indianola and the National Balloon Museum. We're told its regular balloon regattas are not to be missed!

Des Moines is proud of its agricultural heritage, and its 400-plus factories are dedicated to food production and processing. But this city of nearly 500,000 people actually has a bigger claim to fame: it's the third largest insurance center in the world after London, England, and Hertford, Connecticut. Now we've got nothing against insurance salesmen but...

So what else does Des Moines have? We took a peek at the city's website and were excited to discover it's 'a wonderful place to live, work and visit'. And for residents, 'affordable housing and one of the nations shortest commute times'

# DES MOINES

| Population (year 2000) | 198,682 |
|---|---|
| Males | 96,157 (48.4%) |
| Females | 102,525 (51.6%) |
| Elevation | 955 feet |
| County | Polk |
| Land area | 75.8 square miles |
| Zip code | 50309 - 50321. |
| Median resident age | 33.8 years |
| Median household income | $38,408 |
| Median house value | $81,100 |

| Races in Des Moines | |
|---|---|
| White Non-Hispanic | 79.6% |
| Hispanic | 6.6% |
| Other race | 6.2% |
| American Indian | 0.8% |
| Two or more races | 2.2% |
| Black | 8.1% |
| Ancestries | |

German (21.5%), Irish (12.7%), English (9.3%), United States (6.8%), Italian (3.9%), Norwegian (3.8%)

| For population 25 years and over in Des Moines | |
|---|---|
| High school or higher | 83.0% |
| Bachelor's degree or higher | 21.8% |
| Graduate or professional degree | 6.5% |
| Unemployed | 6.7% |
| Mean travel time to work | 17.5 minutes |

| For population 15 years and over in Des Moines | |
|---|---|
| Never married | 28.2% |
| Now married | 50.9% |
| Separated | 1.7% |
| Widowed | 6.5% |
| Divorced | 12.7% |

7.9% Foreign born (3.1% Latin America, 2.6% Asia, 1.6% Europe)

| Crime | |
|---|---|
| Violent Crime risk | 9 murders (4.5 per 100,000) |
| Property Crime risk | 1,676 burglaries (840.6 per 100,000) |

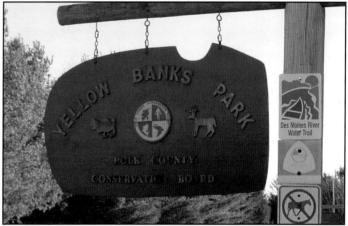

makes it one of the most desirable places in the Mid West. Then there's the international airport which, despite its name, only caters to domestic flights.

In the summer of 2005, the locals were gearing up for the 20th anniversary of the town's twinning with Saint-Etienne, the French industrial sprawl that would come close to top of the list of Gallic crap towns. Other than that, a new street re-surfacing project and the mosquito spraying program appeared to be conspiring to keep the locals inside once again.

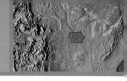

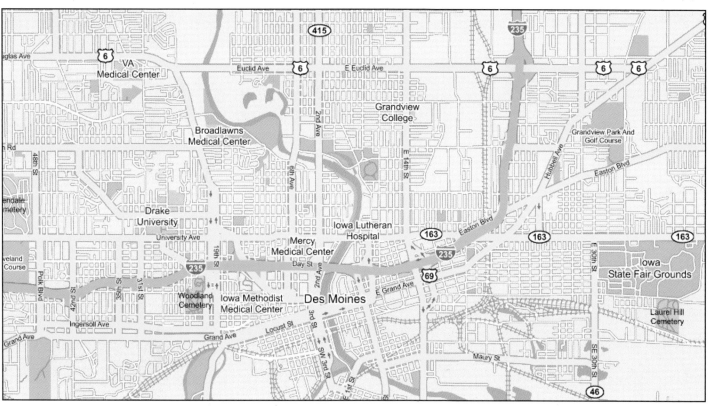

### ELLSWORTH, KANSAS
*Motto: 'Wickedest cowtown in the West'*

It's plain why the Great Plains are losing their population. They're, well, just too dead plain. So several towns from Kansas to North Dakota have resorted to desperate measures to prevent the dusty winds simply blowing them off the map. We've picked on one, in our characteristically arbitrary fashion, and we're sure that the townspeople will accuse us of being unfair to them. But Ellsworth, Kansas, does pretty well sum up the reasons why folk tend to take a one-way ticket

outta here.

Kansas lacks interesting things to do, that's sure, but it also lacks interesting things to look at. There are no mountain peaks, gorges, mighty rivers, waterfalls; it's just monotonously flat. And slap bang in the middle of it, surrounded by endless wheat fields, is Ellsworth.

Once it boasted of being 'the Wickedest cowtown in the West', situated beside the Union Pacific railroad track, at the end of one of the Texas cattle trails. Ellsworth County's population grew to 15,000 but has now shrunk back to 6,000 – with Ellsworth 'city' itself down to a teeny 2,100. One reason for this sad state of affairs is that fewer people are working on the land. Another is that bored college leavers can't wait to join the rural brain drain, and once they've tasted city life, they never return. The result is an accelerating exodus, as services decline and even more people leave.

In desperation, Ellsworth is now advertising a 'Welcome Home Plan' for young families to come and live in the place. The bribes being offered are free land on which to build, help with a home loan and free utility installation. The town will even help fresh arrivals with the deposit on their new home, the size of the gift dependant on the number of children they are bringing to the local school. The only qualifications for acceptance seem to be American citizenship or a bank account.

| Population (year 2000) | 2,965 |
|---|---|
| Males | 1,688 (56.9%) |
| Females | 1,277 (43.1%) |
| Elevation | 1550 feet |
| County | Ellsworth |
| Land area | 2.1 square miles |
| Zip code | 67439 |
| Median resident age | 40.0 years |
| Median household income | $35,625 |
| Median house value | $47,000 |

| Races in Ellsworth | |
|---|---|
| White Non-Hispanic | 85.9% |
| Hispanic | 3.9% |
| Other race | 0.9% |
| American Indian | 0.9% |
| Two or more races | 1.6% |
| Black | 7.6% |
| Ancestries | |
| German (35.5%), Irish (9.0%), English (8.5%), Czech (6.9%), United States (6.2%), French (3.4%) | |

| For population 25 years and over in Ellsworth | |
|---|---|
| High school or higher | 85.8% |
| Bachelor's degree or higher | 15.8% |
| Graduate or professional degree | 5.9% |
| Unemployed | 4.1% |
| Mean travel time to work | 14.1 minutes |

| For population 15 years and over in Ellsworth | |
|---|---|
| Never married | 22.5% |
| Now married | 53.4% |
| Separated | 1.9% |
| Widowed | 9.9% |
| Divorced | 12.2% |
| 1.6% Foreign born | |

| Crime | |
|---|---|
| Violent Crime risk | 0 murders (0.0 per 100,000) |
| Property Crime risk | 41 burglaries (629.3 per 100,000) |

Not too selective, then.

Despite this open-arms welcome, there has been no repeat of the Land Grab that brought settlers rushing to this state a century ago. Ellsworth's director of economic development, Anita Hoffhines, says that the handful of families who were first to answer the town's call had been attracted by the clean air, a good school, lack of crime, and 'Christian values'. She says: 'The scheme best suits those wanting to get away from the big cities. But they'll have to be willing to move out of their comfort zone. If they expect to have a Starbucks, a sushi bar and a movieplex, it will never happen.'

And that is the problem with Ellsworth and places like it. People who leave the cities may worry about having to take a pay cut to come to Ellsworth, where the main employers are an industrial valve manufacturer and the local prison. But that's no problem, because when newcomers get here they find there is nothing to spend their money on anyway. At the

Crossroads Diner, a young waitress succinctly summed up the life that awaits the optimistic newcomers: 'You go to work, you go home, you play bowls, you go the bar. And that's it. I'm not joking.'

We don't want to malign the little town, because its failings are common to this part of the world. And it is, after all, trying to do something dramatic to reverse its fortunes. We wish it well. But even the pro-active Ellsworth Chamber of Commerce cannot disguise the fact that there's not too much fun to be had here.

Take their 'Annual Events in and around Ellsworth'. The entry for January reads: 'Not much going on. Check out a good book from the J.H. Robbins Memorial library.' February mentions a minor event in another town. The same goes for March. But for Ellsworth, there's only one entry, and it reads: 'Finish the book.'

Three months to finish a book? They must be slow readers in Ellsworth, because there's nothing else to do in the place – and that's official.

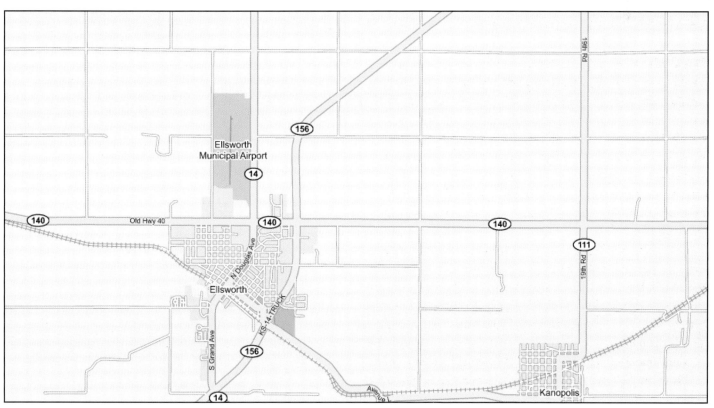

## BATON ROUGE, Louisiana
*Union, justice and confidence (state motto of Louisiana)*

'Busted flat in Baton Rouge, heading for the train…'
At least Kris Kristofferson was headed for the train LEAVING this busted, flat, Bible-belt hellhole of gimcrack buildings, sub-standard bars and people whose chips about the rather more bustling New Orleans down the Interstate are so big they practically lean over.

'Situated on the Mississippi River, Baton Rouge represents the best of Louisiana's vibrant culture,' lies the town's official website. 'The state capital is a thriving city that is home to both LSU and Southern University and numerous businesses and industrial facilities. Known for its great people, its unique food and its lively music, it has something for everyone – including a local government that cares.'

The reality is, of course, different. Mediocrity is reflected along with the harsh glare of the midday sun from streets pockmarked from lack of care and repair.

The one thing that Baton Rouge can justifiably boast about is the Louisiana State Capital building, an art deco glory that stands amid 50 acres of gardens. But it serves only as a reminder of how corrupt (or in some case, mad) the leaders of this state have been. The capital building is a monument to Governor Huey Long, the demagogue who ordered its construction in 1931 and was assassinated inside it four years later.

His worthy successors included Jimmie Davis, recalled for writing the song You Are My Sunshine and for riding his horse up the steps of the place rather than for any political gifts. Another incumbent of that office was Governor Eddie Edwards, who was sentenced to jail in 2001 for extortion. Also upholding the finest traditions of the Old South was David Duke, a state representative who ran for governor, but was better known as Grand Wizard of the Ku Klux Klan. He was jailed for fraud in 2003.

The high-minded motto of this state is 'Union, justice and confidence'. The politicians seem to have formed a union of confidence tricksters until justice finally caught up with them.

Baton Rouge was so named because when French explorers first came upon the site, they found poles smeared in blood to delineate the hunting grounds of the native Houmas and Bayougoulas tribes. The area appeared on French maps as 'Baton Rouge' meaning 'Red stick'.

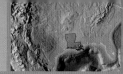

# BATON ROUGE

| Population (year 2000) | 227,818 |
|---|---|
| Males | 108,255 (47.5%) |
| Females | 119,563 (52.5%) |
| Elevation | 53 feet |
| County | East Baton Roug |
| Land area | 76.8 square miles |
| Zip code | 70801 - 70836. |
| Median resident age | 30.4 years |
| Median household income | $30,368 |
| Median house value | $94,700 |

| Races in Baton Rouge | |
|---|---|
| White Non-Hispanic | 44.7% |
| Hispanic | 1.7% |
| Other race | 1.8% |
| American Indian | - |
| Two or more races | 1.0% |
| Black | 50.0% |

**Ancestries**

French (8.9%), English (6.3%), German (6.2%), Irish (5.7%), United States (4.2%), Italian (3.9%)

| For population 25 years and over in Baton Rouge | |
|---|---|
| High school or higher | 80.1% |
| Bachelor's degree or higher | 31.7% |
| Graduate or professional degree | 12.8% |
| Unemployed | 8.3% |
| Mean travel time to work | 20.9 minutes |

| For population 15 years and over in Baton Rouge | |
|---|---|
| Never married | 39.3% |
| Now married | 40.6% |
| Separated | 2.8% |
| Widowed | 7.2% |
| Divorced | 10.1% |

4.4% Foreign born (2.2% Asia, 1.0% Latin America, 0.7% Europe)

| Crime | |
|---|---|
| Violent Crime risk | 59 murders (25.8 per 100,000) |
| Property Crime risk | 4,070 burglaries (1781.1 per 100,000) |

You might think that nothing much has changed, because blood still runs regularly into the dank earth of this steaming place. Louisiana is second (after Nevada) in the list of 'Most Dangerous States in the USA'. It's a ranking (worked out by rating murders, rapes and other major categories against the national average) that the state manages to achieve year after year. Among the 225,000 population of Baton Rouge itself, crime runs at exactly double the US average.

Perhaps this is because there is little else to do in Baton Rouge but rob, rape and murder your neighbours. Click on the visitor website section in July (when this entry was compiled) and the prospective tourist planning his trip to Baton Rouge is greeted with an awesome choice of... nothing at all. No culinary events, no historical events, no musical performance, family fun or even antique fairs.

Perhaps that is by design. Being the state capital, Baton Rouge tries to distance itself from the fun and frivolity of that action-packed sin city 'N' Awlins' downriver – and manages it handsomely by sending the casual visitor into the North American equivalent of the Aboriginal dream-time trance. All one can hope for is waking up to find that the train that old KK sang about is waiting at the station to whisk you away to somewhere that's more interesting.

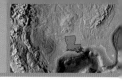

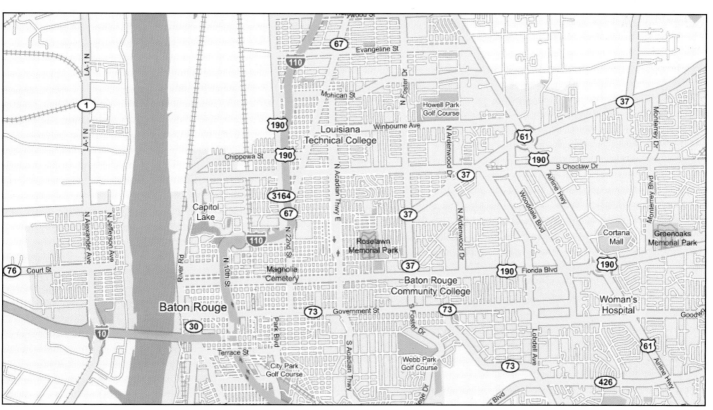

### ABERDEEN, MARYLAND

*Manly Deeds, Womanly Words
(state motto of Maryland)*

Pretty explosive place, Aberdeen. God only knows what the 15,000 or so residents are breathing, drinking, eating as they try to exist in this, one of the most polluted places in the United States. In short, the entire region is a dumping ground for everything that does bad things to a nation's people as well as a nation's enemies. It has experienced years of military and industrial pollution. Where do we begin?

During World War I, the site, first known as the Gunpowder Reservation, produced and filled gas shells. It became Edgewood Arsenal in 1918 and fell under the control of the Ordinance Department when it became part of the new Chemical Warfare Service. Large quantities of chemical agencies were produced. Aberdeen got worse in World War II when it was redesignated the Army Chemical Center. Edgewood now conducts research and development, testing, procurement, production and mobilization planning of chemical material.

Residents near the Aberdeen Proving Ground – described as a US Army Garrison but boasting a huge area designated to such people-friendly activities as the US Army Chemical and Biological Defense Command and US Army Medical research Institute of Chemical Defense – describe the place as 'Hell, hell, hell.'

There is a pervading atmosphere of suspicion and fear in this place, even though the local economy depends to a degree on its citizens tending the poisonous plant in their midst. More than 10,000 civilians are employed at APG, compared

with only 4,700 military personnel, which means that twice as many ordinary folk as Army guys are exposed to this deadly stuff. You'd think they'd keep it in the family a bit more.

Growing concern for the community led to endless meetings to secure a 'clean up' in 1991. Talks dragged on, as only the Department of Defense knows how to stretch them. Aberdeen didn't really get the facts about what all this war garbage was doing to them. And then came 9-11, which prompted Deputy Defense Secretary Paul Wolfowitz to issue a memo instructing DOD employees to protect 'sensitive but unclassified information' that could be 'compiled to reveal sensitive conclusions'. No, we're not sure what he means either. What we do know is that the long-suffering people of Aberdeen lost their right to know just exactly what was poisoning their lives every day.

Organizations such as the Working Group on Community Right-to-Know have joined the people's fight. Their aim is simple: 'To prevent pollution, people need adequate information. With information, communities can better demand accountability from government.' The DOD, however, doesn't believe it is accountable to anyone. It doesn't feel bad that Aberdeen's groundwater and at least 11 drinking wells are contaminated with perchlorate, an ingredient in rocket fuel used at Aberdeen Proving Ground for years. Perchlorate is a particularly nasty pollutant that moves rapidly through soil and groundwater and can cause thyroid tumors and disrupt thyroid hormone levels during pregnancy leading to mental retardation, loss of hearing and speech, birth defects and other problems in infants and children.

To be fair on the DOD, they do ensure a timetable of entertainment in Aberdeen. In 1994, 40 non-stockpile munitions, including sarin mustard and phosgene, were

| | |
|---|---|
| Population (year 2000) | 13,842 |
| Males | 6,579 (47.5%) |
| Females | 7,263 (52.5%) |
| Elevation | 83 feet |
| County | Harford |
| Land area | 6.4 square miles |
| Zip code | 21001 |
| Median resident age | 36.8 years |
| Median household income | $39,190 |
| Median house value | $109,400 |

| Races in Aberdeen | |
|---|---|
| White Non-Hispanic | 63.5% |
| Hispanic | 3.4% |
| Other race | 1.4% |
| American Indian | 1.3% |
| Two or more races | 3.5% |
| Black | 27.4% |
| **Ancestries** | |
| German (16.7%), Irish (10.0%), United States (8.6%), English (8.5%), Italian (3.4%), Scottish (2.3%) | |

| For population 25 years and over in Aberdeen | |
|---|---|
| High school or higher | 77.9% |
| Bachelor's degree or higher | 15.6% |
| Graduate or professional degree | 6.5% |
| Unemployed | 3.6% |
| Mean travel time to work | 25.5 minutes |

| For population 15 years and over in Aberdeen | |
|---|---|
| Never married | 27.5% |
| Now married | 50.2% |
| Separated | 3.5% |
| Widowed | 8.3% |
| Divorced | 10.5% |
| 4.5% Foreign born (2.2% Europe, 1.7% Asia) | |

| Crime | |
|---|---|
| Violent Crime risk | 1 murder (7.1 per 100,000) |
| Property Crime risk | 113 burglaries (804.4 per 100,000) |

unearthed and four of them were detonated in the open, just a few miles from the local population and boaters on Chesapeake Bay.

It is hardly surprising that, according to the US Census Cancer Mortality by State, Maryland has a higher rate of cancer than most of the country, with a reported 193 deaths per 100,000. (Only Delaware with 195 and the District of Columbia with 230 beat that rate – and anyway look at how close they are to the Chesapeake Bay.)

Of course, it is the little people that the big bully boys hurt most. Low-income residents rely on food from the bay to supplement their diets. Thousands eat fish, crabs and snapping turtles – all nicely seasoned with toxins such as dioxin.

If it all wasn't so chilling, we might even be able to raise a smile at the Aberdeen Proving Ground's Hotel Finder. We can't believe anyone would wish to spend a night within a 100-mile radius of this chemically charged catastrophe of a city. Yet the APG's message is: 'Welcome! The US Army's Aberdeen Proving Ground is located in northeastern Maryland near the inland end of Chesapeake Bay. We charge NO SERVICE FEES and our hotel location information and unique codes will save you time and money.'

Is there something in the air that attacks not only the

health of the people of Aberdeen, but their morals too? Property crime levels here are higher than Maryland's average. So too are violent crime levels. Theft is a popular pastime. Because of the city's location – on the north end of the mid-Atlantic region and bisected by Intercity-95 – drugs, weapons and all illicit proceeds destined for points south of New York City routinely transit the city through Baltimore, Aberdeen's major seaport just 25 miles away. Baltimore itself contributes to a substantial amount of international drug trafficking and carries the dubious distinction of being one of the most heroin-plagued cities in the nation for over the past ten years.

So that is the tale of poor polluted, benighted Aberdeen. Named after a proud Scottish city, this is a place whose institutional posioners must have hearts of stone.

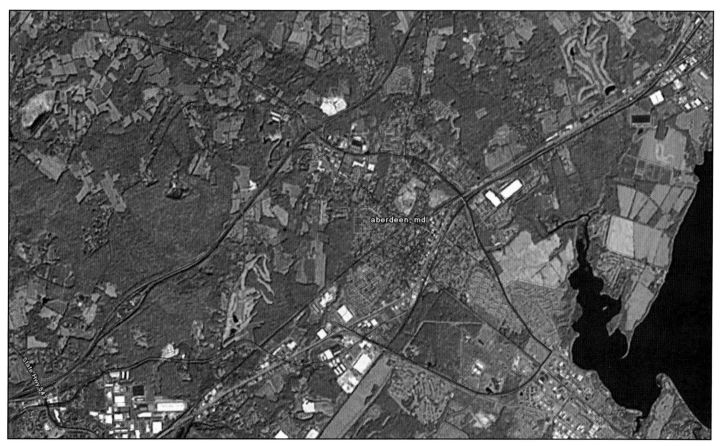

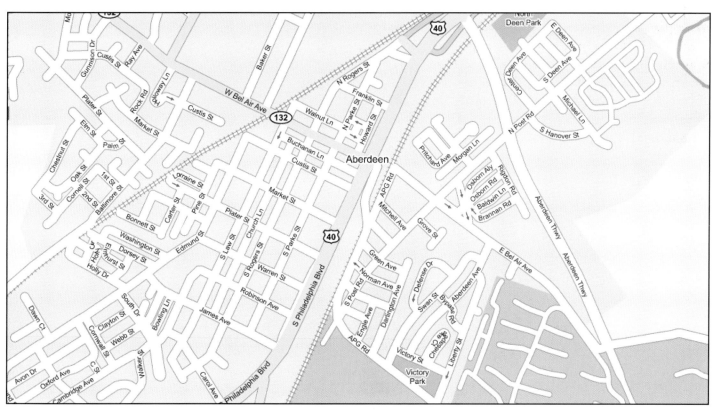

## ACCIDENT, MARYLAND
*Unofficial motto: 'Lack of interest/apathy'*

Accident is a town waiting to happen. Well, at present, you couldn't really call it a proper town. With a population of just 353 at the last count, and snuggled into a total area of one half a square mile, Accident seems to be more of a mirage than a real place.

Yet we now have it on good authority that it really does exist (one of our researchers having recently returned with the joyful news), nestling near Deep Creek Lake in northern Garrett County, the westernmost county of Maryland. It even has its own website, though sadly this is not the mine of information one would wish for. Log on to 'News' and you find the message: 'There is no news to report.' Log on to 'Events' and displayed before you are the words: 'There are no events to report.

Visitors may get the feeling that everyone is sleeping on a 24/7 basis. But lo, then you discover that once a year Accident

wakes up with its 4th of July Homecoming sponsored by the Volunteer Fire Department. The event includes a parade, 'patriotic activity', entertainment 'throughout the day', hay rides, games, art and craft shows, 'fine food and beverages' and a walking tour of the town – the latter, no doubt, accomplished by simply turning round and facing in the opposite direction.

We stumbled on Accident by accident – honest – while trying to avoid a large traffic jam in Western Maryland on July 4. And, wow, were we excited. Sadly, we were too late for the early morning church service and flag raising ceremony that kicks off the annual freedom bash. But we arrived just in time for a moving speech by a Vietnam Vet and we wandered around an impressive display of military uniforms in the Fire Hall. Members of Accident Cultural and Historical Society and the delightfully named Flowery Vale Garden Society were on hand to answer lots of questions. The Accident Concert

Band launched into an afternoon of music and we bought 'I Love Accident' buttons for all of our friends.

But the highlight of the day was a visit to one and only historical structure: a garden shed with a chimney built around 1800. We shouldn't really call it a shed; it is actually a log cabin with a bit of land which Accident's first settlers, James and Pricilla Drane, made their home in 1800 and planned to turn into a farm. Whether this was a happy move, no official Accident report states. What we do know is that James and Pricilla soon discovered that they could not grow tobacco in Western Maryland because of the cool climate. This was certainly a bitter blow to a couple who were, er, tobacco farmers.

Now the patriotic locals are the first to admit that, aside

| Population (year 2000) | 353 |
|---|---|
| Males | 150 (42.5%) |
| Females | 203 (57.5%) |
| Elevation | 2395 feet |
| County | Garrett |
| Land area | 0.5 square miles |
| Zip code | 21520 |
| Median resident age | 38.5 years |
| Median household income | $22,500 |
| Median house value | $91,500 |

| Races in Accident | |
|---|---|
| White Non-Hispanic | 99.7% |
| Hispanic | - |
| Other race | - |
| American Indian | - |
| Two or more races | - |
| Black | - |
| Ancestries | |
| German (36.8%), English (11.9%), United States (11.6%), Irish (6.2%), Italian (5.1%), Scotch-Irish (2.0%) | |

| For population 25 years and over in Accident | |
|---|---|
| High school or higher | 82.6% |
| Bachelor's degree or higher | 18.3% |
| Graduate or professional degree | 10.1% |
| Unemployed | 6.8% |
| Mean travel time to work | 26.7 minutes |

| For population 15 years and over in Accident | |
|---|---|
| Never married | 25.3% |
| Now married | 53.2% |
| Separated | 3.0% |
| Widowed | 14.9% |
| Divorced | 3.7% |
| 1.4% Foreign born | |

| Crime | |
|---|---|
| Violent Crime risk | - |
| Property Crime risk | - |

from July 4, not much really happens in Accident. Most of the houses are hidden in the woods or nestled near Deep Creek Lake, and on any other day of the year you could be forgiven for thinking Accident really is a mirage.

So how did Accident mishap-pen? According to historians, the place can trace its name back to around 1750 when King George II of England paid off a debt to one George Deakins by giving him 600 hectares of land of his choice in western Maryland. Deakins sent out two parties of engineers, with neither party knowing of the other's existence. (See, Accident made its own fun even then). Apparently, when they returned, both parties were amazed to learn they had marked the same oak tree as a starting point and marked off the same acres. Mr Deakins considered this a sign – a happy accident, no less – and duly chose that portion of land, patenting it as 'The Accident Tract'.

Someone once described Accident as 'nothing but woods'. But in fact, the beautiful farmland surrounding Accident is one of its few virtues. What isn't an attractive site is the

county-owned Central Garrett County Industrial Park on the south end of town. The park is anchored by Phenix Technology, manufacturers of electrical motors, and Garrett Container Systems, manufacturer of large shipping containers. Both companies have expanded, leaving very little land available for development in the Park.

While we're on Accident's dark side, now is the time to mention that the town's commercial area is bisected by Route 219, a busy corridor connection between Deep Creek Lake and Interstate 68. Therefore, its main thoroughfare is, as one recent report noted, 'heavily traveled' with automobile and truck traffic.

Oh, and in reference to that report, it is officially called the Community Legacy Strategic Plan. And it makes for fun reading. The report, aimed at creating a purposeful and prosperous future for Accident, lists the place's strengths and weaknesses. Strangely, the industrial park is defined as a 'strength', along with 'sense of community' and 'beauty of area'. Accident's recorded weaknesses are topped by 'lack of participation/apathy', closely followed by 'stagnant population' and 'sewer system'. Strange how the two seem to belong to each other. Another weakness is apparently 'not taking advantage of tourists', which can be interpreted at least two ways.

We digress. Accident has 17 businesses which include two restaurants, one bakery two 'auto-related' and two medical. The place is anything but thriving. There have been declines in the construction and manufacturing jobs which were once the big-earners. Now the tourism industry is proving a popular employer – but in Accident, that isn't enough. Those capable or keen enough to earn larger wages have left the town for pastures new, leaving it with more than the country's average number of lower paid.

Perhaps they have all fled to another state, for Accident's home county of Maryland is not a healthy place to be. It rates sixth in the country in the cancer risk states. There are also massive quantities of chicken manure circulating in the county, but that's way down from Accident, in the Chesapeake Bay area, so it would be unfair to make any chicken shit jokes about the little place. (But did you know, incidentally, that a typical farm raises 200,000 chickens every year, supplying more than enough nitrogen and phosphorus in chicken droppings to fertilize more than 100 acres of crops?)

Anyway, back to Accident. With just 353 people hanging around, it isn't hard to work out a breakdown of the population. There are 138 households and 96 families. The racial make-up is 99.72 per cent white and, intriguingly, a mere 0.28 per cent 'from two or more races.' Just over half of the households are married couples, 37.3 per cent have children under 18, 30.4 per cent are non-families and 21.7 per cent have someone living alone over the age of 65 years.

Want more statistics from Accident? The average age is 38. For every 100 females aged 18 and over, there are only 73.6 males. Which obviously means some gals are gonna miss out. Hence, no doubt, the fact that 12.3 per cent of the households have a female with no husband present.

It gets sadder. Out of Accident's total population, 17.3 per cent of those under the age of 18, and 24.1 per cent of those 65 and older, are living below the poverty line. Yet Accident is officially described as an 'attractive place for retirees' – perhaps because it is nice and quiet and there is nothing to spend your money on.

In fact, it isn't always deadly quiet. For two weeks every summer the North American Academy of Piping School sets up shop at the Hickory Education Center and would-be bagpipers fork out $600 for the privilege of learning to play in the woods. We have it on good authority that sounds of 'skirling' – that's the nasty screechy noise amateurs make when trying to tune up – echo throughout Accident.

But the sleepy locals don't like to complain. This Community Legacy Strategic Plan, which we mentioned earlier, is making a valiant attempt to revitalise Accident – and if that means screeching bagpipes disrupting the peace, so be it.. There is even talk of a Revitalization Task Force. To this end, suggestions for making Accident somewhere you'd want to be include 're-enactments of daily life' (you'd have to find signs of life first), 'pick your own' programmes (we hope they mean fruit), and putting potted plants along Main Street.

Otherwise, this wise report notes, Accident – not the most pro-active place in the USA – might fall foul of one of the many 'threats' it faces. Including (and isn't there a familiar ring about this?) 'lack of interest/apathy...'

### MELROSE, MASSACHUSETTS

*By the sword we seek peace, but peace only under liberty (state motto of Massachusetts)*

A local newspaper report on a rash of drug overdoses in Melrose, Massachusetts, began with the question: 'Why Melrose? … Why now?' The real question nowadays should be: 'Why Melrose? … Full point.'

Actually, we know why everyone in Melrose feels the need to seek solace in mind altering illegal substances. We probably would too if we were forced to live in a town with no alcohol. There are no bars, no discos, no restaurants selling anything worth drinking and not even a liquor store.

Now we are aware from our history books that the Puritans founded Massachusetts. They first sailed in on the Mayflower back in 1620 after being persecuted for their religious beliefs in Britain. We can only guess that some of them settled in Melrose and, while its liberal big sister Boston took to drink with a gusto, the tut-tut Puritan influence remains to this day in poor Melrose.

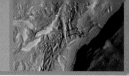

| Population (year 2000) | 27,134 |
|---|---|
| Males | 12,757 (47.0%) |
| Females | 14,377 (53.0%) |
| Elevation | 133 feet |
| County | Middlesex |
| Land area | 4.7 square miles |
| Zip code | 02176 |
| Median resident age | 39.4 years |
| Median household income | $62,811 |
| Median house value | $254,400 |

| Races in Melrose | |
|---|---|
| White Non-Hispanic | 94.5% |
| Hispanic | 1.0% |
| Other race | - |
| American Indian | - |
| Two or more races | 1.4% |
| Black | 0.9% |
| Ancestries | |
| Irish (35.3%), Italian (22.4%), English (13.1%), German (5.6%), French (4.8%), French Canadian (3.8%) | |

| For population 25 years and over in Melrose | |
|---|---|
| High school or higher | 91.6% |
| Bachelor's degree or higher | 40.1% |
| Graduate or professional degree | 15.0% |
| Unemployed | 2.0% |
| Mean travel time to work | 28.4 minutes |

| For population 15 years and over in Melrose | |
|---|---|
| Never married | 27.8% |
| Now married | 56.5% |
| Separated | 1.4% |
| Widowed | 7.4% |
| Divorced | 6.9% |
| 6.1% Foreign born (2.8% Europe, 1.7% Asia, 0.8% North America) | |

| Crime | |
|---|---|
| Violent Crime risk | 0 murders (0.0 per 100,000) |
| Property Crime risk | 73 burglaries (265.7 per 100,000) |

This town of Melrose, just seven miles north of Boston, began life as a tiny settlement in 1633 (although not chartered as a city until 1899) and its name is said to be due to a resemblance to the scenery of Melrose, Scotland. We have to assume the settlers were blind, rather than blind drunk. Or maybe they too had been taking exciting hallucinogenic substances. For anyone who has visited the beautiful Scots Borders town of Melrose, with its exquisite abbey and gentle riverside setting, will fail to notice any similarity.

Unlike its idyllic transatlantic namesake, the Massachusetts Melrose expanded through manufacturing – its proudest products including metalwork, leather goods, clothing and rubber shoes – which funded the building of some fine Victorian homes dating from the late 1800s.

Its past influences its make-up now. White non-Hispanics dominate the 28,000-strong population (94.5 per cent), with all other categories having minimal appearances. Ancestries are predominantly Irish, Italian and English. The good folk of Melrose are generally well educated (91.6 per cent high school

or higher; 15 per cent graduate or professional degree) and unemployment (at 2 per cent) is low. Whereas in much of this book, the crime figures are depressing, the official figures for Melrose begin with: 'Murders 0 (0.0 per 100,000).'

So what's wrong with the place?

Absolutely nothing, according to the Melrose Mirror, a local newspaper that goes to great pains to assure its readers that they reside in the greatest city in America. The paper invites their 'Random Thoughts' and is rewarded with essays on 'Library gets new flagpole' and 'Quilting is my hobby'. One contained a parable that proved just what a super-dooper city Melrose is. To quote (sorry, we mean To gush):

'Take a walk along the main street and be ready to respond to the many smiles and "howdys" you will receive along the way. I think that the pleasant smiles of our citizens reflect the attitudes of the offices and the officers who are responsible for the care of the city proper and its citizens. They are always ready to lend a helping hand.

'One day I saw three little children leave the YMCA with their mother who was carrying a sled. The youngsters insisted that she was to ride on the sled and they proceeded to run and slide down East Foster Street on the sidewalk with Mommy dragging her feet so that no one was in harms way.'

Hmmm. To quote a local: 'I'm afraid mom sleding down East Foster Street is about as exciting as it gets here. There is absolutely nothing to do. We've got a boring main street full of boring fast-food joints and that is just about it. Anyone unlucky enough to be born in Melrose gets the hell out at the first opportunity. It's a total dump.'

We can only assume that's why there has been a rash of drug overdoses. Some people really are that desperate to check out of town.

# MELROSE

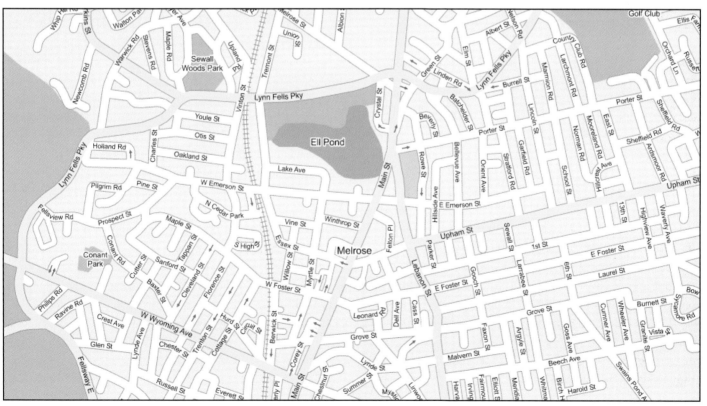

### SPRINGFIELD, MASSACHUSETTS
*Motto: 'The Comeback City of America'*

It is nicknamed 'The Comeback City of America', which is wrong on two counts. It's attempt at a comeback from the depths of recession and depression hasn't worked. And no-one visiting would ever come back.

You have to be amongst America's obsessed basketball nuts

to even set foot in the place, because Springfield is where the game was invented – probably because bouncing and throwing a ball was the only thing bordering on the skilful and creative that anyone could ever do here. No matter where you wander in this urban mess, and no matter how hard you try to escape them, signs pointing to the Basketball Hall of Fame are always in the line of vision.

What is now Springfield was founded as a fur trading post in 1636 by William Pynchon on land bought from the Indians. Five years later, it was named in honor of Pynchon's English birthplace – which is fitting, because the English Springfield has since been subsumed into the city of Birmingham, in the heart of the grimy industrial Midlands. In the eighteenth century, the American Springfield harnessed the power of the Connecticut River, and mills of all varieties sprouted. In the nineteenth century, it became a major railroad center and experienced another industrial boom.

Those booms have come and gone, leaving a sad legacy. One indication of its demise is the crime tally. The invaluable City-data.com Crime Index marks Springfield at 896.3 – shamefully higher than the US average of 330.6.

| Population (year 2000) | 152,082 |
|---|---|
| Males | 71,802 |
| Females | 80,280 |
| Elevation | 70 feet |
| County | Hampden |
| Land area | 32.1 square miles |
| Zip code | |
| Median resident age | 31.9 years |
| Median household income | $30,417 |
| Median house value | $87,300 |

| Races in Springfield | |
|---|---|
| White Non-Hispanic | 48.8% |
| Hispanic | 27.2% |
| Other race | 16.4% |
| American Indian | 1.0% |
| Two or more races | 4.0% |
| Black | 21.0% |
| Ancestries | |
| Irish (12.6%), Italian (9.3%), French (8.2%), Polish (6.0%), English (4.8%), French Canadian (4.4%) | |

| For population 25 years and over in Springfield | |
|---|---|
| High school or higher | 73.4% |
| Bachelor's degree or higher | 15.4% |
| Graduate or professional degree | 5.9% |
| Unemployed | 8.5% |
| Mean travel time to work | 21.5 minutes |

| For population 15 years and over in Springfield | |
|---|---|
| Never married | 38.4% |
| Now married | 39.9% |
| Separated | 4.0% |
| Widowed | 7.5% |
| Divorced | 10.2% |
| 8.0% Foreign born (2.7% Latin America, 2.6% Europe, 1.9% Asia) | |

| Crime | |
|---|---|
| Violent Crime risk | 12 murders (7.8 per 100,000) |
| Property Crime risk | 3,808 burglaries (2473.3 per 100,000) |

Another result is more physical: today's Springfield is yet another of those US towns that is synonymous with 'industrial' and 'sprawl'. Pretty it is not, with an ugly heart for a city centre that is split by the Connecticut River.

To be fair, the town's literature and website do not try to hide these disfiguring inheritances from the past. The town boasts of its 'multicultural diversity', admits it is a 'city for business', and it hopes for 'new growth in the twenty-first century'. It adds: 'Midway between New York and Boston and on the road between New York and Canada, Springfield is ideally located for travel in all directions.' But presumably only one way – out!

The city is also proud to be home to America's first frozen foods, the Springfield rifle and children's writer Dr Seuss – whom the place must have disturbed enough to write Green Eggs and Ham. There's the Dr Seuss National Memorial Sculpture Garden in his honor, where undoubtedly, amongst the exhibits of his characters, you will find a metallic Cat in a metallic Hat.

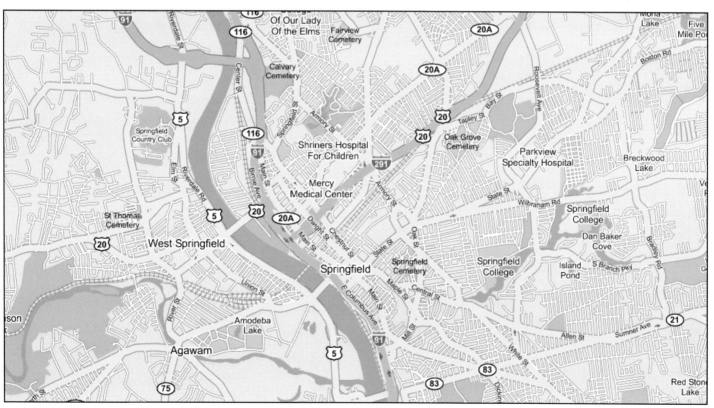

### DETROIT, MICHIGAN

*If you seek a pleasant peninsula, look about you
(state motto of Michigan)*

It spawned Madonna, Eminem, Motown Music and the modern motor car, but back in 1996 Detroit earned itself the accolade of 'world's least appealing travel destination'. Locals – or what's left of them, as people have been deserting this grubby urban mess for years – responded by printing t-shirts saying 'I'm so bad I vacation in Detroit'.

What's changed since then. Very little. Downtown is a no-go zone and the Southern suburbs are just as bad. The cars that made Detroit famous provided the means of escape. Brave tourists venturing into the city are advised to stay in Ann Arbor, its hipper sister city, and to avoid motels around the bus station at all costs.

Henry Ford would be spinning in his grave if he could see his great metropolis now. Boarded up, abandoned buildings

and an eerie ghost-town ambience interspersed with blasts of gunfire are enough to send even the bravest of travellers running for cover. The once-grand Michigan Central train station is surrounded by razor wire. and empty weed-infested lots signify a half-hearted attempt at cleaning up the abandoned slums. In 2005 14,000 buildings were slated for demolition as the city attempted for the fourth or fifth time to re-generate.

Founded as a trading post in 1701 by the French explorer Antoine de la Mothe Cadillac, who lent his name to the car some two centuries later, the place was acquired by the Americans in 1796 , surrendered to the British in the 1812 war and regained the following year by the States. Its name means 'strait' in French, signifying the narrow waterway which marks the American-Canadian border.

A large traffic-choked tunnel leads to Windsor, Ontario, and for many travellers passing through Detroit it is the only thing they want to see in this once grand town. Analysing 400 metropolitan areas in the US and Canada for their book Cities Ranked and Rated, authors Bert Sperling and Peter Sander describe Detroit as 'a lesson in the evolution of urban America'. In other words, it expanded quickly, fell from grace and has now gone to the dogs.

It has always been a transportation hub; carriage and bicycle manufacture having begun in the 19th century, and industry exploded with the advent of the motor car. During World War Two, the city produced military equipment. But by the 1960s, Detroit was on the outs, and people began deserting for the leafy suburbs. Foreign car manufacture knocked Motor City for six, and 1967 race riots signalled the beginning of the end.

| Population (year 2000) | 951,270 |
|---|---|
| Males | 448,319 (47.1%) |
| Females | 502,951 (52.9%) |
| Elevation | 600 feet |
| County | Wayne |
| Land area | 138.8 square miles |
| Zip code | 48201 - 48242 |
| Median resident age | 30.9 years |
| Median household income | $29,526 |
| Median house value | $63,600 |

| Races in Detroit | |
|---|---|
| White Non-Hispanic | 10.5% |
| Hispanic | 5.0% |
| Other race | 2.5% |
| American Indian | 0.9% |
| Two or more races | 2.3% |
| Black | 81.6% |

**Ancestries**

Polish (2.0%), German (1.8%), Subsaharan African (1.8%), Irish (1.5%), United States (1.2%)

| For population 25 years and over in Detroit | |
|---|---|
| High school or higher | 69.6% |
| Bachelor's degree or higher | 11.0% |
| Graduate or professional degree | 4.2% |
| Unemployed | 13.8% |
| Mean travel time to work | 28.4 minutes |

| For population 15 years and over in Detroit | |
|---|---|
| Never married | 43.6% |
| Now married | 31.2% |
| Separated | 4.2% |
| Widowed | 8.3% |
| Divorced | 12.7% |

4.8% Foreign born (2.1% Latin America, 1.6% Asia, 0.6% Europe)

| Crime | |
|---|---|
| Violent Crime risk | 395 murders (41.3 per 100,000) |
| Property Crime risk | 15,096 burglaries (1578.6 per 100,000) |

Today the growth industry is crime. Some 743 people per 100,000 were victms of violent crime last year alone, against the national average of 456. Actually the crime rates are dipping – but that's more to do with the city's shrinking population. The metropolitan sprawl, which includes neighbouring Flint, has 4.4 million residents but the city center's population has dropped from 2 million in the 1950s to 951,000 in 2000.

Public transport is practically non-existent, because the city fathers saw no reason to provide trains or subways when the motor car was king. Instead it lists amongst its achievements America's first mile of concrete pavement in 1909, the first traffic light in 1915 and the first city freeway in 1942.

So what does one do in Detroit? Personally we'd recommend the Henry Ford Museum – but that's because it's several miles away in the leafy suburb of Dearborn. Seriously though, it's worth the visit to see the limo President John Kennedy was assassinated in, the Lunar Rover used on the Apollo space mission and the bus in which Rosa Parks was travelling in Montgomery, Alabama, in 1955 when she refused to give up her seat to a white person and sparked the civil rights movement.

Rosa Parks is revered in Detroit, where 81 per cent of the population is African American, and she has a road named after her. It's a couple of blocks from the Motown Historical Museum, which was once called Hitsville USA, and is home to Berry Gordy's Motown recording studios.

The pokey studio where the likes of Diana Ross and the Supremes, Smokey Robinson and the Jackson Five cut their first hits still remains. But Berry and his stars – like every other sensible person from Detroit – long ago got the hell outta town.

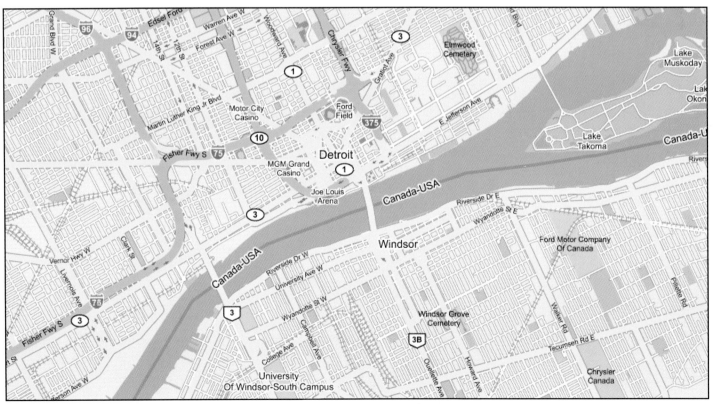

## PHILADELPHIA, MISSISSIPPI

*By valor and arms*
*(state motto of Mississippi)*

Philadelphia, Mississippi, is the town that, by rights, should have died of shame. No such luck — although, to all appearances, it has long been in its death throes.

Its grim racial history made Philadelphia infamous way back in 1964 with the murder of three civil rights workers, a crime that was the inspiration for film Mississippi Burning. It took four decades before proper justice was at last seen to be done, when in 2005 one of the perpetrators was finally convicted.

But whereas it was a single, extreme act of bigotry that put Philadelphia on the map, the fetid climate and rank poverty of the town suggests that it could just as easily be wiped off again. Which would be a pity, because this place has a noble history.

The Choctaw Nation have lived in this part of the world

for at least 400 years. A proud tribe, in 1831 they refused federal demands to abandon their ancestral homeland in favour of Indian Territories in Oklahoma, hiding out in swamp and forest while the US government took 63,000 square miles of their lands. They are more prominent citizens these days, developing businesses, creating an industrial park and operating the state's largest casino on their tribal land. Uniquely among Native Americans, they have retained their language, and 90 percent of tribal members speak their native tongue, with English as a second language.

The rest of Neshoba County, where the Choctaw live, have a less proud history. This town of Philadelphia, about 100 miles north-east of Jackson, has a population of 7,300, made up of 55 per cent White and 40 per cent Black, with an average age in the mid-thirties and a strange imbalance of 55 per cent female and 45 per cent male. As of the last survey, the per capita income for the city was $15,787, with 28 per cent

of the population below the poverty line. And to prove things are not getting any better, 41 per cent of those under the age of 18 are living below the poverty line.

This is not too unusual for Mississippi, of course. It is the state that consistently comes top in the table of 'Least Livable States', ranked by 43 data categories. According to the latest census, Mississippi has the fifth lowest median income in the United States. But it's worse if you're black; the per capita income of black Mississippians is about half that of the whites. And in a state where Blacks constitute 36 percent of the total population, they make up about 75 percent of the prison population.

So, as we know, with poverty comes crime, ignorance, mistrust and hatred. When three young civil rights workers

| Population (year 2000) | 7,303 |
|---|---|
| Males | 3,276 (44.9%) |
| Females | 4,027 (55.1%) |
| Elevation | 424 feet |
| County | Neshoba |
| Land area | 10.6 square miles |
| Zip code | 39350 |
| Median resident age | 36.5 years |
| Median household income | $26,438 |
| Median house value | $56,200 |

| Races in Philadelphia | |
|---|---|
| White Non-Hispanic | 54.9% |
| Hispanic | 1.5% |
| Other race | 0.5% |
| American Indian | 2.6% |
| Two or more races | 1.2% |
| Black | 40.1% |
| Ancestries | |
| United States (14.0%), Irish (5.4%), English (5.1%), German (2.2%), Scotch-Irish (2.1%) | |

| For population 25 years and over in Philadelphia | |
|---|---|
| High school or higher | 70.9% |
| Bachelor's degree or higher | 18.0% |
| Graduate or professional degree | 6.3% |
| Unemployed | 9.1% |
| Mean travel time to work | 16.3 minutes |

| For population 15 years and over in Philadelphia | |
|---|---|
| Never married | 28.9% |
| Now married | 44.6% |
| Separated | 2.8% |
| Widowed | 11.8% |
| Divorced | 12.0% |
| 0.9% Foreign born | |

| Crime | |
|---|---|
| Violent Crime risk | - |
| Property Crime risk | - |

— James Chaney, 21, Andrew Goodman, 20, and Michael Schwerner, 24) — were murdered in Philadelphia in 1964, it made national headlines but was not considered at all out of place in Mississippi. After all, the slayings of 14-year-old Chicago youth Emmett Till in Money in 1955, of Medgar Evans, the state's NAACP (National Association for the Advancement of Colored People) chairman in Jackson in 1963, and of civil rights supporter Vernon Dahmer in Hattiesburg in 1966 all went unpunished.

The three murdered in Philadelphia — there as part of the Mississippi Freedom Summer, a civil rights initiative to register black voters — went missing after they had gone to investigate the burning of a black church. That same day, they had been stopped near Philadelphia and taken to jail for a supposed speeding violation. Local Ku Klux Klansmen were tipped off and, when later released, the three were ambushed, murdered and their bodies buried nearby. In 1967, seven men were convicted of conspiracy, although none served longer than six years. Eleven others walked free, one of them Klansman

Edgar Ray Killen. But in June 2005, Killen, then aged 80, was brought back to court and finally jailed as a murderer.

So has anything changed in this little Mississippi town? .Some lawyers and journalists close to the case allege that at least seven others involved in the killings are still alive and free. Ben Chaney, brother of victim James Chaney, said after the trial that the Black community still suffered in Philadelphia, adding that: 'Blacks are the last to get hired and the first to get fired.'. And local civil rights leader Leroy Clemons described the town, rather diplomatically, as having 'economic shortcomings'.

The faded shop fronts are the most graphic indicator of the decline of the place, although the Philadelphia Chamber of Commerce does its best to look on the bright side. It boasts: 'Blessed with natural beauty and small-town charm, Neshoba County and Philadelphia offer the best in recreation, relaxation, and entertainment with events like the annual Neshoba County Fair and Choctaw Indian Fair, the Pearl River Resort and an excellent system of public parks. The area offers outstanding 18-hole golf course facilities at the Dancing Rabbit Golf Club on the Choctaw Indian Reservation and the Philadelphia Country Club. Come take a tour of our fair city.'

Perhaps something is being done at last to revamp Philadelphia's image and consign its shameful past to fading memory. After all, who would wish to remind the world of its ignorance, bigotry, persecution and easy recourse to violence?

Well, Philadelphia Chamber of Commerce, for one. Their office has produced a glossy brochure urging visitors to come and gawk at its bloody history. With a map showing where the three young men were murdered and buried, tourists are invited to join 'a journey toward freedom'. The title of this hypocritical pamphlet capitalizing on the victims of the Civil Rights Movement is: 'Neshoba County, African-American Heritage Driving Tour: Roots of Struggle, Rewards of Sacrifice'.

Someone else's sacrifice… but let's cash in anyway.

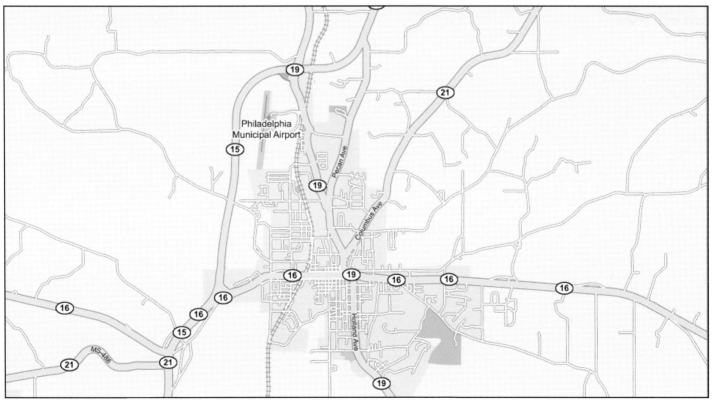

## BRANSON, MISSOURI

*The welfare of the people shall be the supreme law (state motto of Missouri)*

Ah, Branson. The billion dollar 'leisure vacation destination' with its non-stop spectaculars, state-of-the-art stages and shows that just go on and on and on and...

We mentioned Branson to a friend of ours. 'Home to the Osmond Family Theatre and a host of other musical venues featuring people you've vaguely heard of but can't quite picture,' was the reply. Then came the afterthought: 'Basically this is Nashville for old people with the early-bird specials and other fast food all mushed up so the old folk with false teeth – or no teeth at all – don't have to worry about chewing.'

The good people of Branson might dispute all this. After all, with the average age of inhabitants being 43, it has to be the influx of the REALLY aged that's bringing the place down. Yes, Branson is certainly on the map when it comes to turn-up-and-watch entertainment, but it's lost its way in the real world.

Let's, for a start, look at how Branson compares with the rest of Missouri. Even the word 'average' is too good for the place. The median household income is below state average. The number of college students is below state average. And because the millions of visitors and the emphasis on having a good time would drive any sensible person mad, it is no wonder that the length of stay in Branson is officially 'significantly below' state average. Anything in Branson above state average? Yes, the number of unemployed is above state average; property crime is above state average; violent crime is above state average. We've already mentioned the average age of Branson. Naturally enough, that's above state average too.

So with the statistics nicely in place, let's take a closer look at Branson. One of the state's top tourist attractions, it is home to 45 theaters and (following completion of a monster of a complex in 2005) 110 shows, buckets of fishing, several theme parks and music resounding from every corner. More than seven million visitors a year stop by. Hence, as we have already noted, several thousand inhabitants move on elsewhere as quickly as possible. Have we mentioned yet just how many people actually try to live in Branson? It's around 6,000. Yes, just 6,000, all no doubt spending most of their time hiding under the duvets in this little mountain town. The place was growing by six per cent a year in the Nineties but that has slowed to a mere one per cent, and we wondered why.

Branson glories under the name of Ozark Disneyland. (Ozark, because Branson nestles among the Orzark lakes. I don't think we need to explain the Disneyland bit). The town's proud Mission Statement is: 'The City of Branson is committed to its citizens and to those who visit here, to ensure a safe and environmentally sound community... We look to tomorrow, remembering yesterday, dedicated to excellence today.'

That's all rather grandiose, considering you're talking about a city whose culture and style boasts the Baldknobbers Jamboree as its longest-running show. It is in its 46th season, it is billed as Branson's First Show, and is still packing 'em every night in to its 1,500-seat theatre. 'Come see a show of country, bluegrass, gospel, patriotic music, beautiful costumes and Droopy Drawers Jr,' scream the billboards. Or as Baldknobbers Jamboree singer and guitarist Dennis Mabe says (and he should know): 'Day or night, our little town of Branson, Missouri, just may hold more stars than anywhere else in the universe.'

| Population (year 2000) | 6,050 |
|---|---|
| Males | 2,810 (46.4%) |
| Females | 3,240 (53.6%) |
| Elevation | 722 feet |
| County | Taney |
| Land area | 16.2 square miles |
| Zip code | 65616 |
| Median resident age | 43.0 years |
| Median household income | $31,997 |
| Median house value | $123,900 |

| Races in Branson | |
|---|---|
| White Non-Hispanic | 92.0% |
| Hispanic | 4.3% |
| Other race | 1.5% |
| American Indian | 1.5% |
| Two or more races | 1.6% |
| Black | 0.8% |
| **Ancestries** | |
| German (18.7%), English (14.5%), Irish (11.9%), United States (10.4%), French (4.1%), Dutch (2.9%) | |

| For population 25 years and over in Branson | |
|---|---|
| High school or higher | 83.3% |
| Bachelor's degree or higher | 20.8% |
| Graduate or professional degree | 6.5% |
| Unemployed | 8.8% |
| Mean travel time to work | 16.0 minutes |

| For population 15 years and over in Branson | |
|---|---|
| Never married | 17.8% |
| Now married | 56.7% |
| Separated | 1.8% |
| Widowed | 9.9% |
| Divorced | 13.8% |
| 3.5% Foreign born (2.0% Asia, 0.6% Europe, 0.5% Latin America, 0.4% North America) | |

| Crime | |
|---|---|
| Violent Crime risk | 0 murders (0.0 per 100,000) |
| Property Crime risk | 133 burglaries (2185.0 per 100,000) |

Now what would Ruben Branson make of all this? It was he, back in 1882, who opened the first general store. From then on, the place attracted settlers who took a shine to the fertile land, abundance of game and fishing in the White River. In 1895, little Branson's tomato crops were thriving and a cannery was built. It was the completion of the Iron Mountain and Southern railroad in 1903 that brought Branson into the real world – or the unreal one, depending on which way you look at it. People from miles away wanted to come and explore what was still an unspoiled location, and soon an area was designated as a town under the direction of Charles Fulbright, president of the Branson Town Company. There was a bit of a tussle when it was discovered that another businessman, a Mr B. B. Price, wanted to put his own town there, but eventually Mr Fulbright won and the name Branson was saved for posterity.

Come 1904 and Branson had two saloons, a rooming house, two doctors and several other businesses as well as the General Store, and within a decade the town had become a thriving little tourist hotspot, with the lake attracting keen fisher folk and the commercial ice plant, soft drink bottling plant and candy and ice cream factories attracting a lot of money. Records show that an average 27,000 visitors visited Branson during the summer of 1913, as the stage was set, we can aptly say, for its future in the entertainment industry.

And it is entertainment, unremitting entertainment, that has given Branson its fun and fast reputation. This is where we came in. The growth of Branson's show time is really down to CBS, whose 60 Minutes programme featured the place some years ago. This led to the real entertainment explosion, and now the building and showbiz just goes on and on.

Take April for instance. That's the month when Branson

annually. What can you find to spend so much money on? Yep, you guessed it…

According to the Drug Rehabs organisation: 'Drug trafficking organizations control a large majority of the distribution of methamphetamine, cocaine, marijuana, and heroin in Branson. Various organizations continue to traffic in cocaine and heroin. Crack Cocaine continues to be readily available in all urban areas of the city. In addition, small toxic methamphetamine laboratories are found in Branson.'

That's the sleazy side of Branson. The calm, quiet side is reflected in the waters of Lake Taneycomo which flows through the city. Sadly, we jest – for tranquillity is just anathema to the city fathers. The lake is scheduled for a 'water show of spectacular proportions' that can be seen from Branson Landing, and, since the company responsible boasts the Bellagio Hotel in Las Vegas, Disney Marketplace in Orlando and Universal Citywalk in Universal City, California, it's guaranteed to be anything but peaceful. Branson Landing doesn't escape either; it is earmarked for one of the country's 'most attractive and dynamic mixed-use projects' comprising a hotel, retail, convention center, condominium and yes, of course, theatre space.

The curtain, it seems, will never come down on Branson, Missouri. But the town that aspires to become a rival to Las Vegas has a lot of catching up to do. Vegas is, after all, is a byword for everything gawdy, tawdry, tacky, brash and bad-taste. Branson isn't as good as that.

kicks into 'high gear' with Branson Fest, a five-day festival. It is also the month when the 'internationally-awarded' Silver Dollar City Theme Park opens, with the first of its four seasonal festivals, World Fest, bringing in hundreds of performers from around the world. Then there's Dolly Parton's Dixie Stampede, complete with six tons of real live buffalo leading the stampede nightly. There's also the Sullivan Shows, the Welt Resort, the Jim Stafford Theater and, as from July 2005, The New Lakes Theater. Away from theaterland, there's the Powder Keg that explodes constantly at the Silver Dollar Theme Park and the Branson Balloon, in which 40 folk can take to the air at any one time and enjoy aerial views of the Ozarks. The Titanic Museum and Attraction is the newest happening at Branson.

Don't think the fun stops in winter. That's when you have the BransonFest (in March) and the Ozark Mountain Christmas (in November and December) 'to ensure year-round tourist traffic'.

Of course, there has to be somewhere to put up all the fun-seeking folk who visit Branson. The sensible people who live there sure ain't having anything to do with them. It's a good job, then, that there are over 18,000 hotel rooms available – especially when you know that Branson's little population swells to over 100,000 every single day.

Those visitors have created a $1.7 billion tourism industry with more than $50 million in sales tax revenue generated. The total retail sales revenue for the county is over $1 billion

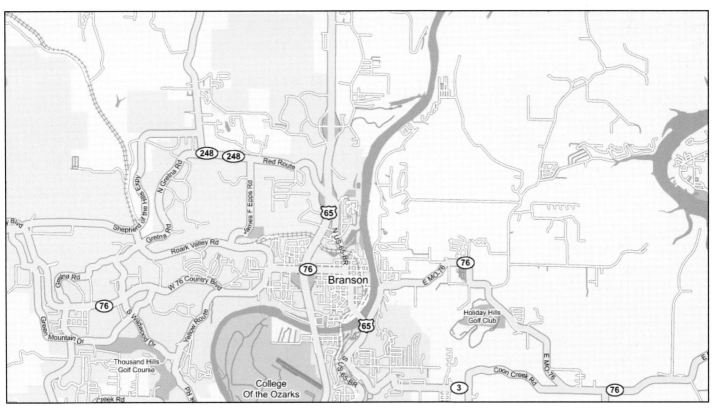

### BUTTE, MONTANA
*'Oro y plata' (Gold and silver) (state motto of Montana)*

'Hey guys, come and have a look at this!' says one thrilled tourist on a viewing platform at Butte's Berkeley Pit. Is he witnessing a great testimony to man's excavational skills? Or a slice of history that has us awe-struck? Shucks no. He's gawping at the most toxic stretch of water in the United States. It's here, right in Butte, which for some dumb reason is pronounced 'beaut', as in thing of beauty.

The question on our lips is: Why? Berkeley Pit is a stinking, horrid mass of poisoned water in a disused mine. It could win prizes for size, being 1,800 feet deep, 5,600 feet wide and 7,000 feet long. It could certainly win awards for controversy, with the clean-up brigade who want rid of the water-logged mass coming up against the traditionalists who believe that one day it can all be put back just as it was in the days when Butte was 'the richest hill on earth' teeming with mineral seams.

Gray, black, a literal pit of despair, is how Butte can be summed up. Abandoned pits line the hillside, together with slagheaps and old buildings, the remains of the copper-mining industry.

Butte's mining industry might be dead, but it refuses to let it rest in peace. Outside the World Museum of Mining is a collection of rusting machinery and the museum's 35-building Hell Roaring Gulch re-creates a cobbled-street mining camp complete with church, schoolhouse, Chinese laundry, saloon and bordello. Bordello? Ah, yes. Those miners needed some light relief after hours in the dark. Sadly for these fellas, when the last pit closed down in 1982 (after much rioting) the last brothel closed with it.

One local, Rudy Gircek, tried to inject some fun into the old town by opening the Dumas Brothel Museum. The Dumas was built as a brothel in 1890 and stayed in business

| Population (year 2000) | 33,892 |
|---|---|
| Males | 16,755 (49.4%) |
| Females | 17,137 (50.6%) |
| Elevation | 4462 feet |
| County | Pondera |
| Land area | 716.1 square miles |
| Zip code | 59750 |
| Median resident age | 38.9 years |
| Median household income | $30,516 |
| Median house value | $75,900 |

| Races in Butte | |
|---|---|
| White Non-Hispanic | 93.7% |
| Hispanic | 2.7% |
| Other race | 0.6% |
| American Indian | 2.9% |
| Two or more races | 1.4% |
| Black | - |
| Ancestries | |
| Irish (27.4%), German (18.2%), English (15.3%), Italian (6.3%), Norwegian (5.5%), French (5.1%) | |

| For population 25 years and over in Butte | |
|---|---|
| High school or higher | 85.2% |
| Bachelor's degree or higher | 21.9% |
| Graduate or professional degree | 6.9% |
| Unemployed | 6.7% |
| Mean travel time to work | 14.2 minutes |

| For population 15 years and over in Butte | |
|---|---|
| Never married | 23.9% |
| Now married | 53.4% |
| Separated | 1.1% |
| Widowed | 9.6% |
| Divorced | 12.0% |
| 1.6% Foreign born | |

| Crime | |
|---|---|
| Violent Crime risk | - |
| Property Crime risk | - |

until that doomed day in 1982. For a while, it was the only surviving building of a once thriving red-light district, and tours gave visitors a fascinating glimpse into underground 'bedrooms' accessible through tunnels that connected with the uptown business district.

We were tempted to rush along and take a peek at this piece of significant social history. Unfortunately, the place closed down for good in May 2005 due to local apathy and to burglars stealing most of the museum's artefacts...

Some people think we are being mean about Butte, especially as it strives to be hospitable. With its large Irish population, the place hosts the biggest St Patrick's Day in the Rockies, with an estimated 40,000 people passing through. If that counts as green culture, then all we can say is that the place could do with a few trees.

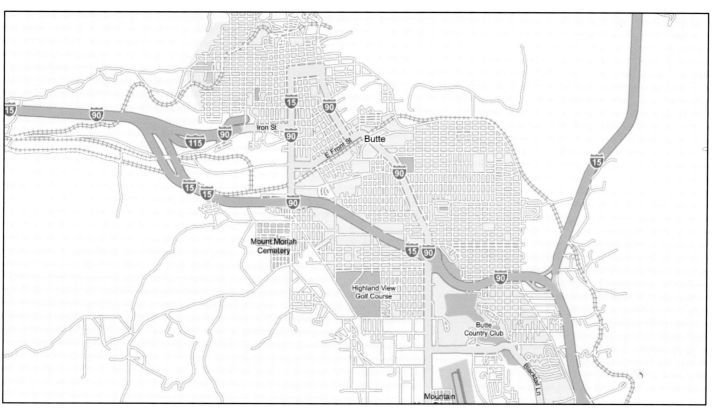

## LINCOLN, NEBRASKA
*Motto: 'The Prairie capital city'*

**M**ention Lincoln, Nebraska, and the following words instantly come to mind: 'Penis of the Prairies.' OK, OK, so the phrase refers to the 400ft-high Art Deco central tower of this, the state capital, and its topping of a 20ft statue of a sower (a David-like figure sowing seeds) on a pedestal of wheat and corn. The erection is particularly phallic and fittingly described -- but we kinda like 'Penis of the Prairies' so let's allow it to encompass all that is Lincoln.

Incidentally, the American Institute of Architects rate the four-tiered tower as the fourth modern architectural wonder of the world, alongside India's Taj Mahal and England's Parliament building. The Institute really should get out more.

On the other hand, what should not be getting out in Lincoln is hazardous waste. The town is obsessed with the stuff, judging by the amount of literature on the subject engendered by the city and university authorities. Stop any

man in the street and he could probably tell you exactly how much toxic matter had been collected that very morning. They all loved the tornado of 2004 because it meant fanatical hazardous waste groups and Lincoln-Lancaster County Health Environmental experts could spend two weeks collecting all that filthy detritus. Just for the record, the happy gatherers collected 12,175 pounds of pesticides alone.

Other poisons permeate the place. The drug methamphetamine is the greatest narcotic threat to the city of Lincoln, and experts say that the increase in both illegal and legal Hispanic workers is to blame. Says one report: 'The drug is available in almost every community. Hispanic drug trafficking organizations are flooding most Hispanic communities with methamphetamine...' Those ever-wary watchdogs at Drug Rehabs.org agree, saying: 'Methamphetamine produced in clandestine labs is also readily available in many communities. With the vast amount of

farms across the city and limited law enforcement resources, this area is prime for exploitation.'

Chillingly, there have been no fewer than 16,763 violent drug criminals arrested in the last few years. Official reports also show that during 2003, property crime levels in the Lincoln area were higher than Nebraska's average. So too, were violent crime levels -- no doubt making up a good proportion of the 5,606 that, according to latest figures, were committed throughout the whole state.

Given the above statistics, it is encouraging to learn that Nebraska's motto is 'Equality before the law'. And while we're on the subject of 'famous last words', let us remember the wise pronouncement of Thomas Rogers Kimball, Advisor to Nebraska Capital Commission, who once said: 'The capital of

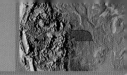

| Population (year 2000) | 225,581 |
|---|---|
| Males | 112,361 (49.8%) |
| Females | 113,220 (50.2%) |
| Elevation | 1189 feet |
| County | Lancaster |
| Land area | 74.6 square miles |
| Zip code | 68502 - 68532 |
| Median resident age | 31.3 years |
| Median household income | $40,605 |
| Median house value | $104,100 |

| Races in Lincoln | |
|---|---|
| White Non-Hispanic | 87.8% |
| Hispanic | 3.6% |
| Other race | 1.8% |
| American Indian | 1.2% |
| Two or more races | 2.0% |
| Black | 3.1% |
| Ancestries | |
| German (39.7%), Irish (12.7%), English (11.0%), Czech (5.8%), Swedish (5.0%), United States (3.9%) | |

| For population 25 years and over in Lincoln | |
|---|---|
| High school or higher | 90.2% |
| Bachelor's degree or higher | 33.3% |
| Graduate or professional degree | 11.2% |
| Unemployed | 3.8% |
| Mean travel time to work | 17.1 minutes |

| For population 15 years and over in Lincoln | |
|---|---|
| Never married | 33.4% |
| Now married | 50.6% |
| Separated | 1.1% |
| Widowed | 5.1% |
| Divorced | 9.8% |
| 5.9% Foreign born (3.0% Asia, 1.3% Latin America, 1.2% Europe) | |

| Crime | |
|---|---|
| | 6 murders (2.7 per 100,000) |
| | 1,970 burglaries (872.3 per 100,000) |

a state is the outward sign of the character of its people.'

The creation of Lincoln as state capital was not an easy one, however. The place, originally called Lancaster, was selected as state capital in 1867 only if folk agreed to change its name to Lincoln in honor of old Abe. Choosing Lancaster/Lincoln did not please the territorial authorities in Omaha, who wanted to retain their town as capital and couldn't see why a village with only 30 residents should claim the title. Such was its wrath that the move of all official documents and even office furniture to Lincoln had to take place in the middle of the night to avoid ugly clashes. But would proud Omaha have ever agreed to change its name to win the honor?

Well, Lincoln won, and Lincoln grew, and of recent years it has been flourishing, although, as we have seen, much of it is bad. Throughout the 1990s, Lincoln's population grew by about 18 percent, and in latter years there has been an annual rate of 1.4 per cent. The number of Hispanic workers has nearly tripled in the last ten years. What woos them to Lincoln? The answer: the charms of more than 165 meat-

packaging and poultry plants. There are also 55,000 farms citywide.

We assume the good folk of Lincoln don't mind sharing their homes with total strangers as, although the population is increasing, the number of houses to accommodate them is going down. So much so that, according to the official statistics, in the year 2000 not a single new one was built. Perhaps much of the population is happily roosting amongst some of those 55,000 farms.

Lincoln prides itself on being culture city. It does abound with colleges, universities, schools, museums and art galleries, but when we sent out one of our spies, she reported back that Lincoln is grim with a capital 'G' rather than brimming with culture with a capital 'C'.

Major plans are afoot to revitalise Lincoln's downtown. Originally the place to shop and work, the area has lost his shine as locals choose to live further from the city's core and the God that is the automobile allows them to drive some distance to spend their money. Downtown Lincoln struggled

particularly through the 1980s and 1990s as the major retailers upped and left. If the redevelopment goes ahead, it would include new businesses, a park and a $50m entertainment arena. A 'sister project' to breathe new life into downtown Lincoln is the Antelope Valley Project, which would take 20 years to complete at a cost of $240 million. Its major aim is to eliminate the flood threat from Antelope Creek, which flows along downtown's eastern edge, thus freeing hundreds of acres of floodplain for new roads, bridges and other concrete structures.

Supporters of the plan see it as 'an opportunity for redevelopment, economic growth and job opportunities'. Critics like Quintin Fish, manager of First Carburetor & Tyre Inc, say quite simply: 'I don't really see a need for it.' Mr Fish, like many others, don't like the idea that 49 businesses, 47 homes and privately-owned buildings will have to be demolished to make way for the new Antelope Valley. Perhaps they need not fear; already, there are problems finding the funds for the project.

Good things DO happen in Lincoln. There's the Nebraska State Fair, with 'daily pig races, pickles and pioneers'. There's the Farmer's Market every Saturday in the Historic Haymarket area of town. And every night, the students give downtown a bit of its buzz back as they hit the bars and eateries. The 76,000-seater Memorial Stadium attracts football fans. But some say it is more like a gladiatorial ring because of the bloody and brutal reputation of home team the 'Big Red' Cornhuskers.

Around 225,600 people live in Lincoln. And to give the place its due, a huge number (over 90 per cent) have benefited from a high school or higher education. But it all begs the question: if you are so bright, how come you live in Lincoln? Or, if you no longer live in Lincoln, what have you done since?

A good question. Lincoln's most famous son is Richard Bruce Cheney. Our Washington correspondent tells us that he became 46th Vice-President of the United States of America. But have YOU heard of anything he has actually DONE?

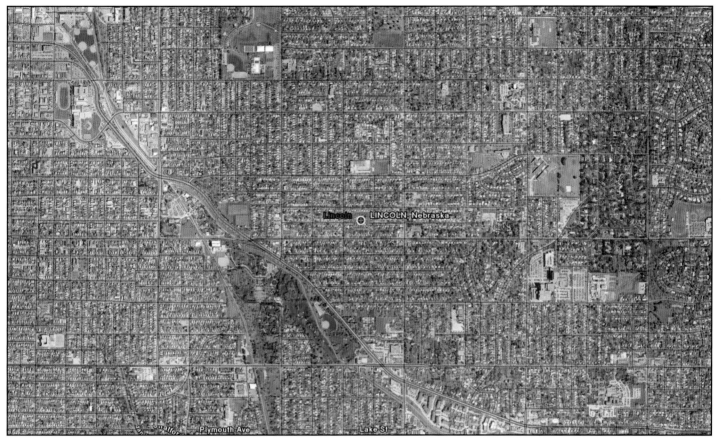

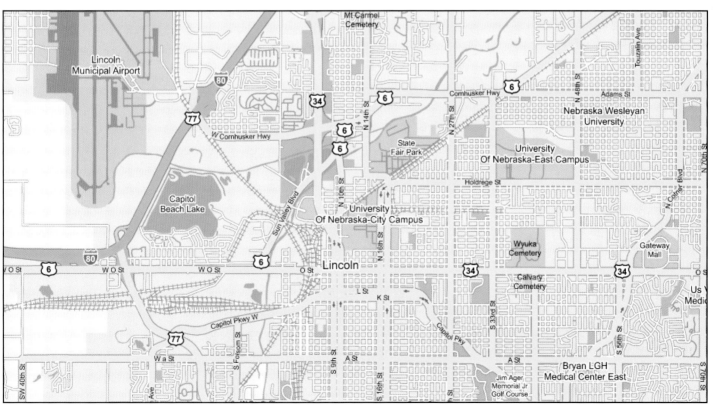

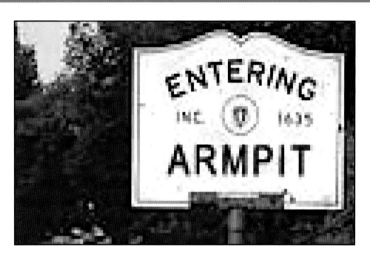

## BATTLE MOUNTAIN
*Motto: 'Battle Born'*

We all believe what we read in the newspapers, don't we? Even when one of the most respected in the land calls your home town 'the armpit of America' because it is such a BAD, BAD place to live? The dubious honor was bestowed on Battle Mountain, Nevada, in the Washington Post in December 2001 by humor writer Gene Weingarten. (It was a joke. Of sorts.) He cited the Nevada town for the armpit award for its 'lack of character and charm', its 'pathetic assemblage of ghastly buildings and nasty people', and its location 'in the midst of harsh and uninviting wilderness'. Sharlene Peterson, executive director of the Battle Mountain Chamber of Commerce, was less than swift to hit back when Weingarten forewarned her about the intended title. Ms Peterson apparently agreed: 'We're just a dying, ugly little mining town without a real identity. It could be an opportunity.' Later she added spiritedly: 'Okay, maybe we're

an armpit. If so, we're shaven and clean and sweet-smelling because out here in the desert, we're arid, extra dry!' If, after all this, you can be bothered to locate Battle Mountain, grab a map and look for Interstate-80 and then go about 218 miles east of Reno. That really is about as much as you'd want to know about the place.

Named after a mining company in 1866, Battle Mountain's fragile economy is still based on mining and ranching. It is home to 2,999 residents – and, as the town website coyly says, there's 'always room for one more!'. Among the inhabitants are descendants of Basque pioneers, who celebrate their northern Iberian heritage with a winter festival and a summer picnic. With more long-term claim to the territory are the local Shoshone tribe, who own and operate the Battle Mountain Smoke Shop on Front Street, a gas station specializing in native crafts, as well as tobacco and fireworks.

All of these good folks of Battle Mountain are no doubt smart, peace-loving people, and, being such a small town, specific population analysis has not been undertaken. However, there are some statistics for the great state of Nevada that at least throw a light on some of Battle Mountain's near neighbours.

In 2005, Morgan Quitno Press, the state and city rankings organisation, produced a pair of interesting tables. Its list of 'Most Dangerous States' is based on six crime categories: murder, rape, robbery, aggravated assault, burglary, and motor vehicle theft. Nevada came top. Morgan Quitno also awarded the 'Smartest State' designation on the basis of 21 factors that measure how a state compares to the national average. The farther below the national average a state's education ranking is, the lower (and less smart) it ranks. Nevada rated 49th – which is pretty dumb, only New Mexicans being rated

| Population (year 2000) | 2,871 |
|---|---|
| Males | 1,464 (51.0%) |
| Females | 1,407 (49.0%) |
| Elevation | 4512 feet |
| County | Lander |
| Land area | 1.8 square miles |
| Zip code | 89820 |
| Median resident age | 31.7 years |
| Median household income | $42,981 |
| Median house value | $79,600 |

| Races in Battle Mountain | |
|---|---|
| White Non-Hispanic | 71.4% |
| Hispanic | 23.6% |
| Other race | 11.8% |
| American Indian | 3.9% |
| Two or more races | 3.7% |
| Black | - |
| Ancestries | |
| German (17.5%), Irish (12.7%), English (9.8%), United States (7.3%), French (4.3%), Italian (3.0%) | |

| For population 25 years and over in Battle Mountain | |
|---|---|
| High school or higher | 79.2% |
| Bachelor's degree or higher | 13.6% |
| Graduate or professional degree | 3.7% |
| Unemployed | 10.2% |
| Mean travel time to work | 24.7 minutes |

| For population 15 years and over in Battle Mountain | |
|---|---|
| Never married | 22.9% |
| Now married | 60.0% |
| Separated | 1.9% |
| Widowed | 3.9% |
| Divorced | 11.2% |
| 12.4% Foreign born (10.6% Latin America) | |

| Crime | |
|---|---|
| Violent Crime risk | - |
| Property Crime risk | - |

dumber.

Perhaps it's something to do with the rarified air. Battle Mountain itself is more than 4,500ft above sea level and, according to the town's publicity officer, 'offers year-round access to vast public lands where residents and travelers alike can hike, camp, hunt, and fish without ever seeing another soul'.

The lack of souls is the reason for the pleading desperation evidenced in the first words one reads on the Battle Mountain Chamber of Commerce website: 'We are actively seeking new businesses to locate in our area of north/central Nevada. We're on the railroad and Interstate 80, and we have an exceptional airport. Hundreds of undeveloped acres are currently zoned industrial and commercial, just waiting for your business.' P-l-e-a-s-e someone, it seems to say, come and notice us!

Well, someone did, but unfortunately for all the wrong reasons. The headline said it all: 'We promised to find the armpit of America. Turns out it's only about five inches from the heart.' Underneath, writer Gene Weingarten said his visit

to Battle Mountain had made even its dreariest neighbours 'look like Florence during the Italian Renaissance'. He wrote:

'Take a small town, remove any trace of history, character, or charm. Allow nothing with any redeeming qualities within city limits – this includes food, motel beds, service personnel. Then place this pathetic assemblage of ghastly buildings and nasty people on a freeway in the midst of a harsh, uninviting wilderness, far enough from the nearest city to be inconvenient, but not so far for it to develop a character of its own. You now have created Battle Mountain, Nevada.'

Following the article, letters of commiseration flooded in to the little town. This is a prime example of such empathy: 'Having read Mr. Weingarten's article, my wife and I are thinking of relocating from Central California to Winnemucca (BM's larger neighbour) solely to be closer to people like you. Your attitude in what could have been an otherwise uncomfortable situation has given us hope, comfort and happiness.' Join the rush!

The shock of the article affected the people of Battle Mountain in different ways. Says one: 'The news hit us out of the blue. Some of us got mad and stayed mad. Some of us got mad and then got over it. Gradually most of us have come to

accept this blow to our pride as the "knock of opportunity" – there were Armpit T-Shirts for sale at Mills' Drug within two weeks of the article's publication.'

Some older locals got a bit uppity about having their hometown call an armpit. But, hey, as one observer notes: 'This is America! The land of the free, the brave, and the public relations gurus. The land where even bad press can be turned into something lucrative – or at least fun.' Fun? Maybe, if you consider the Old Spice deodorant people agreeing to sponsor Battle Mountain's 'Festival of the Pit'. (Armpits, smelly, deodorant, geddit?) Those in Battle Mountain who saw the joke were happy enough to participate in the Tossing the Deodorant competition and Sweaty T-shirt contest (along the lines of a Wet T-shirt contest but... we guess you don't need too much information). Other highlights included the Armpit Beauty Pageant and the Quick Draw anti-perspirant contest. Being dubbed the Armpit of America

does kinda force you to share the joke. The town has erected billboards along I-80 reading 'Battle Mountain, Voted the Armpit of America by the Washington Post' and 'Make Battle Mountain Your Next Pit Stop'.

Which is a bit of an improvement on what Gene Weingarten found when he drove into the place in the winter of 2001 to research his infamous prose. Above a gas station was the highest structure in this flat little town – a 40ft sign that, fully illuminated, should have read: 'SHELL'. The 'S' had burned out.

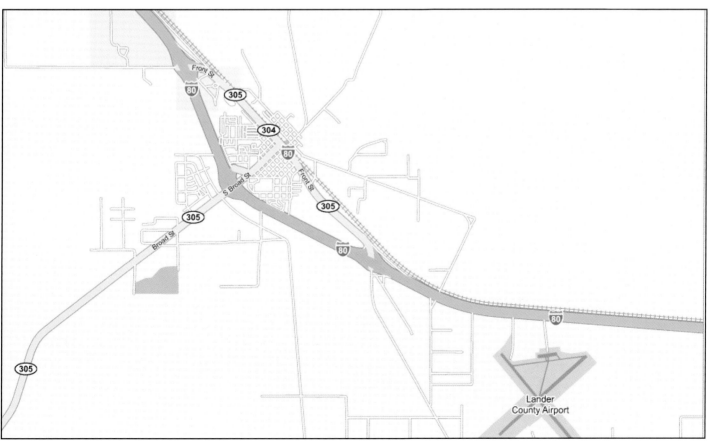

### KEARNY, NEW JERSEY
*Liberty and Prosperity*
*(state motto of New Jersey)*

Before there was fast food, there was Kearny – home of the gristle pie, fatty sausage and other assorted culinary disasters. Kearny is a collection of wannabe Jocks living not far from Manhattan but a long way from Glasgow. St. Andrew's flags appear everywhere, just in case the visitor didn't get the Scottish theme from the aforementioned appalling cuisine on offer.

A town of about 40,000 people named after Civil War general Philip Kearny, the civic website boasts: 'Kearny is a vibrant and prosperous residential, commercial and educational community with citizens working cooperatively to revitalize the town. It has safe and harmonious neighborhoods; a clean, attractive and healthy natural environment; efficient public facilities and services; visually pleasing, pedestrian-oriented streetscapes; a true Town Center downtown; mixed-

use commercial areas; and convenient transportation systems.'

In reality, it is a vapid Nowheresville, choc-a-bloc with all the depressing cultural icons of modern-day America, like Dairy Queen, Burger King and McDonalds, all vying with one another to sell more junk food to a population that can't get enough.

But let no-one say it doesn't have culture. A recent sample of the summer delights being staged there included a seminar entitled 'Understanding Memory Loss', 'Summer Classes in Basic Crochet' and 'Dog Park Open Discussion'.

It is a mystery to most as to why so many Yanks claiming Scottish forebears come to be washed up in Kearny – though, as long as they can get their heart attacks on a plate from the Scots shops on the main drag, they remain relatively happy with the American dream.

The greatest influx of Sweaty Socks (as the English call their northern neighbors the Jocks) seems to have been as the

result of the Clark Thread Company of Scotland extending its activities to the former colonies by erecting four large mills in Kearny between 1875 and 1890. Kearny was incorporated as a town soon afterwards.

According to those inestimable number-crunchers of City-Data.com, the present population is predominantly White Non-Hispanic (60.3%) with, at the other end of the statistical scale, Black (4.0%) and American Indian (0.6%). City-Data also analyses the ancestries of the good folk of Kearny and, confusingly, comes up with: Irish (13.4%), Italian (12.1%), Portuguese (11.8%), Polish (7.8%) and German (6.2%).

With so many citizens of supposedly Irish and European ancestry, how come the town has become known for its Scottishness? Influential friends and neighbours, perhaps...

| Population (year 2000) | 40,513 |
|---|---|
| Males | 20,901 (51.6%) |
| Females | 19,612 (48.4%) |
| Elevation | 125 feet |
| County | Hudson |
| Land area | 9.1 square miles |
| Zip code | 07032 |
| Median resident age | 34.7 years |
| Median household income | $47,75 |
| Median house value | $158,200 |

| Races in Kearny | |
|---|---|
| White Non-Hispanic | 60.3% |
| Hispanic | 27.3% |
| Other race | 10.0% |
| American Indian | 0.6% |
| Two or more races | 4.3% |
| Black | 4.0% |
| Ancestries | |
| Irish (13.4%), Italian (12.1%), Portuguese (11.8%), Polish (7.8%), German (6.2%), United States (2.8%) | |

| For population 25 years and over in Kearny | |
|---|---|
| High school or higher | 70.9% |
| Bachelor's degree or higher | 17.4% |
| Graduate or professional degree | 6.6% |
| Unemployed | 6.8% |
| Mean travel time to work | 30.6 minutes |

| For population 15 years and over in Kearny | |
|---|---|
| Never married | 33.0% |
| Now married | 50.9% |
| Separated | 2.5% |
| Widowed | 6.7% |
| Divorced | 7.0% |
| 38.2% Foreign born (18.7% Latin America, 13.4% Europe, 5.0% Asia) | |

| Crime | |
|---|---|
| | 0 murders (0.0 per 100,000) |
| | 229 burglaries (560.6 per 100,000) |

Scots folk from Manhattan are forced to make an annual pilgrimage to Kearny just before January 25 to buy their Burns Night haggis, a traditional mixture of oatmeal, sheep's heart, lung and lights encased in a lamb's stomach bag. Yum yum.

Kearny's proudest moment, however, was when it played host to Sir Sean Connery, the former James Bond, who was among a group of expats who gathered early one Sunday morning at the Scots Club, a mecca for Scots football fans throughout the north-east of the USA. He was there to watch live coverage of the crucial final fixture of the 2002-2003 season. Apart from his stature and famous face, the shilver-tongued film-shtar stood out from the crowd as he was the only one present wearing a green scarf, indicating his support for the Glasgow team Celtic.

Readers will undoubtedly recall that, on that memorable day, Rangers took on Dunfermline while Celtic played Kilmarnock. You don't? Och, ye puir soul, ye probably have nae heard of Kearny either. In which case, unless you're Scottish, you're missing not one wee thing.

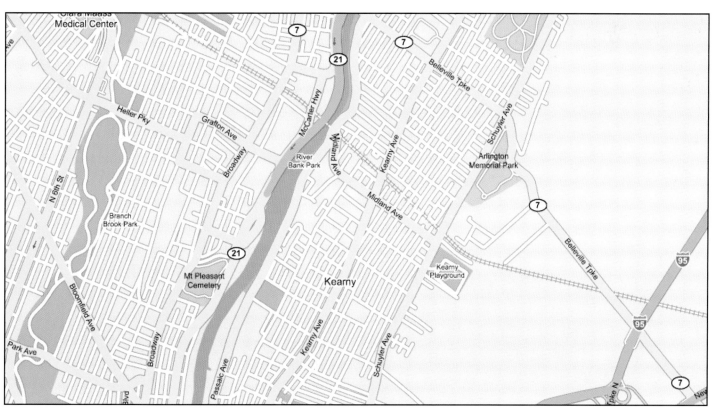

## PENNS GROVE, NEW JERSEY

*Liberty and Prosperity*
*(state motto of New Jersey)*

Penns Grove is now officially New Jersey's most 'distressed municipality' after Newark. That's what the New Jersey Office of Management and Budget says, anyway, and who are we to disagree with this literally sorry state.

Once a thriving fishing community, Penns Grove is now quite derelict. Our visiting spy adds the word 'depressed' to 'distressed', then goes on to elaborate: 'It's a miserable Delaware River town of boarded-up buildings and an abandoned ferry station. Oh, and there's a big hole where a hotel once stood.'

Long gone are the days when sturgeon seemed to jump out of the water and ask to be caught. And when caviar, that salty snack of the moneyed, was an important industry. Well, more than important, because Penns Grove was the only place in the States where the stuff was canned. Now, Penns Grove has a quite different industrial landscape, thanks to chemical giant DuPont Co across the Delaware (more about them later) which soaked up workers and completely changed the area's trading focus. That, together with the building of the Delaware Memorial Bridge, has left Penns Grove is in a very bad way.

Not even the attention of Hollywood has managed to lift the place out of the doldrums. Big-screen tough guy Bruce Willis was raised in Penns Grove and, through his development company Screwball, put up a project to restore some of the sparkle of yesteryear. The plans, knocking around for quite a while, involved a $48.5 million waterfront project which would include the converting of an old bank building

into a restaurant and a Masonic lodge into a nightclub. The riverfront was to be further enhanced with a 90-suite hotel, a four-screen multiplex theatre, a marina and an amphitheate.

Now some might understand that opposition to all of the above might come from those who, while not happy with this sad and bleak place, did not want such an ambitious development. It is strange, however, to learn that local opposition was to the planned 50 single-family homes, which the residents of Penns Grove said just weren't needed! Perhaps the hard-pressed local property owners were all too aware that there was already a ten per cent vacancy rate in their existing houses.

The Die Hard star, who worked at the Dupont plant before making it big, thought he was doing Pernns Grove a favor by offering to 'help the borough get back on its feel and help develop the river to be something everyone can enjoy', but the locals just didn't seem to care. Ultimately, Bruce turned his attentions elsewhere, buying up great tracts of Haley, Idaho, where he and ex-wife Demi Moore both have second homes. He sold his 12 acres of Penns Grove to another developer, who announced plans for a riverside hotel and shopping complex in the summer of 2005.

Once again, the locals have shrugged with indifference. The arrival of an Eckerd drug store and a Dollar Days store in 1996 seems to have been excitement enough for them during this past decade or so.

We seem to be wandering from the point (if there is any) of Penns Grove's existence. But while we may digress, the community may disappear. Through the 90s, Penns Grove's population declined by about seven per cent. Meanwhile, latest figures reveal that crime levels in Penns Grove are higher than New Jersey's average. To be fair (and you've got to admit,

| Population (year 2000) | 4,886 |
|---|---|
| Males | 2,252 (46.1%) |
| Females | 2,634 (53.9%) |
| Elevation | 12 feet |
| County | Salem |
| Land area | 0.9 square miles |
| Zip code | 08069 |
| Median resident age | 30.9 years |
| Median household income | $26,227 |
| Median house value | $72,900 |

| Races in Penns Grove | |
|---|---|
| White Non-Hispanic | 43.0% |
| Hispanic | 39.7% |
| Other race | 17.3% |
| American Indian | 8.1% |
| Two or more races | 2.5% |
| Black | 1.0% |
| Ancestries | |
| Italian (11.4%), German (10.9%), Irish (8.9%), United States (5.3%), English (4.5%), Polish (2.4%) | |

| For population 25 years and over in Penns Grove | |
|---|---|
| High school or higher | 65.6% |
| Bachelor's degree or higher | 7.5% |
| Graduate or professional degree | 1.6% |
| Unemployed | 15.3% |
| Mean travel time to work | 22.8 minutes |

| For population 15 years and over in Penns Grove | |
|---|---|
| Never married | 36.5% |
| Now married | 40.5% |
| Separated | 5.3% |
| Widowed | 7.9% |
| Divorced | 9.8% |
| 3.6% Foreign born (3.1% Latin America) | |

| Crime | |
|---|---|
| Violent Crime risk | 0 murders (0.0 per 100,000) |
| Property Crime risk | 15 burglaries (304.4 per 100,000) |

we do give a balanced account of bad towns) the town's violent crime is less than New Jersey's average, with criminals going in more for larceny-theft, burglary and robbery. This is an interesting insight into more than just the criminal minds of Penns Grove. For quick-cash rather than organised theft is the priority amongst the non-law-abiding citizens.

This is almost undoubtedly down to Penns Grove having a drugs problem. Website Drug-Rehab.org puts it splendidly: 'Penns Grove has one of the highest concentrations of both pharmaceutical and chemical firms in the country. Doctor shopping, employee theft and/or fraudulent phone-in prescriptions remain a source of diversion throughout the city.' Doctors, it seems, also like to help out when they can. Adds the report: 'Intelligence and source information has noticed some questionable prescribing habits of some doctors in their jurisdiction, that seem to be contributing via indiscriminate prescribing and/or sale of prescriptions to known drug abuser.' Apparently, further 'intelligence' (the word doesn't sit easy when talking about Penns Grove) shows that prescription rings based in Philadelphia are travelling to pharmacies in Penns Grove to have their 'scripts supplied.

May we include some more words from Drub-Rehab. org, which puts the town in its proper geographical setting. It describes Penns Close as being situated between the major industrial markets of New York and Pennsylvania and sometimes referred to as the 'crossroads of the east'. The group adds: 'It is a gateway city with major intercity highways, roadways, airports, seaports and other infrastructures capable of accommodating voluminous amounts of passenger and cargo traffic from both the eastern and western parts of the United cities, if not the world. Penns Grove can therefore be considered an ideal strategic corridor as well as a vulnerable corridor for transportation of drug contraband and illicit currency.'

Marijuana and heroin, followed by cocaine are the favoured drugs, the latter especially popular in the 'economically depressed areas' of each southeast county in Penns Grove. Heroin accounts for more admissions to city treatment centers than cocaine, marijuana and all other drugs put together.

All this is a long way from when early settlers first made their home in this riverside enclave. But Penns Grove has never been a hicksville. Originally called Penns Neck, it was so vast that an agreement made on July 13, 1721, split the area into two, Upper Penns Neck tract and Penns Grove. Today, nearly half the population of just under 5,000 is white, with 40 per cent being African American. And despite its all-round derelict reputation – of the mind as well as the environment – the surprising news is that the highest proportion of the population is under the age of 20. The lowest proportion is over 60.

So when they are not in a drug-induced state (or maybe when they ARE in a drug-induced state) what do the people of Penns Grove do to amuse themselves? Each month brings with it highlights of entertainment. In January, there is the Arts Business Institute Weekend Workshop, April boasts 'Remote Control Championships' and September the 'Robotics Extravaganza'. The last two certainly smack of some illicit substance being imbibed by the local residents because we can't find a reference to exactly who the remote controlled and robotics are.

Are we digressing again? Time to return to DuPont Co, which, since its arrival over 100 years ago, has never really had anyone's blessing. Even less now that it wants to add low-level radioactive waste water and infectious wastes to a list of substances eligible for treatment at its plant near the Delaware Memorial Bridge. These low-level radioactive waste waters and infectious liquids would be in addition to a chemical weapons waste disposal plan for the Chambers Works plant in Deepwater, New Jersey. In that environmentally-sound plan, DuPont would treat up to four million gallons of caustic by-products from the destruction of a VX nerve agent stockpile in Newport, Indiana, and discharge the waste water into the Delaware River. Wonder what the fish make of all this? They wouldn't jump out and shout 'catch me' now.

In all, Dupont's application lists around 300 chemicals and compounds that are discharged into the Delaware. No wonder Deborah Heaton, conservation director for the Sierra Club Delaware Chapter, was forced to say: 'The Delaware and New Jersey regulatory agencies need to requite a full environmental impact study and develop a full understanding of what the health impacts are.'

Penns Grove is indeed a funny old place. Poisons in the air, in the water and in its residents – who, by the by, have in their day included 1935 Olympic Gold Medal pole vaulter Donald Bragg (had he been subjected to a whiff of something in the air at Penns Grove?), Chicago White Sox star Eugene 'Dory' Reybold Elsh and actor John Forsythe, who played Blake Carrington in Dynasty.

Penns Grove is indeed a funny old place. Poisons in the air, in the water and in its residents – who, by the by, have in their day included 1935 Olympic Gold Medal pole vaulter Donald Bragg (had he been subjected to a whiff of something in the air at Penns Grove?), Chicago White Sox star Eugene 'Dory' Reybold Elsh and actor John Forsythe, who played Blake Carrington in Dynasty.

Back in the Roaring Twenties, the Ferry Station was the hot place to hang out in Penns Grove. Party animals F. Scott Fitzgerald and his wife Zelda had a mansion on the opposite side of the river, and the glitterati flocked to their wild weekend bashes. We have it on good authority that the beautiful looked pretty damned on their hung-over return journeys. Needless to say, the Greek revival mansion has gone the same way as Penns Grove – it fell into disrepair and was replaced with an industrial jungle.

So there we have it. Penns Grove is a place with no hospital or proper college of its own (six miles away and ten miles away respectively), a low-income, high-as-a-kite community and located in a state that ranks number two in America's list of high health stakes (added cancer risk of 1,400 per 1,000,000), and boasting a map so heavily marked with hazardous waste sites that you might think you're looking at a bug-squashed windscreen.

Now you might think that the Environmental Protection Department is not really doing its job. But it was certainly effective when dealing with developer William Juliano who wanted to build a truckstop near Interchange One of the New Jersey Turnpike. Mr Juliano said his plan was blocked because the area is protected wetlands. Whoever is right in this little episode of New Jersey life doesn't really matter to us. What does is the billboard Mr Juliano put up over the Delaware Memorial Bridge: 'Welcome to New Jersey. A horrible place to do business.'

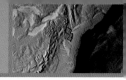

## LOS ALAMOS, NEW MEXICO
*It grows as it goes (state motto of New Mexico)*

If you're a town whose name cannot be spoken, then the future will never look bright. But that's what happened to this place, whose reputation has bombed - quite literally.

Back in 1942, the American and British governments decided to amalgamate the research efforts involved in building the atomic bomb. When it came to finding a location in a sparsely populated area away from the sea and with a reasonable all-round climate, Los Alamos fitted the bill perfectly. The exclusive, private Los Alamos Ranch School was the subject of a government buy-out, and when the final class graduated in 1943, the scientists moved in.

Perfecting - if that is the right word to use - the bomb took two years of top-secret work. During that time, the words 'Los Alamos' were forbidden and newcomers to the area were simply given the address of 109 Palace Avenue to

report to. We all know what happened next, with the horror of Hiroshima and Nagasaki brutal reminders of how humanity is lost in war.

But if that wasn't enough, Los Alamos gained even further notoriety with the construction of the H-Bomb. Spies betrayed its secrets to the Russians, and Los Alamos became a byword for paranoia, treachery and science gone mad.

The gate-house on the road up from Santa Fe (probably the place you'd head straight for rather than linger in Los Alamos) was finally taken down in 1957 after shielding the public from the ranch's secrets for 12 years.

With a record like that, it is no wonder that today Los Alamos boasts a booming laboratory business which is spending over half its billion-dollar annual budget on the research and development of nuclear weapons.

It is not a place where residents feel comfortable saying to outsiders: 'Hey, come and stay.' Extolling the virtues of a town best-known for making weapons which will wipe out

| | |
|---|---|
| Population (year 2000) | 11,909 |
| Males | 5,993 (50.3%) |
| Females | 5,916 (49.7%) |
| Elevation | 7575 feet |
| County | San Miguel |
| Land area | 10.9 square miles |
| Zip code | 87544 |
| Median resident age | 40.2 years |
| Median household income | $71,536 |
| Median house value | $228,500 |

| Races in Los Alamos | |
|---|---|
| White Non-Hispanic | 80.8% |
| Hispanic | 12.2% |
| Other race | 3.0% |
| American Indian | 1.1% |
| Two or more races | 2.4% |
| Black | - |

**Ancestries**

German (19.3%), English (15.7%), Irish (12.6%), United States (5.1%), Italian (3.7%), Polish (3.3%)

| For population 25 years and over in Los Alamos | |
|---|---|
| High school or higher | 96.4% |
| Bachelor's degree or higher | 62.1% |
| Graduate or professional degree | 37.3% |
| Unemployed | 2.3% |
| Mean travel time to work | 14.6 minutes |

| For population 15 years and over in Los Alamos | |
|---|---|
| Never married | 20.5% |
| Now married | 63.2% |
| Separated | 1.2% |
| Widowed | 3.7% |
| Divorced | 11.4% |

8.2% Foreign born (3.5% Asia, 3.0% Europe)

| Crime | |
|---|---|
| Violent Crime risk | - |
| Property Crime risk | - |

the world is a hard act. You could say the Bradbury Science Museum on Central Avenue might be worth a visit, but even there you're invited to press buttons to light up those countries that 'might pose a threat to stability'. Good family fun, huh?

You can't escape the killing fields at the Los Alamos Historical Museum, either. Here you can thrill to an aerial photograph of Hiroshima and another picture of a guy cutting a mushroom-shaped cake.

Los Alamos still likes to think of itself as a wealthy location but it is obviously aware there is no need for expensive places to stay. A lot of the area is still off-limits, which is not particularly good for any tourist industry. There are a couple of boring motels where - surprise, surprise - the main clientele are scientists. And there are a handful of B&Bs, whose guests, one can only guess, are scientists in charge of making the smaller bombs.

With its aggressive and hostile reputation, some might think it a pity that although the whole of Los Alamos was threatened with obliteration in the huge Cerro Grande forest

fire of May 2000, not every building disappeared. Even worse, anything burned to the ground was rebuilt.

All in all, it comes as no surprise that Los Alamos is in the state whose crime statistics make it the most dangerous in the whole of the USA.

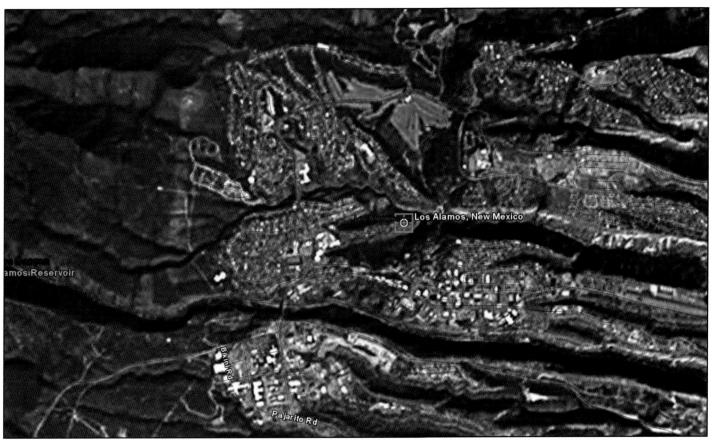

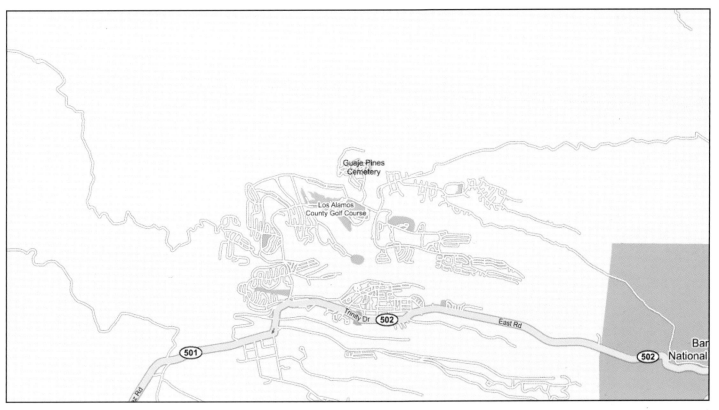

### ROSWELL, NEW MEXICO
*Motto: 'All American City'*

Roswell has twice been chosen as an 'All American City', a designation granted the town by the National Civic League in 1978 and 2002, putting the place in the elite ten two-time winners of this award. We can't argue with the National Civic League, but why Roswell should be particularly honoured as 'All American' is a mystery – when its sole claim to fame is that its best known inhabitants are not American

at all. In fact, they're not even human. They are, of course, aliens. This is the site of one of the most hyped-up conspiracy mysteries of all time – which, after all these years, we will attempt to solve.

At around midnight on July 4, 1947, an unidentified flying object crashed in a storm 75 miles north-west of the town. A principal witness was Jim Ragsdale, who was camping near the crash site and said he had seen the bodies of four small beings. He must have been traumatised by the experience because he waited until 1995 to reveal the fact. Nevertheless, UFO fever had already broken out and has lasted to this day.

Well, we can now reveal the truth about the UFO story that put Roswell on the map of madness. These aliens did not crash attempting to visit Roswell. They crashed trying to escape from it – and for very good reasons, as we shall also reveal.

But just to wrap up the UFO nonsense… In 1994 the Office of the Secretary of the Air Force concluded exhaustive inquiries into whether any government agency 'possessed information on the alleged crash and recovery of an extraterrestrial vehicle and its alien occupants near Roswell'. The Air Force pointed to records that had never been classified, and therefore had been publicly available for

| Population (year 2000) | 45,293 |
|---|---|
| Males | 21,840 (48.2%) |
| Females | 23,453 (51.8%) |
| Elevation | 3573 feet |
| County | Chaves |
| Land area | 28.9 square miles |
| Zip code | 88201 |
| Median resident age | 35.2 years |
| Median household income | $27,252 |
| Median house value | $60,100 |

| Races in Roswell | |
|---|---|
| White Non-Hispanic | 50.9% |
| Hispanic | 44.3% |
| Other race | 21.3% |
| American Indian | 2.1% |
| Two or more races | 3.3% |
| Black | 2.5% |
| Ancestries | |
| German (9.3%), English (8.7%), Irish (7.4%), United States (6.3%), French (1.9%), Italian (1.8%) | |

| For population 25 years and over in Roswell | |
|---|---|
| High school or higher | 73.8% |
| Bachelor's degree or higher | 16.9% |
| Graduate or professional degree | 6.8% |
| Unemployed | 9.7% |
| Mean travel time to work | 16.2 minutes |

| For population 15 years and over in Roswell | |
|---|---|
| Never married | 24.1% |
| Now married | 52.7% |
| Separated | 2.3% |
| Widowed | 9.1% |
| Divorced | 11.8% |
| 10.8% Foreign born (9.3% Latin America) | |

| Crime | |
|---|---|
| Violent Crime risk | 2 murders (4.4 per 100,000) |
| Property Crime risk | 609 burglaries (1337.2 per 100,000) |

decades, proving that the UFO was a balloon-borne research project. Any 'aliens' observed in the New Mexico desert were actually anthropomorphic test dummies that were carried aloft by US Air Force high altitude balloons for scientific research.

But has this made the city leaders of Roswell clam up shamefacedly about their town's notoriety being built on a falsehood? No, they've milked it for every dollar. Once a small ranching town, Roswell is now a byword for lunacy, boasting as its main tourist attraction the so-called International UFO Museum and Research Center, devoted to the 'serious investigation' of visitors from Outer Space.

The giveaway is an admission by the all-powerful Roswell Chamber of Commerce in a website statement that lauds their 'dress a student' program (dress a student as what?) and, of course, the world-renowned Chaves County dental van, while boasting how they've managed to milk a gullible piublic of millions of dollars. The statement reads: 'The fact is that being designated an All America City does not imply that

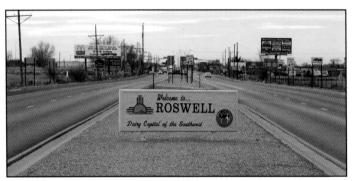

Roswell has no problems or is a perfect city. Rather, it is a recognition that Roswell works collaboratively and collectively to address these issues which are present in our community as in any community. Through local initiatives such as the dress a student program, the Chaves County dental van, and the capitalization of the UFO phenomenon into a $5.2 million industry, Roswell has shown that it is able to overcome adversity with ingenuity and teamwork. It is this community spirit that really counts.'

Since Roswell admits to the community 'issues' it has to 'address', we have no need to labor anyone with the usual litany of criminal behaviour within the population of 44,000 (and falling), where less than seven per cent have any graduate or professional degree and about 10 per cent have no job at all.

After all, how could anyone point an accusing finger at the criminals of Roswell when the city itself is built on a lie. You doubt it? The International UFO Museum and Research Center inadvertently reveals the falsehood when visitors pay their bucks to peer at the grainy filmed 'evidence' of an alien 'autopsy' and peruse the other ludicrous attempts to portray the meanderings of deranged minds as being serious research projects.

For instance, did you know that Neil Armstrong encountered flying saucers on the Moon, and that John F Kennedy was assassinated because he was about to reveal the Roswell secret? And did you know that Roswell was a great place to live?

Much better to drive 75 miles down the highway to Carlsbad and live it up with a subterranean tour of its main attraction: the Nuclear Waste Isolation Pilot Plant, where even more dangerous rubbish is stored than in the whole of Roswell.

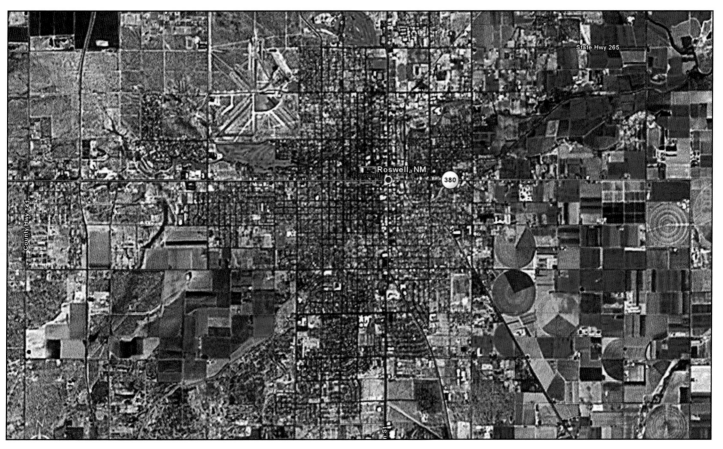

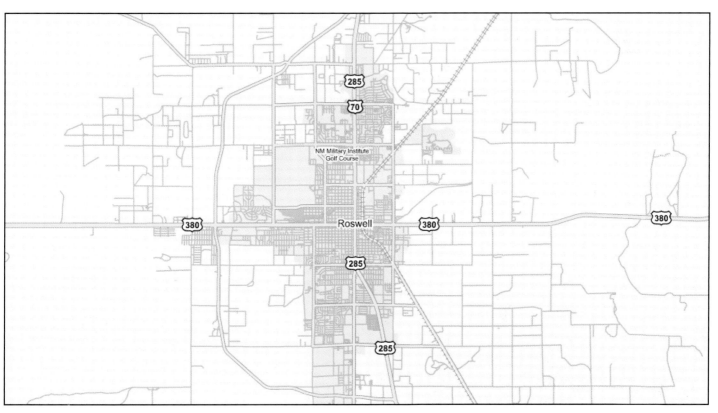

## TRUTH OR CONSEQUENCES, NEW MEXICO
*Motto: 'City of the Sun'*

Truth or Consequences used to be called Palomas Hot Springs until 1950 when it changed its name in honor of a popular radio show of the time. The original game show has long gone and the contestants have grown old and died. Which makes Truth or Consequences a pretty good choice of name for this town – it seems to have suffered a similar fate with the passing of time.

The population of 7,000 is dropping every year. And those townsfolk who do not literally drop dead are increasingly disillusioned and choosing to move on to greener pastures. (And let's face it, almost everywhere is greener than New Mexico, where the climate is so dry that three-quarters of the roads are left unpaved and yet never wash away.)

We wondered what the reasons were for this exodus, and the New Mexico official state statistics provide some of the answers. Here in Truth or Consequences, the truth can

be brutal... incomes, house prices and education levels are way below the state average. While the median age of its inhabitants, at 49, is significantly above normal, along with the number of people institutionalised.

Sure you can snap up a spacious home for as little as $35,000 but most people live in trailer parks scattered willy-nilly around the one-stop-light town. Bargains abound in the supermarkets – for some reason, soft drinks and canned foods with expired sell-by dates are always on sale at knockdown prices.

Drugs are also cheap – which is, by default, the reason for many of Truth or Consequences' woes. The town sits on I-25, the main drug route from Mexico, and its relatively isolated position in the desert has made it a haven for dodgy chemists creating crystal methadine to ship out across the South West.

But like so many things in Truth or Consequences, even the drug makers are below average. It's not unusual for illegal

bathroom laboratories to explode – as true crime author John Glatt discovered when he spent three weeks there investigating a serial sex killer. Loud bangs, followed by shooting flames and fleeing speed freaks, provide more entertainment than, say, the Hot Springs Bakery or the annual Truth or Consequences radio show fiesta.

So, aside from the transient druggies, elderly bikers and new-age hippies who hang out on street corners terrifying the occasional tourist silly enough to venture into town, who actually lives here? Again, the state statistics tell us that the number of Hispanics (27.4 per cent) is significantly above New Mexico's average while the number of African Americans (0.6 per cent) is way below normal.

At an elevation of 4,242 feet, Truth or Consequences, in

| Population (year 2000) | 7,289 |
|---|---|
| Males | 3,586 (49.2%) |
| Females | 3,703 (50.8%) |
| Elevation | 4242 feet |
| County | Sierra |
| Land area | 12.7 square miles |
| Zip code | 87901 |
| Median resident age | 48.0 years |
| Median household income | $20,986 |
| Median house value | $66,500 |

| Races in Truth or Consequence | |
|---|---|
| White Non-Hispanic | 69.1% |
| Hispanic | 27.4% |
| Other race | 9.4% |
| American Indian | 2.8% |
| Two or more races | 2.7% |
| Black | 0.6% |
| Ancestries | |
| German (13.0%), English (11.6%), Irish (11.3%), United States (8.1%), French (4.1%), Scotch-Irish (3.1%) | |

| For population 25 years and over in Truth or Consequence | |
|---|---|
| High school or higher | 74.2% |
| Bachelor's degree or higher | 13.2% |
| Graduate or professional degree | 4.9% |
| Unemployed | 8.5% |
| Mean travel time to work | 17.0 minutes |

| For population 15 years and over in Truth or Consequence | |
|---|---|
| Never married | 18.1% |
| Now married | 49.9% |
| Separated | 1.7% |
| Widowed | 14.5% |
| Divorced | 15.7% |
| 5.4% Foreign born (4.4% Latin America, 0.7% Europe) | |

| Crime | |
|---|---|
| Violent Crime risk | - |
| Property Crime risk | - |

the county of Sierra, covers just 12.7 square miles. With a low median household income (in 2000 it was $20,986 a year), the main 'industries' providing employment are officially listed as: educational, health and social services (22.0%): arts, entertainment, recreation, accommodation and food services (17.8%); Retail trade (11.1%).

There are no specific figures, however, for one of New Mexico's greatest growth industries: crime. The state has a Crime Index of more than 5,000 reported incidents per 100,000 people – ranking it as the third highest in the nation. For violent crime, New Mexico excels, with a reported incident rate of 757.9 per 100,000 people – fourth among the states. It also ranks fourth for crimes against property. For aggravated assaults, it is third, as it is for forced rapes. But it shamefully slumps down the scale when it comes to murders, scoring only a fifth.

In this morass of iniquity, Truth or Consequences boasts of being the 'City of the Sun', a slow but quaint sanctuary in a busy world. To some who have passed through, the town

157

center has been reported as having 'an old fashioned charm' enhanced by such places as Joe's Barber Shop and the Hot Springs Bakery. In reality, it is a transient area full of chrystal meth addicts, drunks and – as author Glatt discovered while researching his book Cries in the Dark – a three-man sheriff's department fighting a losing battle against crime.

He charitably points to a few old springs, spas and bath houses scattered around the town to justify its original name of Palomas Hot Springs but complains that – along with the broken-down old pick up trucks that litter the side streets – they have all seen better days.

So how come it decided to change its name? For centuries the area's thermal springs had drawn native Americans, notably the Apache chief Geronimo, in whose honour the Geronimo Springs Museum on Main Street boasts a life-sized statue. But therein lies a clue to the town's pandering after cheap fame – for alongside is every snippet of information you never wanted to know about Ralph Edwards, presenter of the long-defunct radio show Truth or Consequences.

Back in 1950, Edwards had promised that any place prepared to change its name would be rewarded by hosting its tenth anniversary edition. The foolish folk of Hot Springs sold their heritage for 15 minutes of tawdry fame and bequeathed it an eternity of toe-curling embarrassment as the town with the silliest name in the USA.

Mind you, it could have been worse. Just 70 miles down the road is another dubious attraction: Trinity, famed as the site of the world's first atomic bomb blast. Why the silly citizens of Palomas Hot Springs should have chosen to name their town Truth or Consequences is a mystery – when they could, with some justification, have renamed it Hiroshima.

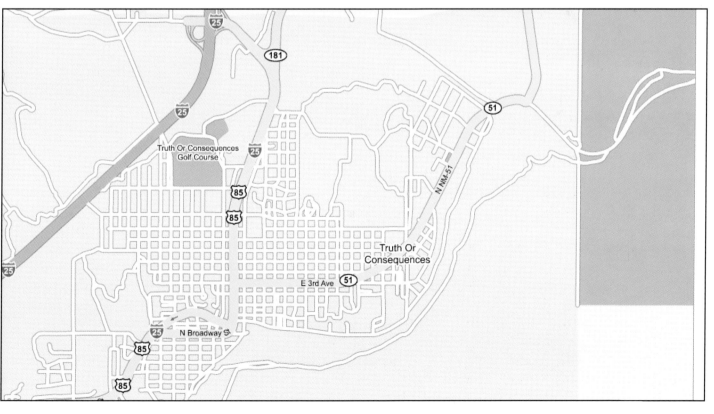

## FLEISCHMANNS, NEW YORK
*Ever upward (state motto of New York)*

An old timer in Fleischmanns, a strange and deeply spooky Catskill Mountain town, recalling happier times, proclaimed: 'Why, if you was to faint, you'd never hit the street, the people were that thick.' Indeed, it was said that during the golden era of train travel, the main thoroughfare resembled New York's perennially packed Times Square and some 10,000 people escaped the city heat for the super cool vacation resort every summer.

So what happened to poor old Fleischmans and where did all the people go? If ever there was a riche- to-rags town, this is it. From 1880 to the 1960s, the town named after a yeast manufacturer was THE glamorous holiday hot spot for the uber-wealthy. And then every kid who'd ever been dragged backwards up a mountain screaming by parents claiming fresh air was good for them exacted revenge. The baby boomers discovered the Hamptons, Florida, the Caribbean, and

Europe… and fled.

Today the only time you're likely to spot anyone in Fleischmanns is on auction night. If broken 1970s televisions, rusting coffee pots or chipped crockery appeal, then this could still be the town for you. The scrubby yard surrounding Robert's Auction House – once the town's grandest hotel – is littered with junk. We'd like to say bargain hunters come from miles around to snap up curios. But sadly the only curiosities here are the black-clad Orthodox Jews picking through the rubble.

The two remaining main streets in Fleischmanns are a hotchpotch of ailing businesses and tumble down houses. The town website proudly boasts that it's the home of the Purple Mountain Press. But investigate cyberspace a bit further and you'll discover that the bookshop has closed and the publishing company has gone mail order. In fact, the one pop-under advert that consistently pops up when you try to log off

is for property foreclosures.

Elsewhere, the Catskills are enjoying a rennaisance. Manhattanites think nothing of driving three hours through snow to enjoy the newly revamped ski resorts, mountain lakes and antique shops. But the latest boom has by-passed poor old Fleischmanns.

The town that once boasted 50 hotels now has just eight scruffy motels and they're all in need of a coat of paint. In 2000 the population was 351 -- in fact, there are so few people that most of them are listed by name on the town website. The median age is 39 and there are 100 women to every 89 men. Interestingly, or maybe not, the men earn an average of $20,208 a year against the womens' $21,563. Ninety-four per cent of the population is white and 18.4 per cent live below

| Population (year 2000) | 351 |
|---|---|
| Males | 166 (47.3%) |
| Females | 185 (52.7%) |
| Elevation | 2268 feet |
| County | Delaware |
| Land area | 0.7 square miles |
| Zip code | 12430 |
| Median resident age | 39.4 years |
| Median household income | $28,500 |
| Median house value | $74,300 |

| Races in Fleischmanns | |
|---|---|
| White Non-Hispanic | 75.8% |
| Hispanic | 19.7% |
| Other race | 1.1% |
| American Indian | 2.0% |
| Two or more races | 2.0% |
| Black | 1.4% |

Ancestries

German (21.7%), Irish (17.1%), Italian (10.5%), Dutch (7.1%), English (6.0%), United States (5.4%)

| For population 25 years and over in Fleischmanns | |
|---|---|
| High school or higher | 71.2% |
| Bachelor's degree or higher | 8.9% |
| Graduate or professional degree | 5.8% |
| Unemployed | 11.5% |
| Mean travel time to work | 22.0 minutes |

| For population 15 years and over in Fleischmanns | |
|---|---|
| Never married | 22.5% |
| Now married | 45.5% |
| Separated | 4.0% |
| Widowed | 14.9% |
| Divorced | 13.1% |

22.8% Foreign born (11.7% Latin America, 9.1% Europe)

| Crime | |
|---|---|
| Violent Crime risk | - |
| Property Crime risk | - |

the poverty line.

Apathy is clearly the main pastime. The town board is considering dis-incorporating and has asked the electorate's opinion. Last time we looked, zero per cent of the population had voted yes, zero no, zero not sure and (surprise, surprise) the total number of people who voted was zero.

It wasn't always this way. Back in 1844, when a General Henry Armstrong leased his 8,000 acres out to tenant farmers, the peasants revolted. The Anti-Rent War, as it was known, led to lease reforms across New York State, and the green and pleasant valley prospered. By 1870, the area was called Griffin Corners, after local lawyer Mattew Griffin. The attorney's fame was short lived – in 1883 Charles F. Fleischmann started snapping up land and commissioned a spectacular house that cost the then enormous sum of $30,000.

The Hungarian born whisky distiller and yeast manufacturer encouraged his family and friends to do likewise, and very soon the town – or village as he insisted on calling it – was renamed in his honor. The Fleischmanns threw money

at everything, even kitting the local brass band out in uniform so it would greet their private train at the railroad station.

Fleischmanns's son Julius was a major league baseball fan and donated a sports park. His greatest discovery was John 'Horius' Wagner, who's sporting prowess earned him the nickname The Flying Dutchman. There's not a lot today to recommend the park, and all that remains of baseball's heyday is Wagner Street, the scruffy main thoroughfare.

It's fair to say the air conditioner helped kill Fleischmanns. In the days before electricity in every home became the norm, New Yorkers escaped to the mountains for the breeze. The grown-ups loved the open spaces; the kids didn't. Bored teenagers grew into wealthy adults, and by the 1970s they were traveling to far more exotic locations.

Then there were the (ahem) arsonists who torched the hotels and once-grand homes after the owners abandoned them. Pyromania was terribly popular for a while, and cynics would say that the insurance rewards weren't bad either.

Today, the biggest crime in Fleischmanns is illegal parking. Despite the utter lack of visitors, there are signs everywhere warning of stiff fines for traffic offenses. The problem for Fleischmanns is that most people ignore the signs and just keep on driving.

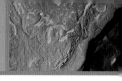

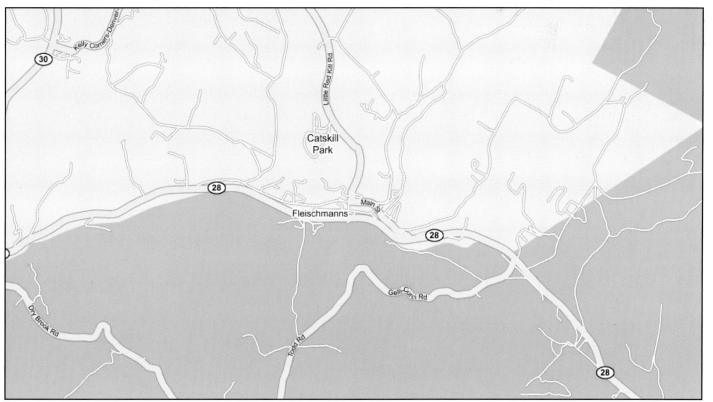

## NIAGARA FALLS, NEW YORK
*Ever upward (state motto of New York)*

Ah, Niagara Falls. Breathtaking views, helicopter rides over the water, honeymoon hotels and Marilyn Monroe. Er, no. That's Niagara Falls, Canada. Stand at the edge of the Horseshoe Falls and cast your eye along the water line. You'll quickly spot its ugly sister across the border, blotting the landscape with electricity plants, crumbling old factories and the occasional chimney belching out smoke. We say occasional because industry – and the acrid black yuk that used to

accompany it – is a thing of the past in Niagara Falls, New York.

Back in the dark ages – 1901 to be exact – the world oooh-ed as the newly harnessed falls provided the electricity for nearby Buffalo's Pan-American Exposition. Dozens of buildings twinkled like proverbial Christmas trees and the good folk of Niagara could have been forgiven for thinking they'd got it made. Then bang, President William McKinley was assassinated while visiting the fair and whatever glory Niagara hoped for disappeared back into a black hole.

While its Canadian sister played to the tourists, New York's Niagara worked hard to create industry. Mills, steel works and military bases provided jobs aplenty, and by the time the New York State Authority's giant new hydroelectric plant was up and running in the early 1960s, the population had swollen to 100,000.

And then the light bulb flickered off. Within 10 years, industry started leaving Niagara – often for the sunnier climates of Arizona and the Carolinas – and the town became known more for its environmental disasters in the Niagara River and Love Canal than its manufacturing.

By 2000 the population had fallen to 55,593, and those who stayed earned on average $26,800 per household, 36 per cent below the national average. In 1995 the locals fought

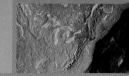

| | |
|---|---|
| Population (year 2000) | 55,593 |
| Males | 26,002 (46.8%) |
| Females | 29,591 (53.2%) |
| Elevation | 618 feet |
| County | Niagara |
| Land area | 14.1 square miles |
| Zip code | 14301 - 14305 |
| Median resident age | 38.0 years |
| Median household income | $26,800 |
| Median house value | $60,800 |

| Races in Niagara Falls | |
|---|---|
| White Non-Hispanic | 75.3% |
| Hispanic | 2.0% |
| Other race | 0.7% |
| American Indian | 2.4% |
| Two or more races | 2.0% |
| Black | 18.7% |

**Ancestries**

Italian (23.2%), German (16.8%), Irish (13.7%), Polish (11.0%), English (8.4%), French (3.2%)

| For population 25 years and over in Niagara Falls | |
|---|---|
| High school or higher | 76.6% |
| Bachelor's degree or higher | 12.5% |
| Graduate or professional degree | 4.8% |
| Unemployed | 10.1% |
| Mean travel time to work | 17.0 minutes |

| For population 15 years and over in Niagara Falls | |
|---|---|
| Never married | 31.7% |
| Now married | 43.6% |
| Separated | 3.2% |
| Widowed | 10.2% |
| Divorced | 11.4% |

5.0% Foreign born (2.2% Europe, 1.7% North America, 0.5% Asia)

| Crime | |
|---|---|
| Violent crime risk | 4 murders (7.2 per 100,000) |
| Property crime risk | 795 burglaries (1427.4 per 100,000) |

back when the US military decided to close Niagara Falls International Airport Air Reserve Station, the biggest Air Reserve base in the US. Their victory was short lived, and in 2005 the base was up for the chop again with the loss of another 642 jobs.

Over the years, Niagara has tried to cash in on the Canadian side's tourism industry – and failed. Locals say it's because commercial flights no longer come into its international airport, the last private carrier having pulled out in 2000. But in fairness, even Oscar Wilde complained about the New York side of the falls. Back in the 19th Century he wrote: 'I was disappointed in Niagara – most people must be disappointed in Niagara. Every American bride is taken here, and the sight of that waterfall must be one of the earliest, if not the keenest, disappointments in American married life.'

In 1885 the environmentalists created America's first state reservation park on the US side. It seemed like a great idea at the time – after all, the falls are one of the seven wonders of the natural world – but it means all building is restricted. So

while Canada has cashed in with casinos and hotels, all the US side has to show for it are some flower beds.

But unless you hit Niagara in the height of summer – for that, read July and August – you won't be sitting in a deckchair enjoying the view. The first freeze of the winter begins in September and the last usually coincides with Memorial Day, the official start of everyone else's summer at the end of May. From Christmas to March, the city is buried under snow – it's the fifth snowiest metropolitan area in America – and wind blowing from Lakes Erie and Ontario means it feels like minus 30 degrees F even when the temperature is claiming to be hovering just above freezing.

Try crossing the Canadian border into New York in the height of winter and you'll be met by sullen-faced guards trudging through snow like South Park cartoon characters. Coach loads of shoppers are regularly pulled from their warm seats and ordered to march to an Eastern European style checkpoint to fill in dozens of forms due to perceived passport or visa irregularities.

If you're wondering why people bother crossing the border,

there is the attraction of a giant retail mall and, depending on the fluctuating dollar, there are bargains to be had at big-name fashion stores. Unfortunately, the jobless locals complain they can't afford designer duds.

Still, it's cheap to live in the area. Bert Sperling and Peter Sander, in their admirable tome Cities Ranked and Rated, put Niagara and Buffalo 370th out of 400 on the house price list. Just $85,000 gets you a nice winter proofed Cape Cod, at a good $100,000 below the average in the North East.

Feeling hungry? We couldn't find a decent restaurant in Niagara itself, but 30 minutes' drive into sprawling Buffalo found us at the Anchor Bar, a dingy watering hole that claims to have invented that great staple of American foods, the Buffalo Wing. They're still made to order (a minimum of 10 cost just under $6) but critics have described the wings as 'forgettable'. Just like Niagara Falls really.

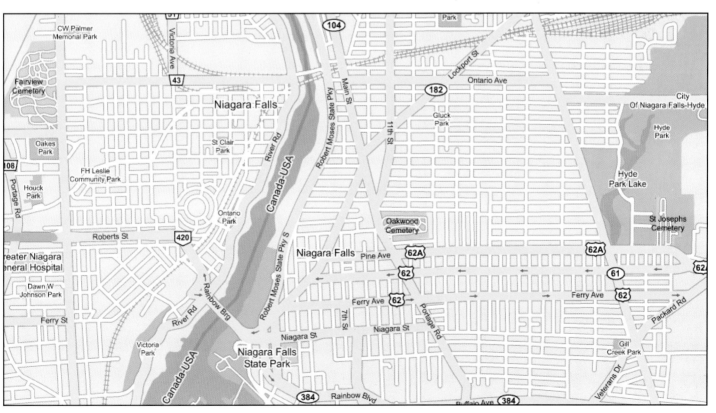

## ROOSEVELT ISLAND, NEW YORK
*Ever upward (state motto of New York)*

A splodge of land in the middle of New York's murky East River so grossed out the Victorian novelist and social reformer Charles Dickens that he cut short his visit to a lunatic asylum and fled. More than a century and a half later, Roosevelt Island still has the same affect on unwary visitors.

The seriously strange town of 5,000 people offers some of

the most amazing views of Manhattan. In return, it provides the Big Apple with a spooky vista of crumbling buildings and the ghostly ruins of a smallpox hospital. Roosevelt Island actually has six structures on the National Register of Landmark Buildings – yet the bureaucrats who run the place have allowed most of them to fall into total disrepair.

It is heart breaking to watch the 1796 Blackwall House fall to pieces. The clapboard house – the sixth oldest in the entire city of New York – sits rotting in the shadow of a new skyscraper built to accomodate nearby hospital workers. Weeds were growing through the roof guttering until the guttering fell off a couple of years ago. The porch is taped off because the wood has rotted, 'Keep Out' signs have been posted to ward off squatters, and the basement has flooded several times. As a local historian tells us: 'The only thing they haven't done to it, is put a match to it.'

Then there's the landmarked smallpox hospital ruins, shored up with girders and surrounded by wire fences to keep unsuspecting visitors out of harm's way. Designed by James Renwick, who also built Manhattan's St. Patrick's Cathedral, it has now fallen beyond repair, and every winter chunks of masonry drop off as the brickwork freezes and thaws.

| | |
|---|---|
| Population (year 2000) | 15,854 |
| Males | 7,455 (47.0%) |
| Females | 8,399 (53.0%) |
| Elevation | - |
| County | Nassau |
| Land area | 1.8 square miles |
| Zip code | 11575 |
| Median resident age | 31.5 years |
| Median household income | $56,715 |
| Median house value | $153,700 |

| Races in Roosevelt Island | |
|---|---|
| White Non-Hispanic | 2.9% |
| Hispanic | 16.2% |
| Other race | 8.3% |
| American Indian | 1.6% |
| Two or more races | 3.7% |
| Black | 79.0% |
| Ancestries | |
| West Indian (14.8%), United States (3.5%), Subsaharan African (2.0%) | |

| For population 25 years and over in Roosevelt Island | |
|---|---|
| High school or higher | 70.6% |
| Bachelor's degree or higher | 14.3% |
| Graduate or professional degree | 5.8% |
| Unemployed | 6.4% |
| Mean travel time to work | 33.9 minutes |

| For population 15 years and over in Roosevelt Island | |
|---|---|
| Never married | 40.1% |
| Now married | 40.5% |
| Separated | 5.0% |
| Widowed | 6.6% |
| Divorced | 7.8% |
| 24.6% Foreign born (23.0% Latin America) | |

| Crime | |
|---|---|
| Violent Crime risk | - |
| Property Crime risk | - |

All that remains of the Municipal Lunatic Asylum is the semi-ruined Octagon administration block – although recently work has begun on two apartment blocks sprouting like ears off the side. Before Dickens fled in horror at conditions in the rest of the loony-bin, he did comment on the magnificent staircase and architecture.

Dickens, no shrinking violet when it came to appalling filth and poverty in his native Britain, had this to say about the asylum and its inmates in 1842: 'Everything had a lounging, listless, madhouse air, which was very painful. The terrible crowd with which these halls and galleries were filled so shocked me, that I abridged my stay within the shortest limits, and declined to see that portion of the building in which the refectory and violent were under closer restraint.'

It wasn't just the lunatics at the asylum who gave the island a bad name. One of the inmates built a lighthouse – one of the few things recently renovated – brick by brick to guide ships past the vicious rip tides at the northern tip. The swirling filthy water was dubbed Hell's Gate after more than

100 ships sank in the 19th century, and even today ghostly sailors are said to haunt the area – along with Mae West, who was incarcerated on the island in 1926 for daring to write and star in a Broadway play called Sex.

Now we know people who actually live on Roosevelt Island – reachable by a strange red cable car featured in the fight scene between Tobey Maguire and Willem Dafoe in Spiderman – and they claim it's a great place to bring up kids. Well yes, there is some scrubby open space, complete with rusty barbecues, and a big white oblong balloon affair with tennis courts inside. Locals, many in wheelchairs and living at the long-time care rehabitilation hospital, insist fish caught in the East River are eatable, though we honestly don't know anyone brave enough to try one. And there are plans afoot to turn the southern tip of the island into a cultural center and park, incorporating the small pox hospital ruins. But unless New York gives the go-ahead soon – and anything relating to poor old Roosevelt Island seems to stay constantly on the back burner – there will be nothing left of the ruins to save.

The 147 acre wasteland, with a small Main Street of apartment blocks resembling Communist Eastern Europe before the Berlin Wall fell, should be one of the prime real estate spots in New York. Sadly, it is not, and to work out why we need to examine the town's history.

The Native Americans called it Minnahanonck, which roughly translates as 'nice island'. Unfortunately, they were the last people to think so. They flogged it for a handful of trinkets in the 1630s to the Dutch, who discovered it was a good place to keep pigs and called it Hogs Island.

The British got their hands on it in the 1660s and named it in honor of New York sheriff Captain John Manning, but he was ultimately banished there after being found guilty of cowardice and treason. When he died in 1885, his stepdaughter Mary Manningham (FOR INFO: Correct) inherited it and renamed it after her husband Robert Blackwell.

Two hundred years later, the family flogged it for the princely sum of $32,000 to the city of New York and it became home to criminals, the sick and the poverty stricken. Prisons, workhouses and charity hospitals sprung up overnight, one of the latter dealing exclusively with venereal diseases. By 1872, there were 11 horrendously overcrowded institutions on the island, which was by then known as Welfare Island.

The first three quarters of the 20th Century saw the island's fortunes plunge even lower. Hospitals moved elsewhere, buildings crumbled and vandals destroyed everything that hadn't fallen apart. The two mile stretch of land – at that point, reachable only by boat – proved popular only with the New York Fire Department, as a training ground because there were so many abandoned buildings.

It stayed a ghostly eyesore until the 1970s when the New York State Urban Development Corporation decided to rename Welfare Island in honor of President Franklin Delano Roosevelt. They built four government subsidized housing blocks for 2,000 'pioneer residents' and promised to renovate some of the landmark buildings.

The Blackwell Farmhouse was restored in the 1980s – only for it to start falling back into disrepair when money for its long-term upkeep failed to materialise. A group of Manhattan residents have paid for the Smallpox Hospital ruins to be floodlit at night – apparently the spooky vista is a talking point at dinner parties among those with Roosevelt Island views – but so far no one seems willing to cough up money to actually save the ruins.

Then there's the tramway – linked by cables to the screachingly noisy, traffic-clogged Queensboro Bridge, which soars above Roosevelt Island effectively blotting the landscape in every direction. It was meant as a temporary measure before the subway arrived, but is still going strong and proves to be one of the few quirky things that attracts visitors to the island.

Sadly, most people do a Dickens, and upon landing take one look at the urban disaster sprawling in front of them and catch the same tram back to Manhattan.

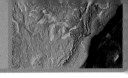

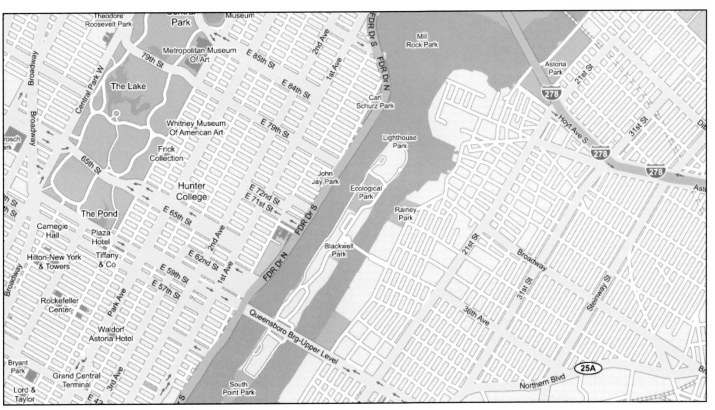

## DURHAM, North Carolina
*Motto: 'Bull City' or 'City of Medicine'*

Otherwise known as 'Fat Chance City' or 'Slim Pickings', Durham prides itself on being the diet capital of the world. Says one who knows – and hates – the place: 'Lourdes for fatties is more like it.'

There are three big weight-loss clinics here and legend has it that some of their more established yo-yo dieters are so scared of going home and piling on the pounds again that they reside at the fat clubs forever. Honest. This wouldn't be such a blight on the already blighted town of Durham if the obscenely obese didn't insist on wearing shorts because of the warm climate. Perhaps the local tourism industry could capitalize on this and have a regular Fatties Parade. A bit like Disney's, only with no-one singing 'I want to Be like You'

Just who benefits from the Dudley and Caroline Beauty Colleges is a terrifying thought. It could be all that nursing, hopes of losing blubber and becoming a beauty that keeps the female population of Durham higher than the male population.

There's another big health aspect that Durham is proud of. The city is the center of the nation's tobacco industry, after farmer Washington Duke came home from the Civil War with the great idea of producing cigarettes. By 1890, he and his three sons had formed the America Tobacco Company, one of the country's most powerful businesses. There were also the tobacco corporations of Liggett & Meyers, R.J. Reynolds and P. Lorillard. Thanks a million Washington; America's health owes a lot to you.

If you are fascinated by that little plant and the habit that causes lung cancer and early death, then drop by the Duke Homestead Historical Site, a museum covering the social history of tobacco farming, complete with demonstrations of farming techniques and tobacco-rolling.

You might agree with us that the introduction of tobacco was one of history's greatest mistakes. If you want another great mistake, how about Durham's nickname of 'Bull City'? John Green of the American Tobacco Company named his product 'Bull' Durham Tobacco after Colman's Mustard,

| Population (year 2000) | 187,035 |
|---|---|
| Males | 89,884 (48.1%) |
| Females | 97,151 (51.9%) |
| Elevation | 394 feet |
| County | Durham |
| Land area | 94.6 square miles |
| Zip code | 27701 - 27713 |
| Median resident age | 31.0 years |
| Median household income | $41,160 |
| Median house value | $126,100 |

| Races in Durham | |
|---|---|
| White Non-Hispanic | 42.4% |
| Hispanic | 8.6% |
| Other race | 4.7% |
| American Indian | 0.8% |
| Two or more races | 1.9% |
| Black | 43.8% |

**Ancestries**

English (8.1%), German (7.2%), Irish (5.7%), United States (5.0%), Italian (2.1%), Scotch-Irish (2.0%)

| For population 25 years and over in Durham | |
|---|---|
| High school or higher | 82.6% |
| Bachelor's degree or higher | 41.8% |
| Graduate or professional degree | 18.3% |
| Unemployed | 5.6% |
| Mean travel time to work | 20.7 minutes |

| For population 15 years and over in Durham | |
|---|---|
| Never married | 37.4% |
| Now married | 44.4% |
| Separated | 3.1% |
| Widowed | 5.9% |
| Divorced | 9.1% |

12.1% Foreign born (6.7% Latin America, 2.9% Asia)

| Crime | |
|---|---|
| Violent crime rate | 28 murders (14.7 per 100,000) |
| Property Crime risk | 3,457 burglaries (1817.4 per 100,000) |

which used a bull in its logo and which Green mistakenly thought was produced in Durham, England. None of this impeded the Bull's incredible success. By the time James B. Duke had purchased the Blackwell Tobacco Company in 1898, Bull Durham was the most famous trademark in the world. It sparked off such popular phrases as 'bullpen' (from a Bull Durham advert painted behind the Yankees' dugout) and 'shooting the bull' (most likely from chewing tobacco). The famous bull's image was painted all over the world, including on the Great Pyramids in Egypt.

Despite the obvious detriment to America's health, it would be churlish of us, at this point, not to mention the $40million gift the tobacco-loving Duke family made to the local college in 1924, helping it to expand into the grand Duke University. The tobacco industry also inspired other Durham-based employment opportunities. The first mill to produce denim and the world's largest hosiery maker were established here.

Long before the aura of tobacco pervaded the town, Durham had seemed to get off to a healthy start. Two Native American tribes, the Eno and the Occaneechi (related to the Sioux), lived and farmed here, and the Great Indian Trading Path ran through the area. Native Americans helped to mould the place by establishing settlement sites, with environmentally-friendly patterns of land use

In 1701 its beauty was chronicled by the explorer John Lawson who called the area 'the flower of the Carolinas'. During the mid-1700s, Scots, Irish and English colonists settled on land granted to John Carteret, Earl of Granville, by King Charles I. The city was named, not after the English town of Durham as is generally supposed, but after Dr Bartlett Durham in the 1800s.

Durham is also known as 'The City of Medicine', possibly

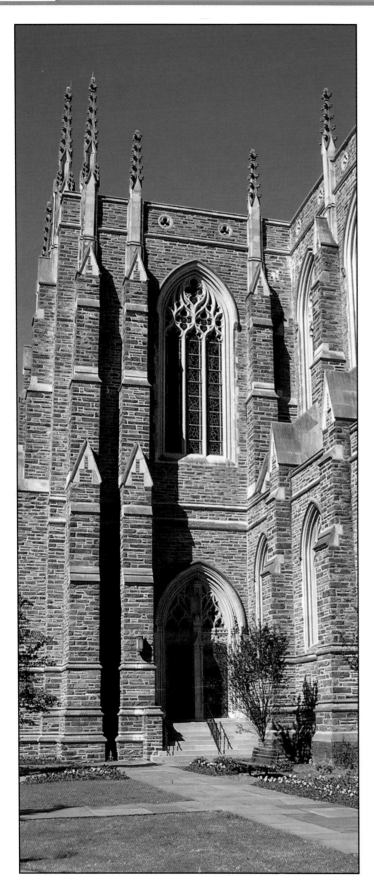

because of the Watts School of Nursing. So it's a great place to be if you are ill. In fact, hospitals are your best bet, accommodation-wise. The hotels downtown are best summed up as anonymous. And whatever you do, move on from the seedy part of town the minute you arrive at the Greyhound station there.

Durham also likes to brag about its black heritage. Today, blacks make up the largest group among its population (43.8 per cent) which is officially accepted as 'significantly above state average'. The Historic Stagville site, seven miles north of the town, gives you an idea of what slavery was all about. Around 80 to 100 African slaves worked on the Stagville plantation and lived in small two-storey houses, one family per room. The huge barn was built by slave carpenters.

It is therefore no wonder that singing the Blues is a popular Durham pastime. The Bull Durham Blues Festival every September attracts artistes from all over America, and visitors help swell the Durham population of 195,914.

The positive points about the place, which we generously include, are that a huge percentage (82.6) of its inhabitants acheived High School or higher education, and that according to the most recent figures, the crimes of rape, robbery, assault, burglary, auto theft and larceny have decreased.

Durham's Brightleaf Square, renovated 15 years ago with its former tobacco warehouses becoming cutesy little shops, is another point in its favour. Amazingly – and somewhat chillingly considering its appeal to the older generation – the average age of a Durham resident is 31. We would like you to tell us why this is. Can it be anything at all with tobacco consumption or the obesity of the town's wheezing, weighed-down, wiped-out elders?

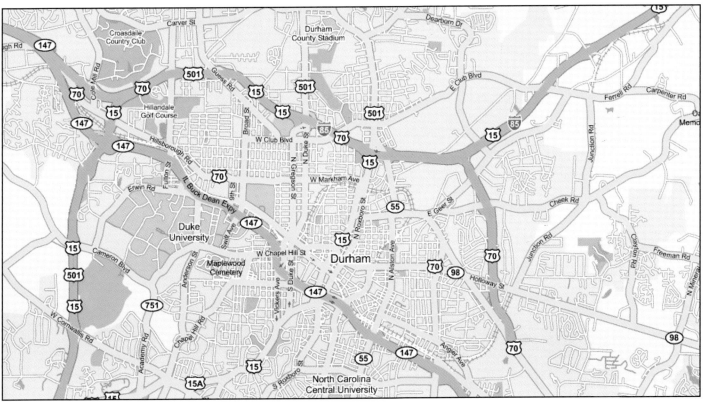

### CHESHIRE, OHIO
*With God, all things are possible
(state motto of Ohio)*

Towns have been wiped out by war, fire, hurricane, flood, even disease. But it is a peculiarity of the American way of life that a town can be wiped off the map by a legal manoeuvre. Yet that is exactly what has happened to Cheshire, Ohio, a community located about 90 miles southeast of Columbus and just upriver from Point Pleasant, West Virginia.

Cheshire, founded in 1863, is now a virtual ghost town, most of its population removed in the space of a few years by the industrial giant that operates a few hundred feet from its City Limits signpost. Most of the inhabitants have moved away, others still cluster nearby, saddened to see their community destroyed.

It has been a filthy business – literally. For years, the citizens of Cheshire had suffered the fallout from the massive

James M. Gavin coal-fueled power plant, owned by American Electric Power. Finally, in a 'David and Goliath' struggle, they determined to fight the energy giant with a landmark environment suit that made legal history.

The town's lawyers put a compelling case: that blue sulfuric clouds regularly escaped from the plant's smokestacks, creating chemical fogs and leaving sooty residue on homes. The effects on human health included sore throats, headaches, eye and skin irritation and even burn marks on lips and tongues. The townsfolk also pointed out that, in the event of a leakage from the plant's ammonia tanks, the local schools would have just six minutes to evacuate their pupils.

Cheshire, therefore, was not a great place to live. But the 221 inhabitants didn't necessarily want to move. They just wanted American Electric Power to stop poisoning them. No such luck. As the legal battle continued year after year, AEP continued pouring its filth into the air.

Then in 2002, the Environmental Protection Agency came to their rescue. It declared the Gavin plant in violation of the

# CHESHIRE

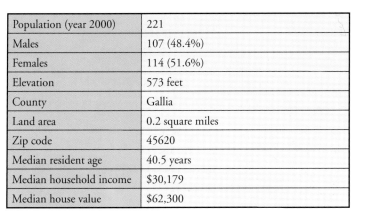

| Population (year 2000) | 221 |
|---|---|
| Males | 107 (48.4%) |
| Females | 114 (51.6%) |
| Elevation | 573 feet |
| County | Gallia |
| Land area | 0.2 square miles |
| Zip code | 45620 |
| Median resident age | 40.5 years |
| Median household income | $30,179 |
| Median house value | $62,300 |

| Races in Cheshire | |
|---|---|
| White Non-Hispanic | 98.2% |
| Hispanic | - |
| Other race | - |
| American Indian | - |
| Two or more races | - |
| Black | 1.4% |
| Ancestries | |
| German (24.4%), United States (13.6%), Irish (8.6%), Scotch-Irish (4.1%), Welsh (3.6%), English (1.8%) | |

| For population 25 years and over in Cheshire | |
|---|---|
| High school or higher | 76.4% |
| Bachelor's degree or higher | 8.1% |
| Graduate or professional degree | 2.7% |
| Unemployed | 11.9% |
| Mean travel time to work | 29.1 minutes |

| For population 15 years and over in Cheshire | |
|---|---|
| Never married | 20.7% |
| Now married | 65.2% |
| Separated | 1.1% |
| Widowed | 6.0% |
| Divorced | 7.1% |
| 0.0% Foreign born | |

| Crime | |
|---|---|
| Violent Crime risk | - |
| Property Crime risk | - |

Clean Air Act and ordered new stringent standards, including the burning of low-sulfur coal.

That concentrated the minds of AEP's high-powered legal team. But they didn't close the plant. In a scenario that could only occur in the USA, American Electric Power made Cheshire an offer it couldn't refuse. With a $20 million community buy-out, it simply paid off the majority of the remaining inhabitants, made them sign a pledge not to sue the company for personal or property damage, boarded up their homes, demolished most of them, sent the former owners packing, and closed the place down.

'It's a sad, sad occasion,' said mayor Tom Rese. 'This is a close-knit community.'

Goodbye Cheshire? Not quite. Some residents aged over 70 sold their homes but got permission to stay in them for as long as they live. A minority of the townsfolk refused to sell at all,

**177**

and subsequent agreements had to be reached to allow them to stay and for Cheshire to remain as a small but extant village.

One of them, 62-year-old Jim Rife, who was born and raised in Cheshire, became the newly installed mayor. He protested: 'AEP told people if they didn't sell, their property wasn't going to be worth anything anyway. If the people had stuck together and refused to sell out, then the deal would not have gone through. I fought against it but there was nothing I could do.'

Before his fellow residents began leaving, however, Rese helped defeat a proposal that would have dissolved the village as a legal entity and began a campaign to annex a contiguous area to the north of the town to re-establish Cheshire and allow it to receive state revenue to pay for services such as law enforcement.

Others among the townsfolk took their compensation cash but, determined to keep family and community intact, remained in the region and planned the rebirth of Cheshire's community spirit in a fresh and cleaner form. And a band of

them vowed to continue the battle against AEP by lobbying and public campaigning.

So, if AEP and their lawyers thought their problems had gone away, they had greatly underestimated the grit of the locals. A group of the area's residents who were not part of the $20 million buyout brought a fresh lawsuit against AEP to try to stop the sulfuric acid that was still being released from the company's stacks. The group, Citizens Against Pollution, alleged the chemical plumes were a 'substantial and imminent threat' to public health.

'Although the Gavin Plant's toxic pollution is harming us and our children, the regulatory agencies have failed to protect us,' asserted Paul Stinson, president of the organization.

So the battle of Cheshire goes on. And despite perfidy, power and poison, the town has not completely died. It is still incorporated and is therefore a legal entity – and as long as some residents hold out, it cannot be closed down.

A local resident recalls with emotion: 'Before the buyout, Cheshire was a nice little place with a town hall, a post office, two churches, one traffic light, a couple of eateries, a gas station and one set of traffic lights. Sure, there were signs at the roadside warning "You are entering a pollution zone" but there was nothing wrong with the place – apart from the poison that American Electric Power was pouring over it.'

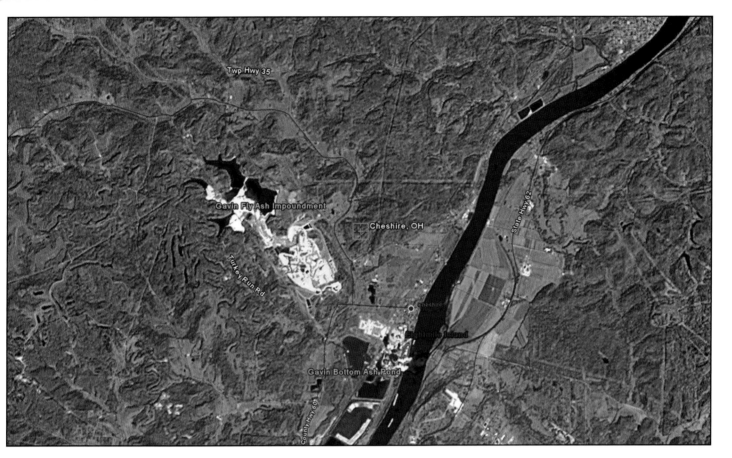

Twp Hwy 35

Gavin Fly Ash Impoundment

Cheshire, OH

Turkey Run Rd

State Hwy 62

cheshire

Big Ohio Island

Gavin Bottom Ash Pond

County Hwy 60-1

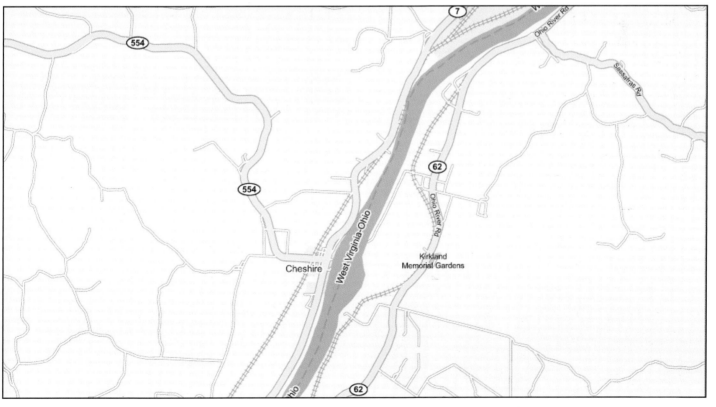

554

7

Ohio River Rd

Sassafras Rd

554

62

Ohio River Rd

West Virginia-Ohio

Cheshire

Kirkland
Memorial Gardens

Ohio

62

## OKLAHOMA CITY, OKLAHOMA
*'The surprise you've been waiting for'*
*(Convention & Visitors Bureau slogans)*

There's only one decent building in Oklahoma City. It's the State Capital and on its pristine front lawn sits a nodding donkey oil rig. There's not a lot to do in Oklahoma except play I Spy Oil Rigs – there are 2000 within the city limits – and the Greco-Roman structure boasts that it is the only capital building in the world that doubles up as a working oil well. It was completed in 1917, 11 years before the oil rush that briefly made OK City a boom town, and when no one had a clue what riches lay underneath.

The arrival of the motor car and Route 66 did nothing to improve downtown Oklahoma, a disappointing mish-mash of non-descript buildings. People simply drove away. Indeed, when we got stuck in Oklahoma for several days, we couldn't find anything to do so we took to driving this way and that along Route 66. Now considered a ghost road and

long-replaced by freeways, we found ruined old red barns, abandoned gas stations, a motel describing itself as 'Amarillo's finest' because it had been used in the Dustin Hoffman movie Rainman and a Native American rest stop with bison out front and bison burgers on the menu inside.

We toured the city's National Cowboy Hall of Fame and Western Heritage Center and popped into a couple of forgetable museums; we ate the same meal several nights running at the one and only half-way decent restaurant; we had a few beers in Bricktown, the so-called happening end of town. Then we tried to find some shops. Maybe we were misled, but we found only the usual malls several miles into the suburbs and that seemed to be it.

Back in 1995, Oklahoma hit the world headlines when Timothy McVeigh and Terry Nichols blew up the Alfred P. Murrah Federal Building with devastating results. Among the 168 people who perished were a group of toddlers in the first

floor kindergarten. A year later, downtown still resembled Belfast at the height of the IRA troubles or Beruit in its bomb happy heyday. Neighboring buildings remained boarded up, shattered windows were left open to the elements and the small, skinny lot where the Murrah Building once stood was a large hole.

Several years on and Oklahoma has turned the lot into a memorial, complete with 168 glass and granite chairs to commemorate the lives of every victim. We're not knocking it. Everything has its place.

So what else has Oklahoma got to offer? Our history books tell us the horror stories. Between 1831 and 1835, President Andrew Jackson ordered the 'Five Civilized Tribes' of Florida and Georgia to relocate to the designated Oklahoma Indian

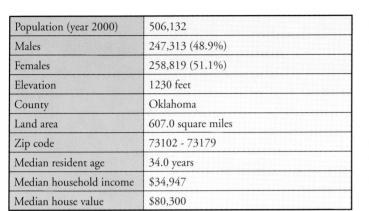

| Population (year 2000) | 506,132 |
|---|---|
| Males | 247,313 (48.9%) |
| Females | 258,819 (51.1%) |
| Elevation | 1230 feet |
| County | Oklahoma |
| Land area | 607.0 square miles |
| Zip code | 73102 - 73179 |
| Median resident age | 34.0 years |
| Median household income | $34,947 |
| Median house value | $80,300 |

| Races in Oklahoma City | |
|---|---|
| White Non-Hispanic | 64.7% |
| Hispanic | 10.1% |
| Other race | 5.3% |
| American Indian | 5.7% |
| Two or more races | 3.9% |
| Black | 15.4% |
| Ancestries | |
| German (11.7%), Irish (9.2%), United States (9.0%), English (8.5%), French (2.2%), Scotch-Irish (1.8%) | |

| For population 25 years and over in Oklahoma City | |
|---|---|
| High school or higher | 81.3% |
| Bachelor's degree or higher | 24.0% |
| Graduate or professional degree | 8.1% |
| Unemployed | 5.3% |
| Mean travel time to work | 20.8 minutes |

| For population 15 years and over in Oklahoma City | |
|---|---|
| Never married | 26.4% |
| Now married | 51.2% |
| Separated | 2.4% |
| Widowed | 6.4% |
| Divorced | 13.6% |
| 8.5% Foreign born (4.6% Latin America, 2.9% Asia) | |

| Crime | |
|---|---|
| Violent Crime risk | 45 murders (8.9 per 100,000) |
| Property Crime risk | 8,405 burglaries (1656.1 per 100,000) |

Territory. Tens of thousands died on the brutal march that became known as the Trail of Tears, and 50 years later the tribes were booted out again to make way for the white land rush.

The cocky souls that beat the land settlement offers and staked their claims early became known as Sooners, a tag that for some reason stuck and is now given to everyone hailing from Oklahoma. The city – it's Choctaw name means 'land of the red man' – has tried to make amends by celebrating its Native American heritage at every opportunity. And, of course, the white man gave us the musical Oklahoma! But let's not go there.

With just over one million people living in the city – described by its Visitors Bureau as 'the newest frontier' and 'the surprise you've been waiting for' – -the official guide books gush about its small town, friendly feel. Its Cost of Living index of 84.3 makes it one of the cheapest state capitals to live in, and house prices average around $96,400, way below the national median of $160,100.

We found a reference book that offered 'mild winters' as an attractive reason for living in Oklahoma. But what about the summers? Long, dusty and hot is what they are – it's not unusual for the thermometer to stay at 100 degree F for 50-day stretches . The city is also famous for its severe storms. For that, read tornadoes and hail.

Oklahoma scores 62 on the tornado risk scale, as opposed to the national average of 19. Consequently, practically every house in the city is surrounded by an unattractive wire fence to guard against twister damage.

The North Canadian River doesn't roar; it rarely even dribbles. For most of the year it's a dried-up ditch. The rolling countryside surrounding the city is attractive, if you like that sort of thing – but only before the drought sets in – and there are a few interesting old farm buildings. But our own personal favourite remains Route 66 … that's where we got our kicks on the way OUT of Oklahoma.

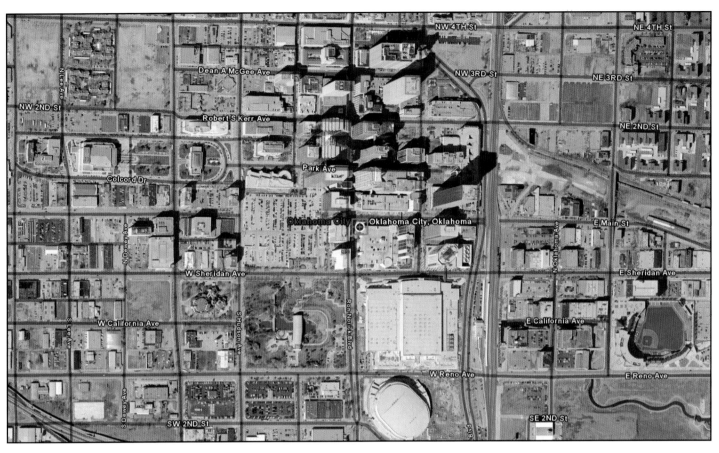

## CENTRALIA, PENNSYLVANIA
*Virtue, liberty and independence (state motto of Pennsylvania)*

You've got to admit it. The people of Centralia certainly have fire in their belly. They've had to. Thanks to a disaster dating back to May 1962, the place has definitely got to go down in the Hall of Flame.

That disaster was a fire. A fire, which after more than 40 years and 40 million dollars, is still burning. The flames, smoke, fumes and toxic gases that came up through the backyards, basements and streets of Centralia practically ripped the town apart.

The fire started in a garbage dump in an abandoned stripping pit near the town and would have extinguished itself had it not been for the large coal vein running under the town. As everyone knows, if a fire is getting low, just chuck on another lump of coal. So you can imagine what happens when there is an endless supply of the stuff that just can't help

igniting.

With an original population of 1,100, Centralia has become something of a ghost (should that be toast?) town. Just 30 people hung around long enough to see most of their community razed to the ground. They were happy enough to live alongside the biggest grate in the world. (It was nothing compared to the horrors of the Black Lung disease men caught from working in mines; with that, you just died young.)

It still seems incredible that anyone would want to live any place where heat from burning coal reaches over 700 degrees Fahrenheit at the surface, where sulphur smoke permeates the air and where buildings are shored up with columns of bricks at their sides. Even when the authorities came along and offered people money to leave their homes, many of the good folk just wanted to stay put.

Says one former Centralia resident: 'Maybe it does seem simple, but as a child of coal country, I know it was not. To

leave the only home many of them knew was worse than anything the fire could do to them. My heart goes out to them.'

Two months after it first started, the Department of Environmental Resources began to monitor the fire. Bore holes were drilled to check its extent and temperature. Some people believed these holes also helped provide a nice little natural draft which boosted combustion.

It is no wonder the people are bitter. Right from the moment the first three families were moved from Centralia on May 22, 1969, the residents have been treated as anything but human beings. First a trench was dug north of the Odd Fellows Cemetery, where fly ash and clay seals were used in an attempt to put out the fire. It didn't work. According to

# CENTRALIA

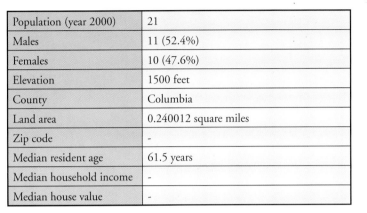

| Population (year 2000) | 21 |
|---|---|
| Males | 11 (52.4%) |
| Females | 10 (47.6%) |
| Elevation | 1500 feet |
| County | Columbia |
| Land area | 0.240012 square miles |
| Zip code | - |
| Median resident age | 61.5 years |
| Median household income | - |
| Median house value | - |

| Races in Centralia | |
|---|---|
| White Non-Hispanic | - |
| Hispanic | - |
| Other race | - |
| American Indian | - |
| Two or more races | - |
| Black | - |
| Ancestries | |
| - | |

| For population 25 years and over in Centralia | |
|---|---|
| High school or higher | - |
| Bachelor's degree or higher | - |
| Graduate or professional degree | - |
| Unemployed | - |
| Mean travel time to work | - |

| For population 15 years and over in Centralia | |
|---|---|
| Never married | - |
| Now married | - |
| Separated | - |
| Widowed | - |
| Divorced | - |
| - | |

| Crime | |
|---|---|
| Violent Crime risk | - |
| Property Crime risk | - |

one observer, if the trench had been dug in three shifts a day instead of one, and if those in charge had considered the work important enough to bust a Labor Day holiday, the fire would have been contained then and there.

In 1980, the US Bureau of Mines' Red Book stated: 'The Centralia mine fire has not been extinguished and has not been controlled.' Within 12 months, 27 more families were moved out at a price less than that which went to those who later begrudgingly allowed their homes to be bought off them.

On February 14, 1981, one resident, Todd Domboski, narrowly escaped death when a hole about four feet in diameter and approximately 150 feet deep opened underneath him. Mr Domboski managed to cling to exposed tree roots until he was pulled to safety. The heat or the carbon monoxide in the breach would have been enough to kill him instantly if he had fallen just a little deeper. It was this incident that first put Centralia's plight in the national media spotlight.

By 1983, the fire was advancing in three or four areas but the government said that trenching the district could cost as much as $660million with no guarantee of success. That was when a buy-out of the remaining homes was proposed. A referendum had 345 homeowners voting to accept the offer

and 200 against. In November 1983, by which time, there was fire under 350 surface acres, $42million was allocated for the buy-out. In 1991 this had increased by three-quarters. Finally, 26 homes along Route 61 were bought out in April that year.

The promises made by the government to extinguish the inferno for good were never kept. It was cheaper to get everyone out by offering cash for the smoke-damaged houses. No-one was interested in what the people themselves really wanted.

When remaining residents put up resistance to leaving, they were hit with a court order to quit their homes by December 1997. Officially, all the people have gone (unofficially, some diehards are still holed up in town) and only the 2,000 homes that haven't been scorched, singed or sent crashing to the ground in flames still remain.

Recalls our former Centralia resident: 'I remember riding in the family car on our way to a local amusement park when I was a child in the mid 1960s. Even then, there would be times where the road we travelled on was closed in a section, due to a subsidence caused by the mine fire. Coal burns and reduces

to ash. The ground above then collapses. I remember not quite understanding what was happening to this town and its people - but now in my late 30s, I understand quite well...'

Yes, Centralia is an awful town – but largely because of the dishonesty of a government that let good, hardworking people down. It is a testimony to how power is abused, leaving the little people in the lurch. In this case, the residents had to leave their homes, families and friends for some strange and often frightening future. It was no wonder they put up a fight.

Today, if you were driving north on route 62 in the heart of the Anthracite coal region of Pennsylvania, you might come across a detour at the top of a hill in a community fittingly called Ashland. If you were to ignore the detour signs and hang the right that 61 takes through Ashland, the first clue that something wasn't right would be the abrupt end to route 61 as it once was. If you were to look to your right and follow a small, slightly less engineered road down and around the close route 61, it would re-emerge at the sad, bad, burned place that is Centralia.

The ruins of Centralia, Pennsylvania, no longer exist on some maps. The presence of a smattering of residents is the reason given for being unable to stop the fire for once and for all. Otherwise, say officials, they could have pushed ahead with plans to dig a 500ft deep trench around the town to try to stop the expansion of the fire into a much larger vein of coal. Ashland, just two miles away, is threatened with a similar fate if the fire can't be contained.

The Commonwealth of Pennsylvania owns the remaining homes in Centralia. So now owners complain that they have a situation where the State owns your house but you still pay property tax.

One local sums it up perfectly: 'This is a small town where coal was once king. But now, with the dead trees littering the once green hillsides surrounding the town, the highways criss-crossed with cracks in them two feet deep and the stench of sulphur smoke rising from the ground, it's more like the devil himself has moved in.'

America would be made up of nothing but abysmal towns if economics over-ruled compassion in the way they have in the case of Centralia.

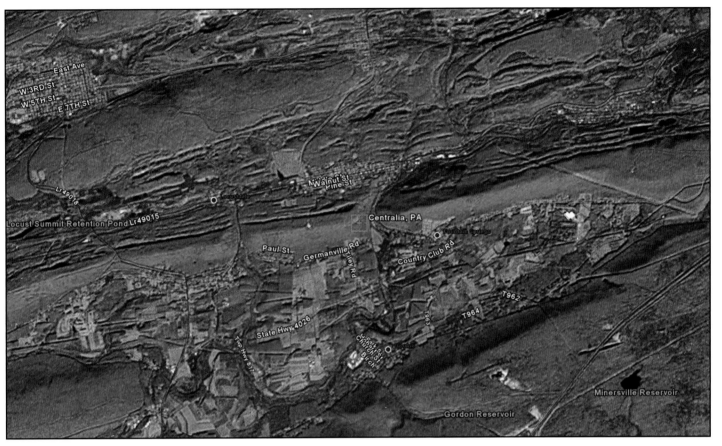

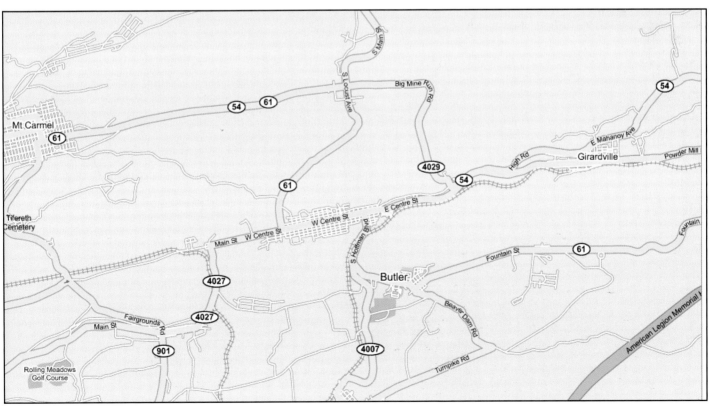

### INTERCOURSE, PENNSYLVANIA
*Virtue, liberty and independence
(state motto of Pennsylvania)*

Intercourse sounds interesting but isn't. The butt of many ribald jokes, droll postcards and schoolkid giggles, you'd expect the place to be at least a little bit of a laugh. But there is no fun to be had here at all.

Part of the motion picture Witness, starring Harrison Ford, was filmed in Intercourse, so you'll quickly gather that this is Pennsylvania Dutch countryside, and Intercourse itself is a town peopled by black-hatted and bonneted religious orders. The name, they will tell you, derives not from what they spend their time doing but from a crossroad where they settled on the Old Philadelphia Pike, earlier known as King's Highway.

Now, if the Amish and other Mennonite orders had stuck by their principles and had turned their back on the modern world, Intercourse would have remained a beautiful backwater

in a land of winding country lanes and immaculate farmsteads in Eastern Lancaster County, 50 miles west of Philadelphia. But rejecting modern life would have meant giving up on the chance to cash in on the celluloid celebrity that the town enjoyed after Witness.

So, of course, we now have the Plain and Fancy Farm, the Amish Experience, Ed's Buggy Rides, restaurants offering 'Pennsylvania Dutch taste sensations', sentimentalised exhibitions of Amish history and 'speciality' shops.

'The Village stands as a clear reminder of our traditional American heritage as people live by a simpler way of life,' boasts the local tourist office. It reports a local B&B innkeeper as saying: 'I've noticed the numbers of our guests who arrive back at the B&B simply excited with a purchase: a corner cupboard, quilt, redwood bird feeder or dried flower arrangement.'

In fact, most visitors come away with nothing as exciting as a redwood bird feeder. They will more likely have visited the olde worlde Amish souvenir store to purchase T-shirts emblazoned with 'Intercourse University' (there isn't one) or a pack of those cringe-making 'From Intercourse Pa' postcards.

How the stricter Amish can square this money-making mickey-taking of their town with the tenets of their creed is difficult to fathom. Of course, many of the more orthodox adherents of the Mennonite Orders have decided they can't. They have already hauled their mule-drawn buggies eastwards to the emptier pastures of Indiana, Iowa and Minnesota, where fewer 'Englishers', 'Yankees' and 'High People' -- names given by the Amish for anyone who is not Amish – are likely to gawp at them from tour buses.

The ones that have remained in Witness country have witnessed a religious ideal turned into a living amusement

| Population (year 2000) | 1,200 |
|---|---|
| Males | - |
| Females | - |
| Elevation | 483 feet |
| County | Lancaster |
| Land area | - |
| Zip code | 17534 |
| Median resident age | - |
| Median household income | - |
| Median house value | - |

| Races in Intercourse | |
|---|---|
| White Non-Hispanic | - |
| Hispanic | - |
| Other race | - |
| American Indian | - |
| Two or more races | - |
| Black | - |
| Ancestries | |
| - | |

| For population 25 years and over in Intercourse | |
|---|---|
| High school or higher | - |
| Bachelor's degree or higher | - |
| Graduate or professional degree | - |
| Unemployed | - |
| Mean travel time to work | - |

| For population 15 years and over in Intercourse | |
|---|---|
| Never married | - |
| Now married | - |
| Separated | - |
| Widowed | - |
| Divorced | - |
| - | |

| Crime | |
|---|---|
| Violent Crime risk | - |
| Property Crime risk | - |

(No census data exists for Intercourse, and therefore information on the population and demographics is unavailable.)

park. They still farm, of course, supplemented by the tourist dollar, and Intercourse is the community center where they bank their cash. The Rough Guide warns prospective visitors: 'Be prepared for a strong smell of horses and cows in much of the county.' But the real smell is from the staple crop now lovingly propagated in this town… greenbacks.

Just for the record, the Pennsylvania Dutch are not Dutch at all; their name is a derivation of 'Deutch', or German. And the likelihood is that Intercourse was not named after a crossroad, but was named after the entrance to an old racecourse nearby – hence 'Enter Course', which evolved into Intercourse when the town was named in 1814.

But what does a name matter? Selling Intercourse is what this community is all about – and there's a name for that.

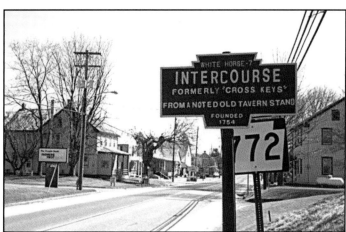

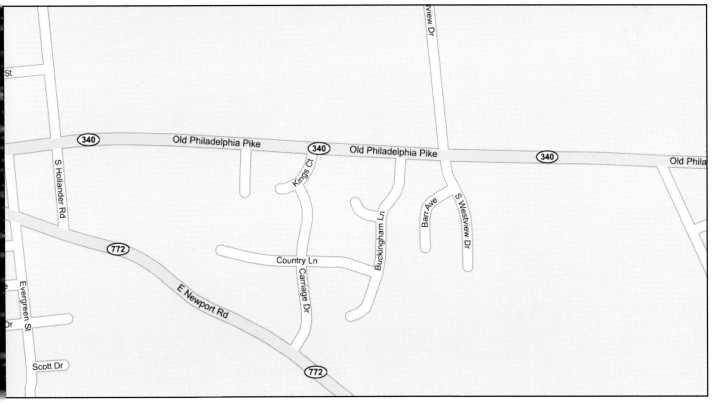

## SCRANTON, PENNSYLVANIA
*Motto: 'The Electric City'*
*Former name: 'Skunk's Misery'*

Scranton is the kind of place where the Deerhunter grew up warped before he went to 'Nam to waste Charlie. Depression hovers like a Black Death miasma over the old coal mines, the industries that served them, and the poor wretches

still forced to live there.

A newspaper once reported it had the highest number of topless bars per capita on the entire Eastern Seaboard, a pole-dancing Narnia-of.the-Dark-Side, where people sport the Stars and Stripes on everything from their pick-up to their dog, yet never seem to question why Uncle Sam stiffed them on the job front.

Perhaps the soporific effects of prolonged noonday mammary exposure, accompanied by Schlitz beer at a dollar a throw, have dulled their capacity for lucid questioning. Scranton has few claims to fame except that Pandora Peaks, the implausibly built porno star of Striptease, peeled her kit off to the delectation of Scranton's downtrodden masses for years before she made it to the fleshmarkets of Hollywood.

With a dwindling number of citizens – in 2000, 76,415 and now estimated to be below 74,712, putting it among the 'Worst 20' of US towns with fastest plummeting populations – Scranton has little appeal as a place to call home. Pennsylvania's fifth most populous city has 18 percent of people under 18, and 12 percent of those 65 and older living below the poverty line.

# SCRANTON

| Population (year 2000) | 76,415 |
|---|---|
| Males | 35,543 (46.5%) |
| Females | 40,872 (53.5%) |
| Elevation | 754 feet |
| County | Lackawanna |
| Land area | 25.2 square miles |
| Zip code | 18503, 18504, 18505, 18508, 18509, 18510, 18512 |
| Median resident age | 38.8 years |
| Median household income | $28,805 |
| Median house value | $78,200 |

| Races in Scranton | |
|---|---|
| White Non-Hispanic | 92.3% |
| Hispanic | 2.6% |
| Other race | 1.2% |
| American Indian | - |
| Two or more races | 1.1% |
| Black | 3.0% |
| Ancestries | |
| Irish (30.3%), Italian (19.4%), German (15.7%), Polish (14.8%), Welsh (6.9%), English (5.8%) | |

| For population 25 years and over in Scranton | |
|---|---|
| High school or higher | 78.2% |
| Bachelor's degree or higher | 15.6% |
| Graduate or professional degree | 5.9% |
| Unemployed | 7.3% |
| Mean travel time to work | 17.6 minutes |

| For population 15 years and over in Scranton | |
|---|---|
| Never married | 31.8% |
| Now married | 45.1% |
| Separated | 2.4% |
| Widowed | 11.8% |
| Divorced | 8.9% |
| 3.1% Foreign born (1.3% Europe, 1.0% Asia, 0.7% Latin America) | |

| Crime | |
|---|---|
| Violent Crime risk | 1 murder (1.3 per 100,000) |
| Property Crime risk | 435 burglaries (569.0 per 100,000) |

Originally a logging town on the Delaware River. Scranton was once a center of the Pennsylvanian anthracite coal industry. During the first half of the 20th century, it attracted many groups of newly arrived immigrants. This heritage is recalled in the Catholic churches that dot the city, which is also home to the University of Scranton, a Jesuit institution with about 4,000 students.

In the past decade, the town worthies have launched several revitilzation campaigns, with the stated aim of 'returning the city to its former glory'. One high point is the Steamtown National Historic Site, a museum that seeks to preserve the history of steam locomotives. But downtown Scranton itself has long ago run out of steam.

Even the train no longer stops in Scranton, where the old Luckawanna Railway Station is arguably the only decent building in town. It has been turned into a hotel – and to all intent and purpose it is way too grand for the locals. There's a fabulously expensive restaurant, the old oak-panelled waiting room is a bar and there's even an outside terrace on what used to be a platform.

But as one traveller who checked in told us: 'Peek from a train carriage-style hotel room window and you will see nothing outside but railway tracks covered by weeds and empty tumbledown buildings.'

But to be fair to the place, it has had some fleeting recognition in popular culture, past and present. Scranton was nicknamed 'The Electric City' for having, in 1886, built the first streetcar system in the US entirely run on electric power. The trams vanished long ago, along with the optimism of the people.

It has three other dubious claims to fame. In March 1965 a truck carrying bananas crashed after coming down a two-mile downhill road that leads into the downtown area. This incident led to the Harry Chapin song ThirtyThousand Pounds of Bananas. Like Scranton, it never figured in any Top Ten.

In 2005, the NBC adaptation of the hit BBC show The Office premiered. The fictional company Dunder-Mifflin portrayed in the show is set in Scranton. In 1999, the Anime series Big O showed Scranton as a city famous for an electricity-generating sea serpent residing in a nearby body of water.

It says a lot for this sullied patch of Pennsylvania that, long before it became a center for logging, coal or steam locomotion, the place that is now the city of Scranton was known as 'Skunk's Misery'.

# SCRANTON

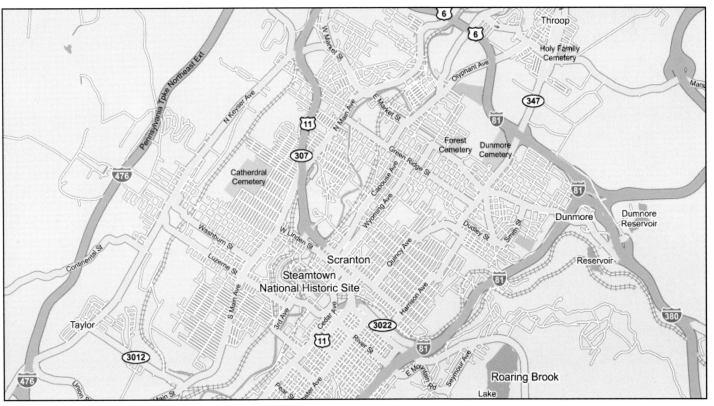

195

## VOLGA, SOUTH DAKOTA.
### *Motto: 'The Town with a Future'*

When people think of the Prairies, it conjures up images of the Wild West, desert, heat and cowboys. Not in South Dakota, it doesn't. The snow starts falling at the beginning of November and it's still on the ground at the end of April. Then, in a flash, it's summer – and with temperatures of 100 degrees F, the drought sets in.

With just 10 people per square mile, the good folk at

the grandly named South Dakota International Business Institute have been trawling Europe trying to entice farmers to emigrate. With that in mind, we thought we'd take a look at Volga, a little town of 1,435 people smack bang in the middle of... er... nowhere.

Land is relatively cheap, at between $1,200 to $1,500 an acre, but any would-be pioneers would need hundreds to make dairy farming viable. Then, of course, you need lots of cows to make the milk that's desperately needed by the large cheese factory 40 miles away. The Business Institute brags that South Dakota doesn't have a state income tax, but there's a very high property tax that works out at around $15 an acre. And that's before Federal taxes.

Locals say Volga is great place to bring up children. Put it this way: they won't be staying out late because there isn't anything for them to do. Actually, we're being unfair. There is the Volga City Community Center, the webpage for which shows an exciting photo of two little boys whooping it up in the swimming pool. The center offers a fun summer program of baseball, softball, basketball, bowling, swimming lessons and story telling. There's also the Boy Scouts and Girl Guides. For the grown ups, the American Legion meets on the third Wednesday of every month, and the Lions Club gets together

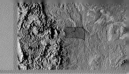

| Population (year 2000) | 1,435 |
|---|---|
| Males | 691 (48.2%) |
| Females | 744 (51.8%) |
| Elevation | 1634 feet |
| County | Brookings |
| Land area | 0.8 square miles |
| Zip code | 57071 |
| Median resident age | 34.4 years |
| Median household income | $41,818 |
| Median house value | $82,000 |

| Races in Volga | |
|---|---|
| White Non-Hispanic | 98.4% |
| Hispanic | - |
| Other race | - |
| American Indian | 0.8% |
| Two or more races | 0.6% |
| Black | - |
| Ancestries | |

Norwegian (39.7%), German (37.5%), Dutch (11.6%), Irish (8.4%), English (6.6%), Danish (6.3%)

| For population 25 years and over in Volga | |
|---|---|
| High school or higher | 91.6% |
| Bachelor's degree or higher | 28.9% |
| Graduate or professional degree | 6.5% |
| Unemployed | 1.2% |
| Mean travel time to work | 13.6 minutes |

| For population 15 years and over in Volga | |
|---|---|
| Never married | 24.6% |
| Now married | 61.4% |
| Separated | 0.0% |
| Widowed | 6.4% |
| Divorced | 7.6% |
| 0.1% Foreign born | |

| Crime | |
|---|---|
| Violent Crime risk | - |
| Property Crime risk | - |

every couple of weeks.

There's one tiny touch of culture in this prairie outpost: a little museum that tells of Volga's history. But there's nothing very romantic about that either, as the various names associated with this town tend to prove. Here we learn that the place was founded by the drearily named Western Town Lot Company, was platted in 1879 by the Chicago and Northwestern Railway as a stopping point on the way to the Black Hills, was originally known as 'Bandy Town', and was renamed Volga after Russia's Volga River (an eccentric allusion to the Great Sioux River that flows nearby).

But Volga does not live in the past. No, not this go-ahead town. Volga residents are so excited at the prospect of newcomers arriving from Europe to farm that they've even dreamt up a motto: 'The town with a future'. So who, we wondered, actually lives here?

Well, there are 691 men and 744 women. Due to the imbalance, perhaps it isn't surprising to discover that 24.6 per cent of the population have never married. But 61 per cent are

wed – and they seem to stay that way. Just 7.6 per cent of the population is divorced and, according to state figures, there is no-one at all who is separated. Perhaps such a state of marital severance is considered just too vulgar in Volga. This could be because life in the town revolves around religion. There are five churches within spitting distance, although the Catholics have to drive the next town, Brookings, to worship.

So what else has Volga got to offer? There's a new truck stop; it's not exactly haute cuisine but it's the nearest thing to a restaurant. And there is a bar, of sorts. The Main Street shops are dedicated to local agriculture. Buying a tractor or fuel isn't a problem in Volga; running out of sugar is. It's 10 miles to the nearest grocery shop in Brookings – considered a BIG city because it has a Walmart on the outskirts.

If you want something special, then it's a 56-mile drive to Sioux Falls, South Dakota's biggest city, with a population of 180,000. That's where you find big shops and restaurants and people who think nothing of driving great distances. Us, we'd drive any distance to avoid Volga, 'the town with a future' – but absolutely no present.

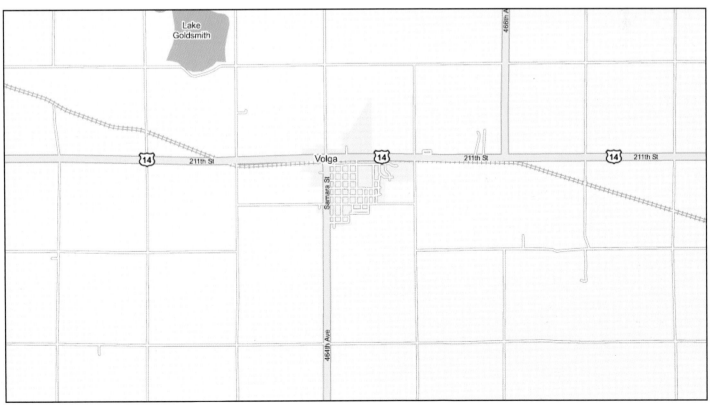

### KNOXVILLE, TENNESSEE
*Motto: 'Dignity and Respect'*

'Good times and good friends await you in Knoxville, a modern Appalachian city with great restaurants, nightlife, museums, shopping, family fun and national championship sports. It's a warm, welcoming place with its own distinct history, vibrant arts community and blessed with the natural beauty of the Tennessee River and the Great Smoky Mountains.'

Well, that's what the Knoxville Tourism website says about the place. Must be right, eh? Hmmm.

Doesn't seem to mention the fact that Tennessee has the eighth worst crime rate in the US. Nor that Tennessee is judged the 46th Most Liveable State in the US. Yep, that's right, there are only three worse ones.

But Knoxville is a place apart, isn't it? An elegant step above its down-at-heel neighbours? The 'good friends' in this 'modern Appalachian city' may beat you up and rob you but presumably they do so with a ready smile and a have-a-nice-day-y'all.

So forget the low-life, let's concentrate on the high life: the 'great restaurants' and 'nightlife'. Pre Prohibition, Knoxville was named as the 'second most sinful' city in America after New Orleans. Those were the days. Well, Prohibition was lifted here in 1971 but try finding a decent drinking hole in or around this town and you could be forgiven for thinking that it's still in force. The one lively road is sadly called Gay Street but there's not much gaiety in the air. Bars in and around Knoxville tend to cater more for the seedy than the joyous.

So what do the good citizens of Knoxville do with their free time? For a start, there is more than an average share of multiplex theaters. Secondly, there is… well, there's not a second, really. Unless you count some of the following attractions.

The much-vaunted 'shopping' is catered for by the predictable shopping malls, of which there are two very large

| Population (year 2000) | 173,890 |
|---|---|
| Males | 82,390 (47.4%) |
| Females | 91,500 (52.6%) |
| Elevation | 889 feet |
| County | Knox |
| Land area | 92.7 square miles |
| Zip code | 37902 - 37938 |
| Median resident age | 33.4 years |
| Median household income | $27,492 |
| Median house value | $78,000 |

| Races in Knoxville | |
|---|---|
| White Non-Hispanic | 79.0% |
| Hispanic | 1.6% |
| Other race | 0.7% |
| American Indian | 0.9% |
| Two or more races | 1.6% |
| Black | 16.2% |
| Ancestries | |
| United States (13.3%), English (10.2%), German (10.0%), Irish (9.9%), Scotch-Irish (3.9%), Scottish (2.5%) | |

| For population 25 years and over in Knoxville | |
|---|---|
| High school or higher | 78.4% |
| Bachelor's degree or higher | 24.6% |
| Graduate or professional degree | 9.5% |
| Unemployed | 6.5% |
| Mean travel time to work | 20.3 minutes |

| For population 15 years and over in Knoxville | |
|---|---|
| Never married | 34.6% |
| Now married | 41.6% |
| Separated | 2.2% |
| Widowed | 8.4% |
| Divorced | 13.3% |
| 3.0% Foreign born (1.2% Asia, 0.9% Europe, 0.7% Latin America) | |

| Crime | |
|---|---|
| Violent Crime risk | 15 murders (8.5 per 100,000) |
| Property Crime risk | 1,717 burglaries (978.7 per 100,000) |

ones. But the main shopping 'street' is Kingston Pike, which runs for about 30 miles and features upmarket outlets like McDonalds and Arby's.

Then there are the aforementioned 'national championship sports'. True, Knoxville was home to the 1982 World's Fair, and if you enter the city from the north, you are still greeted by an impressively huge, though somewhat rusty, gold ball erected to celebrate the event. Knoxsville is also the only place to have a Women's Basketball Hall Of Fame.

Sadly, still on the local law books is the unsporting ruling that it is 'illegal to lasso fish in Knoxville'. So what else can its citizens do for exercise and entertainment these days? Get on the Web and you'll find a prime site is that of the Knoxville Juggling Club ('Dropping stuff on the floor since 1997') which 'meets at the Candy Factory from 7 to 9 p.m. on the second and fourth Tuesday of each month'.

Yes, as the region's Tourism Director boasts, 'East Tennessee is for hearty, fun-loving folks'. Apart from is Dolly Parton's hometown of Sevierville, the area's top tourist attraction is

the Dollywood theme park – 'yep, named after Dolly!', it is at pains to point out in case prospective visitors miss the connection. And within tobacco spitting distance, one can enjoy dodging flying tomatoes in the Famous Tomato Wars, a July highlight of the seed-splattered Grainger County Tomato Festival.

In town itself, the blooming dogwood trees brighten the April landscape during a 17-day cultural celebration at the Dogwood Arts Festival. One of the themes of this parade is 'Marching Through Time', when a riotous and colourful vast crowd of, er, 10 residents dress up in costumes of the period 1880 to 1920 – according to the publicity, 'the years during which most of the development of our area took place'. An accurate statement.

The Mayor of Knoxville's own Vision Statement for the town is to make Knoxville 'America's premier city in which to live, work and raise a family'. To this end, his administration proudly announces as the main headline on its website: 'Knox County Health Department Begins Mosquito Spraying on

June 1.'

What the city can't spray away, however, is the pollution. The place ranks as the twelfth most polluted city in America by the number of particles in the air. Just living there in the smog and filthy, damp air is awaiting death by choking and drowning in one foul swoop.

So if you can't breathe in the place, what can you do? Certainly not venture outdoors. There is hardly a sidewalk in town, and if you did walk, you'd be in danger of being killed. Crimes rates are significantly higher (in many cases, nearly double) than national average for murders, forcible rapes, robberies, aggravated assaults, burglaries, larceny, vehicle threats and arson.

Survive on the mean streets of Knoxville? You haven't a prayer. Well, you have actually.

The key to your salvation is visible as you enter the city from the west, where you are greeted by a giant cross, a

preview of what you will find within the city itself … no fewer than 430 churches.

So that is what the good folk of Knoxville are all doing. Praying for the Good Lord to make life better on the other side. Some well-known names who eventually escaped to the other side from Asphixiation City are Nikki Giovanni, the Princess of Black Poetry, who was born in Knoxville in 1943. The first black federal judge, William Henry Hastie (1904) and Pulitzer Prize winning writer James Agee 1909.) Hopefully, they've got over a mortal existence of life-threatnning criminiality and health-sapping air.

And that's some leap of faith in a dump whose greatest claim to fame is that the mayor from 1952 to 1955 was George R. Dempster, inventor of the Dempster Dumpster.

Knoxville · Knoxville · Gay Street Bridge · Henley Street Bridge · Jersey Ave · Lake · Terrace Ave · James B Karnes Bridge · Stephenson Dr · British Pike

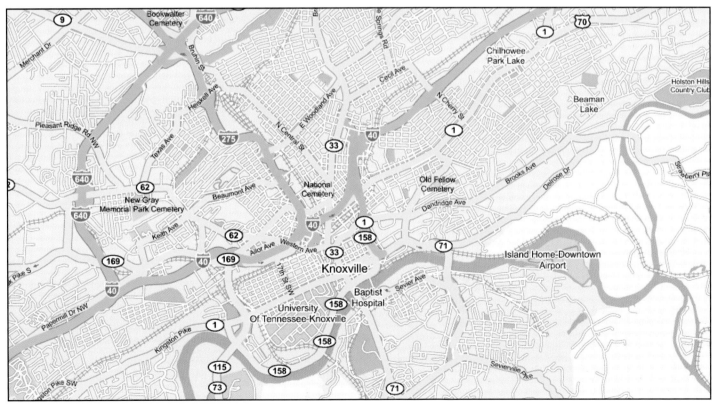

## MEMPHIS, Tennessee
*Agriculture and commerce
(state motto of Tennessee)*

Memphis may be a music 'mecca' but it is also a mystery to us. Its virtues are extolled in the travel 'bible', The Rough Guide to USA. And of course there's Elvis, Blues, soul and rock 'n' roll as well as excellent museums, and a cracking, snapping, popping ambience and night life. Weirdly, Memphis is also the barbecue capital of the nation.

So what's it doing here, you ask. Well, for a start, would you be so handy with a barbecue fork if you knew you were just as likely to be speared on the end of it as that tasty little corn you're cooking up? Or can you truly relax in that bustling, busy atmosphere of the night when something awful is just lurking around the corner?

Memphis, you see, has America's second-highest crime rate. Well that's not as bad has having the HIGHEST, you might say, as you shrug your shoulders and wonder why we've got it in for Tennessee's largest city. Perhaps now is the time to slip in the fact that Memphis's rate of robbery and burglary IS the highest in the US. An English couple staying in the place decided to go for a walk. 'When we told one of the staff at our hotel we were off out, he asked if we wanted to get mugged or killed,' they reported to the folk back home.

Tennessee also got voted in the ten 'Least Livable' states. So, unless you want to point the finger of blame at Nashville (though six million visitors every year can't all be wrong) or Pigeon Forge, home to Dolly Parton's 'fun' park Dollywood (reason enough, together with the five miles of discount shops and motels to stay well away), then Memphis should be man enough to take it on the chin – or chins if you want to make

the comparison with local boy hero Elvis in his latter years.

While we're on the subject of Tennessee as a whole, the place has pretty poor transport connections, with Amtrak only calling at Memphis, and bus travel through the small towns in the east difficult. Not the place to be waiting around for a connection; Memphis is namedyear after year as being in the Top 30 of 'Sweatiest States in the USA'.

Ah, yes, back to Elvis and the Memphis connection. Or as a good friend of ours says: 'Memphis. So OK, it's got Graceland but that's it. Unless you want to count the Peabody Hotel, where every morning there is a big ceremony when a pile of ducks come down the elevator, waddle across the red carpet and climb into the foyer pond. In the afternoon, there's a similar ceremony when they return upstairs. Tennesseans are very proud of this tourist attraction. And did I mention Graceland… that internationally famous shrine that's at the end of a long, nasty road full of used car showrooms and the sort of fast-food joints that Elvis loved so much.'

While we're on the King of Rock 'n' Roll, let's dwell a while on all the Elvis things you can do and see in Memphis. There's Elvis Presley's Heartbreak Hotel just across from Graceland, which has 24-hour Elvis videos in every room, serves peanut butter sandwiches and offers package deals for special Elvis attractions. Graceland – which of course is on Elvis Presley Boulevard – is the surprisingly modest home in which Presley died in 1977. The boulevard is indeed lined with fast-food joints (exactly the ones that killed the King) and Elvis motels but amazingly few Elvis souvenir places. Tours start opposite the house in Graceland Plaza, from where visitors are transported in minibuses through the musical gate in the 'Wall of Love' daubed with thousands of messages from fans. Thence follows an audio tour. The moneyed can buy a 'platinum' ticket to all attractions for $25.25 and take in, not only the house, but Elvis's automobile collection, aeroplanes and the 'Sincerely Elvis' exhibits which include a TV with a bullet hole fired there by the King himself. (He also shot his fridge, stereo and his daughter Lisa Marie's slide thereby single-handedly adding to Memphis's gun crime rate).

Visitors of our acquaintance who did the tour said they found it interesting but added: 'It was all done in annoyingly over-organised style. If you lingered too long in once place, you felt a hand in your back pushing you along.'

Another agreed: 'Yes, they shove you around the ground floor very quickly and before you know it you're be back outside. Of course, everyone wants to go upstairs and view the

| Population (year 2000) | 650,100 |
|---|---|
| Males | 307,643 (47.3%) |
| Females | 342,457 (52.7%) |
| Elevation | 254 feet |
| County | Shelby |
| Land area | 279.3 square miles |
| Zip code | 38103 - 38157 |
| Median resident age | 31.9 years |
| Median household income | $32,285 |
| Median house value | $72,800 |

| Races in Memphis | |
|---|---|
| White Non-Hispanic | 33.3% |
| Hispanic | 3.0% |
| Other race | 1.5% |
| American Indian | - |
| Two or more races | 1.0% |
| Black | 61.4% |

**Ancestries**

English (5.2%), Irish (4.9%), United States (4.5%), German (4.2%), Scotch-Irish (1.7%), Subsaharan African (1.7%)

| For population 25 years and over in Memphis | |
|---|---|
| High school or higher | 76.4% |
| Bachelor's degree or higher | 20.9% |
| Graduate or professional degree | 7.7% |
| Unemployed | 8.6% |
| Mean travel time to work | 23.0 minutes |

| For population 15 years and over in Memphis | |
|---|---|
| Never married | 36.1% |
| Now married | 39.2% |
| Separated | 4.8% |
| Widowed | 7.9% |
| Divorced | 12.0% |

4.0% Foreign born (1.8% Latin America, 1.4% Asia, 0.4% Europe)

| Crime | |
|---|---|
| Violent Crime risk | 158 murders (24.1 per 100,000) |
| Property Crime risk | 15,874 burglaries (2420.2 per 100,000) |

bathroom where Elvis was found dead. But that isn't allowed.

'Outside are the family graves, surrounded by dozens and dozens bunches of dusty and very nasty plastic flowers. There is also a cheap and tacky sign attached to the railings surrounding the graves, explaining that real flowers die in the heat. So they change the plastic flowers every so often on a sort of rotation system!

'Of course, we all wanted bad taste Elvis souvenirs but sadly there weren't any. Perhaps because I'm a not from that part of the world, I wasn't taking the whole thing seriously enough. But you could only buy what I guess the fans consider to be fitting souvenirs to their hero – like little wooden guitars and fridge magnets.'

After Graceland, Memphis's principal shrine to the memory of Elvis is Sun Studio, where he made his early recordings. The building became a scuba-diving store for a while, which not surprisingly didn't do very well due to the lack of nearby places to dive. Today, it is yet another mini Elvis museum.

Presley is the biggest music legend to come out of Memphis, but he is certainly not the only one. Singers such as Otis Redding, Isaac Hayes, BB King and the Staples Singers are all immortalised in the Stax Museum of American Soul Music.

The worst years for Memphis followed the assassination

in 1968 of civil rights activist Dr Martin Luther King. The city went into decline, with downtown blighted by what the Rough Guide describes as 'white flight'. Things only started to pick up in 1990 when money was ploughed into new buildings, attractions and businesses. People in Memphis are particularly proud of Beale Street, now a designated Historic District and tourist haunt, with its Twenties-style facades and signs. (In its Twenties' heyday, Beale was full of vaudeville theatres, concert halls and bars. Much more fun.) But mercifully, the place has long lost its reputation for gambling and prostitution. Or some might say that's when it really was fun time.

One who has visited Memphis certainly doesn't agree with all the shouting about Beale Street's appeal. She told us: 'Beale Street has zero atmosphere. I was really, really disappointed. Beale Street is a sad block-and-a-half that has attempted to turn itself into a theme road. Think International Drive, Orlando – but without signs of life. International Drive is bustling with bars and restaurants and Beale Street has Sun Studios, a couple of bars and that's about it.

'I went there once in the middle of the day and it was deserted. I went there at night and it was deserted. It was August so maybe all the locals were staying inside with their air conditioning. Did I use the word 'deserted?' Well, the streets surrounding Beale Street are all utterly, utterly deserted, too. I was on my own and felt terrified as I walked that block-and-a-half back to the Peabody Hotel.'

There's that song, of course; you know, the one that starts: 'Long Distance Information, give me Memphis, Tennessee...' Well we're still not sure we do want to be given it, despite Rough Guide's waxing lyrical thus: 'Memphis is both deeply atmospheric with its somewhat faded downtown streets dotted with characterful stores and diners and the sun setting nightly across the broad Mississippi.'

We put that in to prove we are fair and unbiased. It doesn't mean we agree. So let's end on our usual sour note. The Mississippi is not called 'The Big Muddy' for nothing. It carried 2lbs of dirt for every 1,000lbs of water. And it floods a lot.

# MEMPHIS

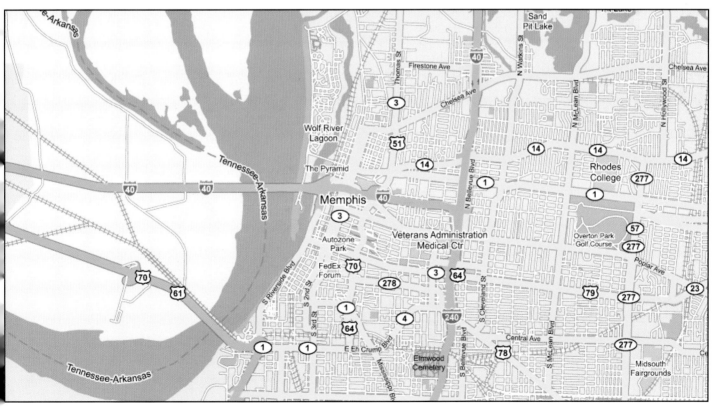

### DALLAS, TEXAS
*Friendship (state motto of Texas)*

Did that historic TV super-soap help put Dallas on any map? The answer is 'Yes', maybe for a couple of years before it was pushed off where it belongs – into obscurity. The eponymous series certainly summed the place up (apart from the glamour and the sex). Good old oil baron JR Ewing was everything that Dallas stands for. Dirty, devious, dollar-grabbing, dire.

There is a saying in Texas (which, incidentally, has the fifth worst crime rate in America) that sums up most feelings about JR's hometown: 'Life is short. Why go to Dallas?' Oh, and did we mention that there actually isn't any oil in the place?

The name Dallas might provoke images of big businesses with equally big, Texan businessmen, but the population of the place has a higher proportion of Hispanic that white office workers. Is that one of the boasts that the Texans in ten-gallon hats like to make? We doubt it, but they do like to ramble on about the size of their state and everything in it. Yet Dallas is small on the notable things that give a city character.

A president was infamously assassinated here, of course, but Deely Plaza, where John Kennedy died in the motorcade in 1963, is surprisingly insignificant when you see it; really just a tiny slip road. And the grassy knoll, on which people were gathered when those fatal shots were fired, is now an anonymous freeway embankment. After the assassination, people visited Dallas for all the wrong, morbid reasons. The infamous murder did provide a great opportunity to cash-in, something Dallas is very good at. The city's Sixth Floor Museum has an audio and visual tour with those never-to-be-forgotten images of Kennedy collapsing into his wife's arms. There's a 'memory book' for visitors to sign. And the killer's 'nest', from where Lee Harvey Oswald fired at the President, has been recreated. The Conspiracy Museum – another desperate attempt to rake in cash from President Kennedy's death – is described in the Rough Guide to the USA as 'a dreadful waste of money'. We have to agree.

Not only a President but the spirit of Dallas itself seemed to die in the ensuing years. The oil boom long ago turned to gloom, and unemployment and crime (in 2002, there were 20,351 burglaries) soared as high as the skyline buildings.

# DALLAS

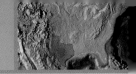

| Population (year 2000) | 1,188,580 |
|---|---|
| Males | 598,991 (50.4%) |
| Females | 589,589 (49.6%) |
| Elevation | 463 feet |
| County | Dallas |
| Land area | 342.5 square miles |
| Zip code | 75201 - 75287 |
| Median resident age | 30.5 years |
| Median household income | $37,628 |
| Median house value | $89,800 |

| Races in Dallas | |
|---|---|
| White Non-Hispanic | 34.6% |
| Hispanic | 35.6% |
| Other race | 17.2% |
| American Indian | 1.0% |
| Two or more races | 2.7% |
| Black | 25.9% |

Ancestries

German (6.1%), English (5.8%), Irish (5.0%), United States (4.1%), Subsaharan African (1.5%), French (1.5%)

| For population 25 years and over in Dallas | |
|---|---|
| High school or higher | 70.4% |
| Bachelor's degree or higher | 27.7% |
| Graduate or professional degree | 9.6% |
| Unemployed | 6.7% |
| Mean travel time to work | 26.9 minutes |

| For population 15 years and over in Dallas | |
|---|---|
| Never married | 34.4% |
| Now married | 45.8% |
| Separated | 3.5% |
| Widowed | 5.4% |
| Divorced | 10.8% |

24.4% Foreign born (19.8% Latin America, 2.6% Asia)

| Crime | |
|---|---|
| Violent Crime risk | 240 murders (19.7 per 100,000) |
| Property Crime risk | 20,635 burglaries (1697.6 per 100,000) |

Apart from one lively cobbled street area of restaurants, everything else is now corporate high rise. No-one ever bothers to go into downtown, which is deserted at night; instead they stay safely and boringly in the suburbs, which sprawl for miles and miles.

The Dallas Cowboys football team has been doing its best to give the place a high profile, an especially admirable effort given that it must often be difficult for them to gulp a clean breath of fresh air. Dallas ranks 14th in the list of shame of the US towns whose atmosphere most affects children's breathing.

It's just not like the famous TV series presented the place. The doings of the Ewings lifted the city's reputation for a while, and the town is desperately trying to hang on to that kudos. The soap, although fading from the screens for good back in 1991, is still a useful source of income, with Southfork Ranch, home of the Ewings, now a small theme park. It fails to mention that the edifice was used for local exterior shots only. Wisely, the stars seldom went near the place; everything else was shot in California – including J.R. himself.

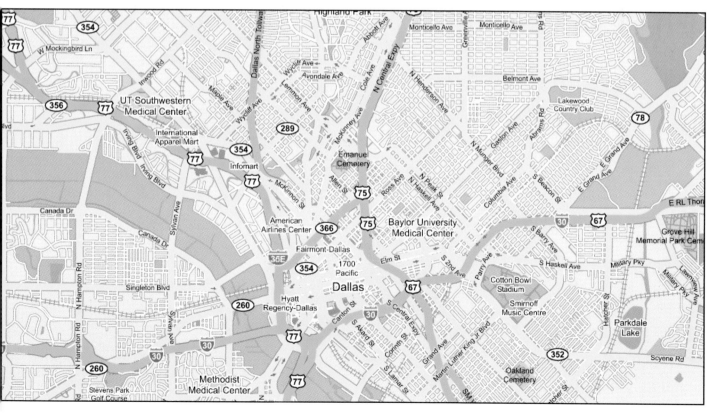

### EL PASO, TEXAS
*Friendship (state motto of Texas)*

Subject of the eponymous 1950s cowboy song that ended in a fatal shoot-out, and once visited by notorious outlaw Billy the Kid, El Paso should be full of character. But it isn't. Instead of whitewashed buildings set in a tight-knit community, El Paso is large and sprawling. Forget those

swinging saloon doors you see on TV. This place is instead a gateway – to dusty gloom in every direction.

El Paso is a town with a split personality. In Texas but almost in New Mexico, it sits on the opposite side of the Rio Grande from its Mexican sister town Cuidad Juarez, the actual border having only been finally resolved in 1963. Now the 600,000 residents of El Paso live uncomfortably alongside the 1.7 million Mexicans across the river, forming the largest bi-national and bilingual megalopolis in North America.

A rich mixture of colours and cultures? Sadly not. This city, which was the second oldest settlement in the US, is now large and sprawling. Instead of a peaceful river frontage, there are belching smelters of copper mills; instead of rolling countryside, there is Fort Bliss army base; and instead of a town center, there are railroad yards. Although the Amtrak train only stops at El Paso three times a week.

The guide books describe El Paso as a 'get-away-from-it-all' retirement haven – but motorists stuck on the one major road, I-40, complain that it is one of hardest places to out of. So much for its 17th-century boast of being the only navigable wagon route through the Rocky Mountains; a few 21st

| Population (year 2000) | 563,662 |
|---|---|
| Males | 267,651 (47.5%) |
| Females | 296,011 (52.5%) |
| Elevation | 3700 feet |
| County | El Paso |
| Land area | 249.1 square miles |
| Zip code | 79901 - 79938 |
| Median resident age | 31.1 years |
| Median household income | $32,124 (year 2000) |
| Median house value | $71,300 (year 2000) |

| Races in El Paso | |
|---|---|
| White Non-Hispanic | 18.3% |
| Hispanic | 76.6% |
| Other race | 18.2% |
| American Indian | 1.2% |
| Two or more races | 3.4% |
| Black | 3.1% |
| Ancestries | |
| German (4.6%), Irish (2.9%), English (2.8%), United States (2.7%), Italian (1.2%), French (1.0%) | |

| For population 25 years and over in El Paso | |
|---|---|
| High school or higher | 68.6% |
| Bachelor's degree or higher | 18.3% |
| Graduate or professional degree | 6.2% |
| Unemployed | 9.2% |
| Mean travel time to work | 22.4 minutes |

| For population 15 years and over in El Paso | |
|---|---|
| Never married | 26.8% |
| Now married | 54.3% |
| Separated | 3.2% |
| Widowed | 6.1% |
| Divorced | 9.7% |
| 26.2% Foreign born (24.0% Latin America) | |

| Crime | |
|---|---|
| Violent Crime risk | 20 murders (3.5 per 100,000) |
| Property Crime risk | 2,553 burglaries (442.9 per 100,000) |

century signposts would help this traffic-clogged metropolis.

City burghers seem to think the temperature is attractive, too. A sweltering 90 to 100 degrees F throughout the summer and constant drought means there is nothing much in the way of greenery. Oh, and on winter nights, the temperature regularly plunges below freezing.

Still, it's cheap to live in El Paso. The average house price is $92,100, way below the national average of $160,100. But most people can't afford to buy – the average family income is $31,932 – and a whopping 42 per cent choose to rent. Five hundred bucks a month ain't bad for a two-bedroom shack.

El Paso's biggest industry is 'apparel manufacturing' – which, to the uninitiated, means cheap t-shirts reading 'My Grandmother went to Texas and all I got was this lousy t-shirt'. Yet despite the clothing industry, there isn't a single shopping mall. Locals swear by the four warehouse clubs that sell monster-sized everything in monster-sized cardboard boxes.

The place has a couple of minor claims to fame. Billy the Kid visited – but only once. That was in 1876 when he got his partner Melquiades Segura out of jail. When it came to being immortalised, Billy went somewhere else to die: Fort Sumner on July 14, five years later. If he called back today, he'd move on equally quickly, having savoured the uninspiring array of bars and eateries.

El Paso has a strange mix of interesting mission churches dating from 1692 and not-so-interesting shops selling cowboy boots and hats. All of this makes us laugh when we hear the local legend that when Wyatt Earp arrived in El Paso he found it too wild and boarded the first train to Tombstone. He should have stayed. El Paso would be brightened up by a good burial.

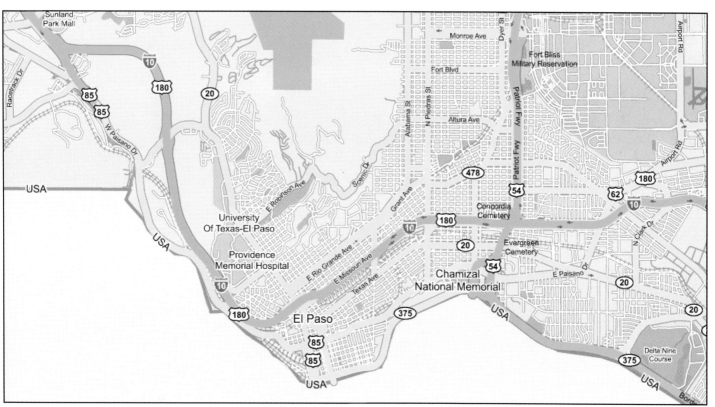

### HOUSTON, TEXAS
*Friendship*
*(motto of the Lone Star State)*

Houston, we have a problem. Well, we don't, actually, but you do. You are a city of large shopping malls, large freeways, large houses – and no heart. For a place so big in a state so big with an ego so big, there really isn't anything of note aside from NASA, to whom the famous 'We have a problem' remark was made by astronaut James A. Lovell during the Apollo 13 Mission.

Now we know why Jim Lovell – echoed on screen by Tom Hanks – made the statement so matter-of-factly. Because dying in the darkness of Space somewhere on the far side of the Moon is infinitely preferable to spending a lifetime in Houston.

Houston is big, that's for sure. Pithily described by the Rough Guide people as 'an ungainly beast of a city', it has a land area of 580 square miles and a population of over two million, of which roughly a third are Hispanic, just under a third non-Hispanic white and a quarter black. More than a quarter of those over the age of 15 are foreign born.

Among this burgeoning population, there is an awful lot of misery – and, it seems, an awful lot of bad people. The well-researched Relocation Crime Lab Index sets a value of 100 as being exactly average across the US. So a value of 150 is pretty bad; a value of 200 means a city has twice the average crime rate; and a value of 273 means that its is a crime-ridden disaster zone. Yes, that latter is Houston's rating, with more than 250 murders, almost 900 rapes, 12,000 assaults and 150,000 thefts of varying degrees. It's frightening to consider that of every 100,000 people living – or, more accurately, attempting to survive – in Houston in 2002 (the latest fully catalogued statistics), 14 were murdered, 39 raped, 612 assaulted and 562 robbed.

It's not much consolation if you are lucky enough to avoid being one of the 24,000 people who suffered auto thefts. Because just driving away from the crime scene that is metropolitan Houston can be equally dangerous: the place ties with San Antonio in the number of drivers experiencing a motor accident – once every 7.8 years. This makes them about a third more likely to have an accident than if you lived in an average American town of normal people.

Mind you, Houston itself is just a giant accident, with no reason whatsoever for its original existence. It was founded by two New Yorkers who, in the optimistic days of 1837, believed

| Population (year 2000) | 1,953,631 |
|---|---|
| Males | 975,551 (49.9%) |
| Females | 978,080 (50.1%) |
| Elevation | 0-90 feet |
| County | Harris |
| Land area | 579.4 square miles |
| Zip code | 77002 - 77099 |
| Median resident age | 30.9 years |
| Median household income | $36,616 |
| Median house value | $79,300 |

| Races in Houston | |
|---|---|
| White Non-Hispanic | 30.8% |
| Hispanic | 37.4% |
| Other race | 16.5% |
| American Indian | 0.8% |
| Two or more races | 3.1% |
| Black | 25.3% |

| Ancestries |
|---|
| German (6.1%), English (5.0%), Irish (4.3%), United States (3.7%), French (1.9%), Italian (1.6%) |

| For population 25 years and over in Houston | |
|---|---|
| High school or higher | 70.4% |
| Bachelor's degree or higher | 27.0% |
| Graduate or professional degree | 9.7% |
| Unemployed | 7.6% |
| Mean travel time to work | 27.4 minutes |

| For population 15 years and over in Houston | |
|---|---|
| Never married | 32.2% |
| Now married | 48.8% |
| Separated | 3.6% |
| Widowed | 5.4% |
| Divorced | 10.0% |
| 26.4% Foreign born (19.4% Latin America, 4.7% Asia) | |

| Crime | |
|---|---|
| Violent Crime risk | 267 murders (13.4 per 100,000) |
| Property Crime risk | 25,108 burglaries (1256.7 per 100,000) |

that this swampy area would one day become the capital of the Republic of Texas. It lost its crown as state capital to Austin in two years later and meandered in the humid doldrums until the last century's oil boom, which created monstrous over-development until coming to a grinding halt in the sudden slump of the early 1980s.

The place has since taken off again and its more recent hectic growth is no doubt one of the reasons why it is such a filthy place, high on humidity and choking with traffic fumes. The organisation Air In Your City Environment Defense, which ranks major population ceneters according to where dirty air affects the greatest number of children places Houston fifth out of 50 American cities.

How do people survive there? They go underground, like Trolls. Beneath the city's central banking area are seven miles of air-conditioned tunnels through which the citizens scurry around, seldom emerging into the smog-filtered sunlight to view the glass and steel and concrete structures that, along with Houston's modern sculptures, are its pride.

What else can we say about this loveless place? A study that looked at the best and worst towns in which to find a mate in the whole of the country put Houston in the bottom ten. That was based on the lack of environments where couples might actually want to leave the safety of their homes to get together. 'Dating venues' such as concerts, coffee shops, bowling alleys and decent bars were all found to be sadly lacking in Houston.

And if you do manage to find a date, another statistic indicates that romance is still lacking beyond the stage of the first kiss. The evidence? Houston is the city with the fewest lingerie shops per capita!

So, Houston figures pretty badly compared with the rest of Texas (Austin was judged the best town in America for dating) and is a statistical crime blot on the rest of the nation. Surely there must be worst places in the world to live?

In 2005, the results of a worldwide Quality of Living Survey were released by Mercer Human Resource Consulting, ranking 215 cities against New York, which was given a rating of 100. The analysis was based on an evaluation of 39 quality of life criteria, including: availability of consumer goods, economic and natural environment, housing, public services and recreational facilities. Cities in Europe and Australasia ranked highly in the survey. In the US, Honolulu and San Francisco came top, while (you guessed it) Houston ranked lowest.

But there is some good news. It convincingly beat off the challenge for the title of the worst city in the world – from Baghdad.

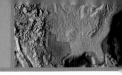

### ROBY, TEXAS
*Friendship (state motto of Texas)*

Welcome to Roby - the richest little borehole in Texas. Bored being the operative word here because there's so little to do that even the tumbleweed looks fed-up as it drifts along the dusty, dry road. Dry, not just from the sun, but because you have to travel 20 miles to get a beer.

Roby's Warhol moment came in 1996 when 43 people in a syndicate picked up 46 million dollars on the lottery. Most of them said it wouldn't change their lives much, which is hardly surprising, because beyond a crap food shop and a crap clothes outlet, there isn't much to do except bet on when it might rain.

The cotton-picking people of Roby – population a tad over 600 – have to go virtually everywhere else for anything else they want to buy not stocked by the hardware store, antiques shops, a grocery and JoAnn's dress emporium.

But then Roby has always been unremarkable.

In 1885 M. L. and D. C. Roby, developers from Mississippi, attempted to get the county government for the newly organized Fisher County to be established at a site they owned in the center of the county. After a bitter struggle with the nearby community of Fisher (now called North Roby), the backers of Roby won the day. In 1886 construction was begun on the county courthouse. That year also the Roby post office and the Roby School opened, and the community had thirteen houses by that summer. By 1900 the community had an estimated 700 inhabitants, four churches, two general stores, a hotel, a restaurant, a bank, and the weekly newspaper, the Fisher County Call.

Roby reached its peak as a trade center for farmers and ranchers in 1950, with 60 businesses and a population of 1,040. But inadequate water supplies had plagued the town from its inception and as the area rural population declined after 1950, Roby also diminished, falling to 784 inhabitants in 1970 and just over 600 by 1990.

After the town's amazingly lucky win in 1996, one antiques shop on the square began hawking wooden signs reading:

'ROBY, Tx,
*Pop. 618*
*576 Po-Folk, 42 Rich!'*

That was because At least one of the 43 winners luckily didn't live within the city limits.

Some years on, the local paper from Austin came back to seek out the technical millionaires – technical because, after the taxman took his bite, they are on some 40,000 bucks a year for the next two decades. Lance Green, one of the 43 winners, now the towns mayor, says the money hasn't changed folks much they're a little calmer when bills come due, but they are still very worried about this years drought. Most

| Population (year 2000) | 673 |
|---|---|
| Males | 300 (44.6%) |
| Females | 373 (55.4%) |
| Elevation | 1961 feet |
| County | Fisher |
| Land area | 0.7 square miles |
| Zip code | 79543 |
| Median resident age | 37.4 years |
| Median household income | $27,031 |
| Median house value | $27,800 |

| Races in Roby | |
|---|---|
| White Non-Hispanic | 73.3% |
| Hispanic | 22.1% |
| Other race | 8.3% |
| American Indian | 0.9% |
| Two or more races | 1.8% |
| Black | 3.3% |

| Ancestries |
|---|
| Irish (12.2%), United States (11.3%), German (9.1%), English (6.4%), Scotch-Irish (4.3%), Scottish (2.1%) |

| For population 25 years and over in Roby | |
|---|---|
| High school or higher | 73.9% |
| Bachelor's degree or higher | 9.7% |
| Graduate or professional degree | 0.8% |
| Unemployed | 4.2% |
| Mean travel time to work | 21.1 minutes |

| For population 15 years and over in Roby | |
|---|---|
| Never married | 21.9% |
| Now married | 55.0% |
| Separated | 1.9% |
| Widowed | 13.3% |
| Divorced | 8.0% |
| 1.2% Foreign born | |

| Crime | |
|---|---|
| Violent Crime risk | - |
| Property Crime risk | - |

winners kept their $7 an hour jobs at the local gin, where Green still works too. Not much had changed and still hasn't. Terry's Cotton Gin, the local industrial Acropolis where the crop is weighed and baled, is still the centre of town, full of good 'ol boys chewing tobacco and moaning, like farmers everywhere, about everything.

Despite the windfall nearly 15 percent of Robyans live under the poverty line, mostly the elderly and the old. But they wouldn't have anywhere to spend their money even if they had some.

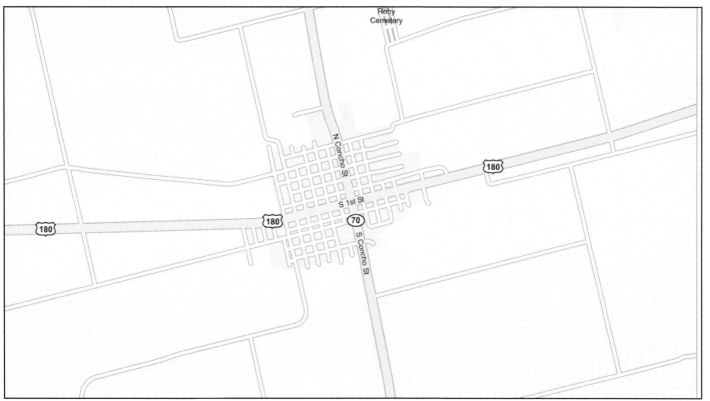

### WACO, TEXAS
*'Home of Texas hospitality' (says visitors bureau)*

When David Koresh decided to coral and then roast his Branch Davidian followers at his nuthouse hideaway on the baked plains outside Waco, the town hitherto famous for beef suddenly became the focus of the world's media.

Much of it was not flattering. Ben MacIntyre, of the London Times, wrote: 'Waco is a one-horse town, and the horse has died.' Pretty soon, Texan types with three ears, four eyes and married to their sisters came a-hunting for him for having 'dissed' their city.

Why bother? Waco is only two letters removed from crap, and even the retards among those who live there must surely know they wallow in the urban equivalent of cowpoke hell.

It is a grid city that has, according to one world-traveled writer: 'The world's most spine-numbingly boring museum, devoted to the macho types who join the Texas Rangers, but who must clearly be gay from the absurd hats they sport. Waco

is a way station to nowhere.'

But we must not prejudge these descendents of a Wild West tradition of virtuous ruggedness. Instead, let's look at some incontrovertible statistics about Waco. With a land area of 85 square miles, the town itself is home to almost 120,000 Waconians, whose median average age is a mere 27 years. Being so young, there is only a small proportion of divorced, separated or widowed. About half the population are white, a quarter Hispanic and a quarter Black, with only one per cent American Indian – a paucity, one supposes, due to those frontier-conquering traditions.

But the more revealing figures are to do with the criminal element among these them. Here, again, we turn to the research gurus who amass statistics on the subject for author David Sperling. His Best Places list has mined recently released FBI Uniform Crime Reports to identify those US cities with the highest and lowest rates of crime. Despite its diminutive

size, Waco gets a dishonourable mention, coming fourth in the chart of 'Worst Medium Sized (pop. up to 500,000) Cities for Crime'. Mostly, it's thieving. But while the larceny rate is high, violent crime is less of a concern, and residents, while patching up their much-burgled homes, can take comfort in the relatively low rates of murder and forcible rape.

'Relatively low' is, of course, no comfort to the victims in the most recent year's crime list available: 14 murders, 58 rapes, 277 robberies, 596 assaults, 2,197 burglaries and 7,143 larceny counts. The City-data.com crime index thereby puts Waco at 647 – almost double the US average of 330.

So 'Welcome to the city of Waco, the home of Texas hospitality!', to quote the town's website aimed at prospective visitors – inviting them to enjoy 'a taste of the Texas history

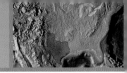

| Population (year 2000) | 113,726 |
|---|---|
| Males | 54,295 (47.7%) |
| Females | 59,431 (52.3%) |
| Elevation | 515 feet |
| County | McLennan |
| Land area | 84.2 square miles |
| Zip code | 76701 - 76711 |
| Median resident age | 27.9 years |
| Median household income | $26,264 |
| Median house value | $53,300 |

| Races in Waco | |
|---|---|
| White Non-Hispanic | 51.1% |
| Hispanic | 23.6% |
| Other race | 12.4% |
| American Indian | 1.0% |
| Two or more races | 2.3% |
| Black | 22.6% |
| Ancestries | |
| German (9.2%), English (6.4%), Irish (6.0%), United States (5.9%), Scotch-Irish (1.9%), French (1.5%) | |

| For population 25 years and over in Waco | |
|---|---|
| High school or higher | 71.6% |
| Bachelor's degree or higher | 18.6% |
| Graduate or professional degree | 7.4% |
| Unemployed | 11.6% |
| Mean travel time to work | 17.6 minutes |

| For population 15 years and over in Waco | |
|---|---|
| Never married | 33.2% |
| Now married | 45.9% |
| Separated | 2.8% |
| Widowed | 7.8% |
| Divorced | 10.3% |
| 8.4% Foreign born (6.9% Latin America, 0.9% Asia) | |

| Crime | |
|---|---|
| Violent Crime risk | 7 murders (6.0 per 100,000) |
| Property Crime risk | 1,875 burglaries (1612.1 per 100,000) |

and hospitality we're famous for' and 'a unique, relaxing getaway from big city hustle and bustle'.

The latter boast is accurate enough. 'Unique' is one way of describing Waco. But as for 'a taste of Texas history', you're better off watching an old movie. Once cattle were rawhided through here on the Chisholm Trail, across the Los Brazos River, but the only longhorns found now are on gaily coloured trucks that park at the foul fast-food joints ringing the city like culinary picket posts. Ask for Texas Beef in the local restaurants and they'll keep you talking while Mungo out back fetches the Mace.

The hotels run to the usual lonesome trail of traveling salesmen everywhere: Quality Inns, Best Westerns and Budget Inns, but perhaps they're all full with fugitives.

On the same Internet page that welcomes guests to Waco with a cornucopia of delights to explore – ie, the zoo, a golf course and a generic anywhere-in-the-world water park – is the information that there are 1,001 pages of active warrants out for people who haven't paid their fines, and those Rangers, with those b-i-i-i-g hats and pointy boots, are still looking for them.

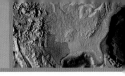

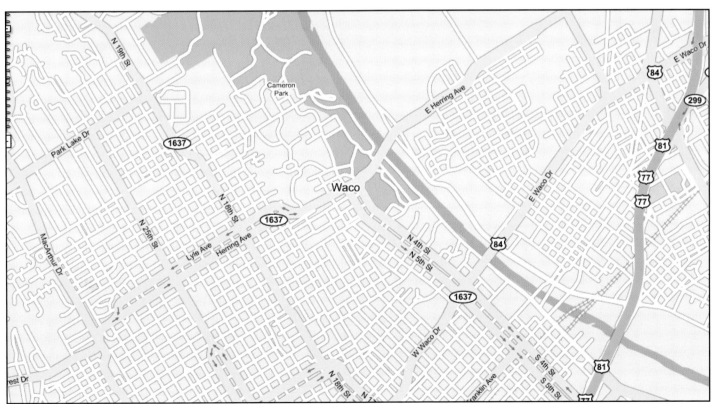

## HILDALE, Utah

*Industry (state motto of Utah)*

Nasty little place Hildale. Full of sinister happenings, kids going missing, corruption, people in power taking advantage of the community's polygamist lifestyle (that's a guy having as many wives as he likes). It's home to the Fundamentalist Church of Jesus Christ of Latter Day Saints. In fact, eerily, it's officially recognised that most residents of Hildale and its twin FLDS enclave, Colorado City, are members of the spooky group. Have to repeat ourselves. Nasty little place, Hildale, sects, sex and secrets.

Where do we begin? Well, the collapse of the Bank of Ephraim is interesting. Regulators said the scandal in June 2004 was all down to bad loans and an alleged multi-million dollar embezzlement scheme. The bank had conducted business with the polygamist community since the 1950s and set up a branch in Hildale in 1995 at the urging of resident Richard Holm, a contractor who built the bank's first office

branch. The Bank of Ephraim regularly made loans to the FLDS members and in 2003 wrote off $1.3 million in bad loans, ending the year with a loss of $778,000.

Because the FLDS church owns all property in the community, residents and business owners used leaseholds to secure loans. At one time, bank officials claimed the bank was on solid footing, though a first-quarter report in 2004 showed a net income of just $30,000. Two members of staff were indicted for embezzlement. Another bank, Far West, took over but initially refused to reopen the Hildale branch, leaving its community, and that in Colorado City, without banking services for a while – which was, we can't help but say, some divine intervention in the workings of a particularly unpleasant sect.

So what sort of town is Hildale? It has a population of 1,895, which is pretty small for a community that thrives on multi-wife relationships, unlawful sexual intercourse and the desire to procreate at every turn. But its population did grow by 43 per cent through the 1990s, so they must be pleased with themselves.

The residents must also be pleased that crime is not an obvious problem. We use the word 'obvious' for good reason – because bads things do happen but are not always openly acknowledged. Anyway, officially, figures for 2003 show there was only the occasional theft. There were no murders or manslaughters, robbery, motor vehicle theft or arson.

Offcially, too, there were no forcible rapes. But the sexual appetites of the menfolk of Hildale are such that little is thought of having intercourse with a juvenile. There don't seem to be any official figures for that. But it is a disturbing fact that the average age for females in Hildale is 14. years.. The average for males is 12 years. This makes the median resident age 13 years – officially described, rather inadequately, as 'significantly below state average.'

Throw in a sprinkling of middle-aged guys, a handful of over-60s and an average household of eight people, and you have the unsavoury snapshot that is Hildale.

Of course, the place is more of a polgamistic congregation than a town. Seated 5,042 above sea level, its nearest town is the Colorado City mentioned above, just over a mile away. Despite being in different states – Colorado City is in Arizona – the two places cozy up nicely with each other, as you would imagine.

These two border communities were established at the turn of the century when the mainstream Mormon church (LDS)

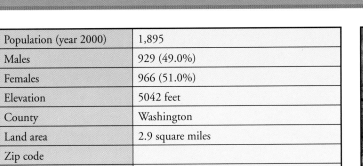

| Population (year 2000) | 1,895 |
|---|---|
| Males | 929 (49.0%) |
| Females | 966 (51.0%) |
| Elevation | 5042 feet |
| County | Washington |
| Land area | 2.9 square miles |
| Zip code | |
| Median resident age | 13.1 years |
| Median household income | $32,679 |
| Median house value | $80,000 |

| Races in Hildale | |
|---|---|
| White Non-Hispanic | 95.9% |
| Hispanic | 1.0% |
| Other race | 0.8% |
| American Indian | 1.2% |
| Two or more races | 0.8% |
| Black | - |

| Ancestries |
|---|
| English (67.9%), United States (14.8%), Swedish (5.8%), German (4.4%), Danish (2.8%), Dutch (1.2%) |

| For population 25 years and over in Hildale | |
|---|---|
| High school or higher | 73.2% |
| Bachelor's degree or higher | 8.8% |
| Graduate or professional degree | 1.9% |
| Unemployed | 2.4% |
| Mean travel time to work | 16.7 minutes |

| For population 15 years and over in Hildale | |
|---|---|
| Never married | 27.3% |
| Now married | 67.1% |
| Separated | 1.1% |
| Widowed | 2.4% |
| Divorced | 2.1% |
| 0.2% Foreign born | |

| Crime | |
|---|---|
| Violent Crime risk | 0 murders (0.0 per 100,000) |
| Property Crime risk | 1 burglary (51.9 per 100,000) |

outlawed the practice of polygamy. Fundamentalists who disagreed with the church moved to the border region to avoid possible prosecution by government authorities. The need for a bolthole was reinforced in 1935 when the Utah Legislature elevated 'unlawful cohabitation' from a misdemeanor to a felony , which made the border town look more attractive as a place where practitioners of plural marriage could step across the Utah line quickly to avoid arrest. Despite the move, there have been two major 'raids', one in 1941 and another in 1953. Another half dozen are long overdue.

The FLDS adherents believe their doctrines will afford them space within the highest level of heaven. Apparently, you need at least three wives to achieve this. It does not, however, seem to afford them a decent education to take with them. The number of college students and those with a bachelor's degree or higher is significantly below state average, which is a depressing reflection on how the young people are encouraged to couple at an age when they should be at college. Thus, it tends to be the older population – those who probably led a more orthodox lifestyle before becoming committed to the FDLS cause- – who boast a High School education. or college degree.

The population of Hildale is, of course, predominantly white with just a smattering of American Indian, Hispanic and other races. The population live in houses which, according to the statistics, are older than average. And not surprisingly, the houses in Hildale have more rooms than any other town in the rest of Utah.

The polygamy beliefs of the FLDS have been described as 'something very disturbing, illegal, immoral and traumatic to most of the people involved'. Indeed, there are many stories that support this. One girl born into the FLDS family ran

away but was brought back, then kept locked in one room for three years until finally making a successful break for freedom.

As many as 400 teenagers – some as young as 13, and collectively known as the 'Lost Boys' – have been forced out of Hildale and Colorado City over a period of just four recent years. Their 'crimes' include wearing short-sleeved shirts, listening to CDs, watching TV or going to the movies. Some were given as little as two hours' notice before being driven out of the community and left like unwanted pets along the road. The authorities say the teenagers aren't really being expelled for committing petty offences but rather to reduce the competition for women.

The man making these decisions is FLDS leader – or 'prophet', as he likes to call himself – Warren Jeffs. This God-fearing pillar of local society is reputed to have 70 wives, one of the more recent of whom was just 17 when she gave birth to his baby. In June 2005, Jeffs was indicted on charges of arranging a marriage between a 28-year-old man who was already married and a 16-year-old girl. Just before this, a Utah judge froze the assets of the United Effort Plan, the FLDS trust that owns most of the homes and land in the polygamous towns.

There is very little community spirit in Hildale. The

nearest hospital is 44 miles away. There is only one restaurant, the Mark Twain Family Diner, but a lot of construction businesses and one school. Because 74 per cent of the 300 pupils are 'low income', the Phelps School relies heavily on Federal money for support. The FLDS make nearly all critical decisions on how their 1,300 youngsters are taught but townspeople themselves contribute little to the cost of educating their children.

Strange, then, that a supporter of the sect should state: 'Education is important to the fundamentalists with about 1,500 students enrolled in elementary and secondary schools in the two communities. College also is considered important and the United Effort Plan often financially assists students to attend college and apply their skills for the common good.'

It sounds comforting to learn that Hildale does have its own city police station. Until you discover that eight police officers were indicted for having sex with juveniles. Does this sound the place described by Douglas D. Alder and Karl F. Brooks in their History of Washington County? 'Hildale-Colorado City has grown in numbers, prospered financially, and gained confidence as a religious community. Members of the two towns are usually easily identified by their modest dress, conservative hairstyles, and lack of makeup. Due to their common large family structure, many can get a real bargain when they purchase a family pass to some events being held in the area. The median family income is low, partly because family incomes have to be divided among so many.'

So yes, Hildale. Sects and the city. A nasty little place. Last words from Dan Fischer, a former FLDS member and now a dentist living outside Salt Lake City: 'There is a virtual Taliban down there. You tell people this stuff happens and they don't believe it.'

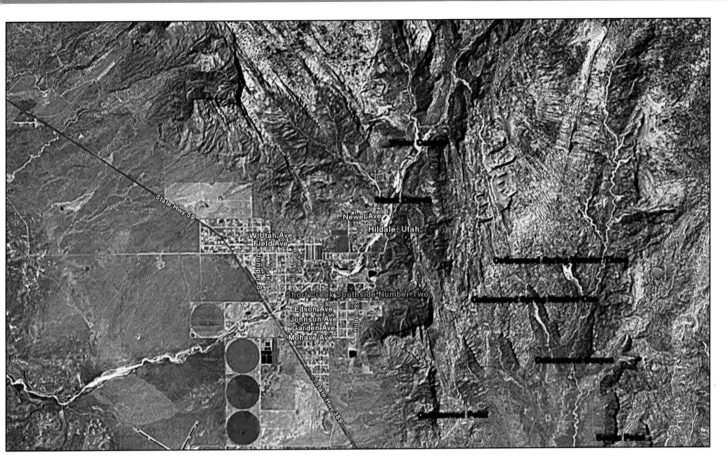

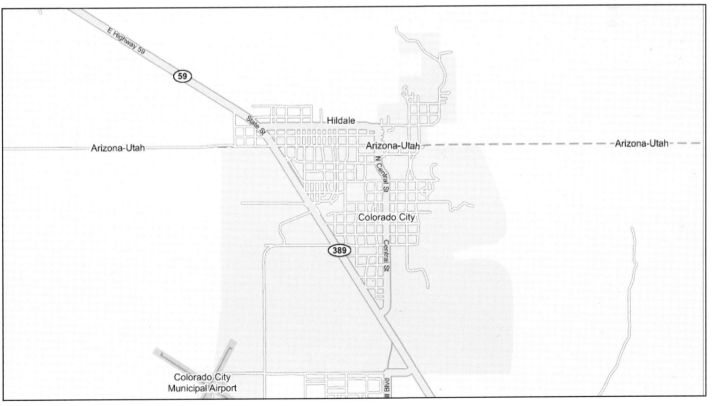

### VIRGINIA BEACH, VIRGINIA
*Motto: 'Live the Life'*

It was a close run thing. Most of us now converse in (a sort of) English. It could have been so different, and we might now all (yes, ALL) be speaking Spanish…

The first English settlers touched land just north of what is Virginia Beach in 1607 before moving on to Jamestown, which they judged to be safer from rape and pillage by the

swarthy soldiers of Spain. If they could have foreseen the aesthetic rape and commercial pillage that we, their successors, have perpetrated on the coastline 400 years later, the consciences of the English would surely not have permitted them to stay and sully the state of their historic visitation.

Virginia City is a summer resort that has grown out of all proportion to become the largest city in the state, thereby defacing a long sandy beach with the erection of drab hotels, chain eateries, noisy bars and dingy nightclubs. Stretching back from Atlantic Avenue are 40 blocks of further downtown sprawl.

The 440,000 or so people who live in Virginia County must count their blessings, however. They have on their doorstep two of America's greatest bastions against the weaknesses of the flesh and the soul. The first is the Association for Research and Enlightenment Center, which celebrates the pioneering work of Edgar Cayce, a pioneer of Extra-sensory Perception in the early years of the last century. While in one of his deep trances, Cayce, known as 'the Sleeping Prophet', could cure the illnesses of anyone anywhere in the world. (Communications weren't quite as good in those day, so his adherents had to take on trust his success rate.)

| Population (year 2000) | 425,257 |
|---|---|
| Males | 210,524 (49.5%) |
| Females | 214,733 (50.5%) |
| Elevation | 15 feet |
| County | Virginia Beach |
| Land area | 248.3 square miles |
| Zip code | 23451 - 23464 |
| Median resident age | 32.7 years |
| Median household income | $48,705 |
| Median house value | $123,200 |

| Races in Virginia Beach | |
|---|---|
| White Non-Hispanic | 69.5% |
| Hispanic | 4.2% |
| Other race | 1.5% |
| American Indian | 1.0% |
| Two or more races | 2.7% |
| Black | 19.0% |

**Ancestries**

German (13.7%), Irish (12.4%), English (11.8%), United States (7.3%), Italian (5.6%), French (2.9%)

| For population 25 years and over in Virginia Beach | |
|---|---|
| High school or higher | 90.4% |
| Bachelor's degree or higher | 28.1% |
| Graduate or professional degree | 8.9% |
| Unemployed | 4.1% |
| Mean travel time to work | 23.9 minutes |

| For population 15 years and over in Virginia Beach | |
|---|---|
| Never married | 25.5% |
| Now married | 57.1% |
| Separated | 3.2% |
| Widowed | 4.7% |
| Divorced | 9.5% |

6.6% Foreign born (3.6% Asia, 1.5% Europe, 1.1% Latin America)

| Crime | |
|---|---|
| Violent Crime risk | 12 murders (2.8 per 100,000) |
| Property Crime risk | 2,285 burglaries (529.2 per 100,000) |

Nowadays, ESP exponents try to work the same miracles themselves in regular 'testings' at the center.

Not sold on the psychic scene? Well, more conventional sanctuary and salvation is at hand. Virginia Beach is also home to evangelist and politician Pat Robertson's Regent University. Robertson, founder of the Christian Broadcasting Network, established the college as 'the nation's academic center for Christian thought and action'. But the word of God is balanced with the some down-to-earth materialism. When we visited Virginia Beach, ex-Presidential candidate Steve Forbes, editor-in-chief of business magazine Forbes, began his teaching role at Regent University with a heavenly talk on 'Innovation and Entrepreneurship'. He identified 'the rule of law, sound money, low taxes, ease of entry into business, and reduction of trade barriers as the five basic principles of economic progress'.

The Good Lord is surely smiling down wryly at the academy's Christian exhortations to fiscal fulfillment – and to the Devil with the meek, who may one day inherit the Earth but not while fundamental evangelists rule in Virginia Beach.

The proximity of a collegiate of moral crusaders is perhaps the reason for one of the city's stranger regulations. It has enacted an anti-cruising law that forbid motorists to drive past the same location twice within three hours. So, if you're a dad with a car full of kids, that semi-naked beach blonde you just cruised past on Atlantic Avenue is safe from your advances. But if you just missed that one empty parking place, don't turn back or you're booked, buddy!

Mind you, why anyone would wish to drive past anywhere in Virginia City more than once is a mystery. Calling itself 'the world's largest resort city', this metropolitan monument to tackiness is, in reality, one long snarled-up traffic jam.

Gas fumes mingle with the smell of really nasty food. For

some reason, Virginia Beach prides itself on catering for the junk food lover's every whim and there's a gawdy painted take away or greasy looking cafe every few yards. For an area that prides itself on the proximity to the sea – Virginia Beach is surrounded by sprawling naval bases and shipbuilding yards that have seen better days – decent fish restaurants are few and far between.

Even if you wanted a quiet meal, it would be impossible. In the height of summer, the place has to rate as one of the noisiest towns ever. Music blares from every bar, screeching videos of surfing competitions and bungee jumping (hello, this is America not Australia) vie with thumping disco and hip hop as drinkers spill out onto the sidewalks.

New York travel writer R.W. Apple returned to Virginia Beach after an absense of nearly 50 years and was flabbergasted by the transformation. Neatly summing up what had happened, his brother-in-law said: 'The foreigners and other come-heres did it.' Turns out the Europeans at the nearby NATO HQ in Norfolk have, along with the military personnel at the seven surrounding bases, stamped their idea of seaside on us. Cotton candy, silly hats, buckets and spades are all very well in Britain's Blackpool on a wet Sunday afternoon or Spain's Costa del Sol … but did those old foes of 400 years ago really have to continue with the rape and pillage of our coastline?

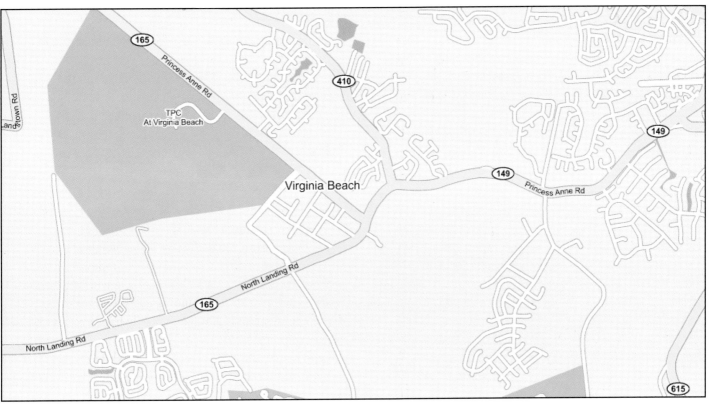

## CASPER, WYOMING
*Motto: 'Oil Capital of the Rockies'*

There isn't much room left for criticism from the outsider when the good people of Casper have done it all adequately themselves. '...poor job opportunities, poor child care, poor health care, many social issues (divorce, crime substance abuse), the large number of single parents and families in poverty...'

These are just some of the failings aired about itself at one of the town's public meetings. On top of all this, local colleges have a hard time recruiting students, and those that are recruited flee the place as soon as their education is competed.

There are many 'Help Wanted' signs swinging merrily at Casper's oil companies (its main industry) that have been there for months. No-one wants to fill the jobs, even if the pay is $22 an hour. Apparently, one of the main reasons for this is the state's substance abuse problem. Indeed, Casper

does have a bit of a drugs problem, with that old favourite, methamphetamine, being the most popular. But one suspects apathy, rather than addiction, stops many people in Casper thinking too seriously about employment.

Casper is a predominantly white community with just a smattering of other races. Its population has grown, especially through the 1990s, and now totals 49,644. 'Dreary Casper, halfway up Wyoming on I-25 may not seem an obvious place to visit,' states our old friend Rough Guide to the USA, adding that its only stop-off allure is the fact that it is 150 miles from anywhere of comparable size. (And has a good number of washrooms perhaps?).

For many years, there has been a debate going on between Casper and the capital, Cheyenne, over which is Wyoming's biggest and most important city. Fans of Casper like to boast that it has Wyoming's biggest shopping center, the Eastbridge Mall, and a 'host of recreational activities to keep Casperites entertained and educational and cultural opportunities to keep

# CASPER

| Population (year 2000) | 49,644 |
|---|---|
| Males | 24,191 (48.7%) |
| Females | 25,453 (51.3%) |
| Elevation | 5140 feet |
| County | Natrona |
| Land area | 23.9 square miles |
| Zip code | 82601, 82604, 82609 |
| Median resident age | 36.1 years |
| Median household income | $36,567 |
| Median house value | $84,500 |

| Races in Casper | |
|---|---|
| White Non-Hispanic | 91.3% |
| Hispanic | 5.4% |
| Other race | 2.0% |
| American Indian | 1.6% |
| Two or more races | 1.6% |
| Black | 0.9% |

**Ancestries**

German (24.9%), Irish (14.8%), English (13.7%), United States (7.9%), Norwegian (5.0%), French (4.1%)

| For population 25 years and over in Casper | |
|---|---|
| High school or higher | 89.1% |
| Bachelor's degree or higher | 22.1% |
| Graduate or professional degree | 7.3% |
| Unemployed | 4.9% |
| Mean travel time to work | 15.8 minutes |

| For population 15 years and over in Casper | |
|---|---|
| Never married | 23.9% |
| Now married | 54.7% |
| Separated | 1.3% |
| Widowed | 6.8% |
| Divorced | 13.4% |

2.0% Foreign born (0.7% Latin America, 0.7% Europe, 0.4% Asia)

| Crime | |
|---|---|
| Violent Crime risk | 2 murders (4.0 per 100,000) |
| Property Crime risk | 435 burglaries (875.1 per 100,000) |

them enlightened.'

Why then, is this place, located in Wyoming's Natrona County and known as the 'Oil Capital of the Rockies', not a good place to be? For a start, one year's figures show Casper's property crime levels were higher than Wyoming's average and a double-figure tally of 'forcible rape' is an unpleasant statistic in the city. Throw in four murders and almost 100 aggravated assaults and you get the impression people get pretty mad at each other a lot of the time.

The history of the place shows that this state of affairs is nothing new – and is how Casper got its name. A group of fur traders built a cabin here in 1812, and Mormons built a ferry crossing of the North Platte River in 1847. Settlers heading west to seek gold were hampered by skirmishes with the Arapaho, Lakota and Cheyenne tribes, and in one of them, a Lieutenant Caspar Collins died trying to rescue a fellow soldier. He took a wrong turning, ended up in an Indian throng and was found shot full of arrows. It seems unfair that he attained misspelled immortality when his name went

through dispatches as 'Casper'.

The town of Casper was established on a wave of criminality -- indeed, the first public building was a jail. The air was filled with the sound of gunfire, residents slept light and vigilantism was rampant. Things got even worse when oil was struck in the huge Salt Creek Field in 1889. It is recorded that 'with the oil came coarse workers, dishonest businessmen, prostitutes, gambling and other threats to polite society'.

Mercifully, an influx of farming and ranching families ensured that schools and churches emerged between the saloons. Women were only permitted to walk on the left of Main Street, across from the saloons, and laws were passed to prevent the discharge of firearms within the city limits. The town boomed until 1929, when the Wall Street crash triggered Depression and the population diminished by half.

Today, Casper is sort of back in business, but as the Rough Guide states: 'It still hasn't completely shaken off the signs of harder times.'

The reason, perhaps, is that the city seems to suffer from a unique phenomenon. It doesn't like to ask for help with its problems. At one of Casper's public meetings, it was generally agreed that 'Wyomingites are socially lazy or too proud to ask for or recognize the need for societal assistants' and that 'one reason for this failure may be our belief in "taking care of our own" and our deep-seated resistance to relying on the federal government.'

It's an admirable quality to want to pull yourself up by your bootstraps, but not so smart when your 'own' are living in poverty and there isn't enough money to buy boots.

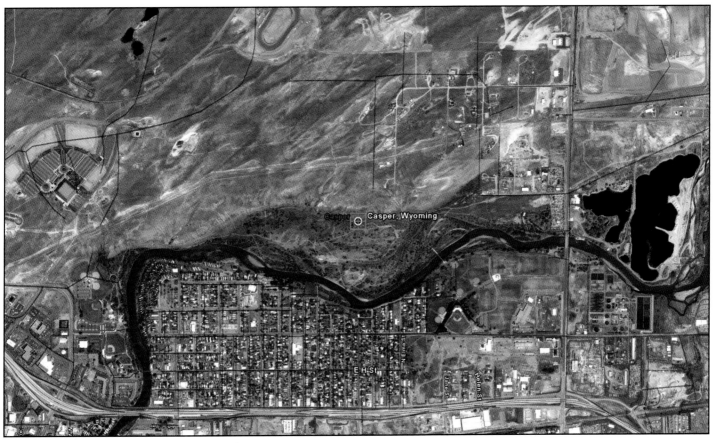

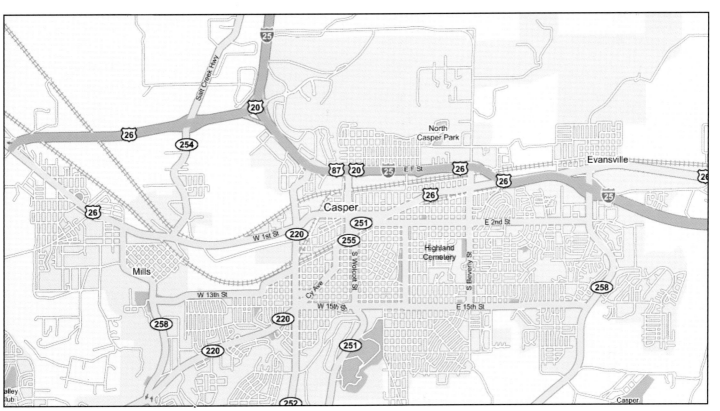

# INDEX